absence
of
closure

By
Gustav Schonfeld

PREFACE

A vision has haunted me recurrently for many years, a recycling short film clip, if you like. It began soon after our liberation from the concentration camp at Muhldorf in Germany. Jews are on a chopping block. God slams his fist down into the crowd. The impact kills many, injures many, and sends the rest flying to all parts of the world. The survivors pick themselves up. All are impaired. Strangely, many are kneeling, in grateful prayer to God for having kept them alive. Other survivors look at them askance, wondering how they can be thankful to a cruel God who permitted his fist to slam into his "Chosen People" in the first place.

I see another series of recurrent images, encompassing much of the twentieth century. The common citizens of Europe, Jews and non-Jews alike, are negotiating a seemingly unending series of dangerous rapids in fragile kayaks. At one time or another nearly all the kayaks turn over; some are righted, some founder. Many people are hurt and many are drowned. Yet non-Jews, even as they are negotiating the hazardous rapids along with their Jewish neighbors, take the time and trouble to leave the relative safety of their own kayaks to overturn the boats carrying the Jews, risking their own safety to do so. During the Second World War the desire to turn over Jewish boats reached the stage of madness. Why?

It did not start with Hitler. For the past eighteen hundred years, European Jews were a barely tolerated minority. Their security, always tentative, was dependent on the tolerance of their non-Jewish neighbors. They had no army to protect them and no land of their own as sanctuary. They were driven from land to land and perforce became the displaced "wandering Jews" of anti-Semitic legend, "verifying" for the Gentiles that their Jewish neighbors were too cosmopolitan, too internationalist, too conflicted in their political loyalties to be trusted as citizens.

I became one of those displaced Jews during the middle years of the twentieth century and I have been angry about it for decades. My mother grew up in Hungary; her losses were greater than mine and she was angrier than I. She used say, "I hate the Hungarians worse than the Germans. I had nothing to do with the Germans before the Second World War. What they did to us was 'impersonal.' But Hungary was my country. My father raised me to be a Hungarian patriot. He served the Kaiser, of Austria-Hungary in First World War. I spoke their language, learned their myths and tales, and sang their songs. When we sang the national anthem I would get goose bumps. They handed my child, my mother, and other family members over to the Germans to be killed."

No one need be surprised by our anger. After all, anger is a universal human response to insult and injury.

A man and I are seated next to each other at a doctors' dinner in an elegant country club. The surroundings are elegant. The table is exactingly set with fine linen, crystal, and silverware. All of us are wearing suits and neckties. My neighbor is disheveled, short, and chubby, speaking English with a distinctly German accent. I ask him, "Where are you from? He replies, "I have been in diaspora in the United States for over thirty years." Startled, I say, "Most people are grateful to be the United States, and do not speak of it as a diaspora, but as a refuge. Why do you consider yourself to be in diaspora?" He says, "I am from Sudetenland, in the western Czech Republic. We were kicked out by the Czechs after the Second World War and forced to live in East Germany."

He is reciting the story of millions of ethnic Germans who had resided for many generations in the Sudeten region of what was the Austro-Hungarian Empire before the First World War. After that war, the Sudeten, land and people, were included in the newly formed Czechoslovakia. This disparaged their national honor. They protested, schemed, and performed acts of sabotage with the aim of undoing the "humiliation" imposed on them by the Versailles Treaty. In 1939 Neville Chamberlain, prime minister of Great Britain, representing the League of Nations in negotiating with Hitler over his demands for more territory, agreed to the dismemberment of Czechoslovakia in return for a promise that there would be no war. He returned to Britain relieved, saying there would be "peace in our time." My dinner partner and his fellow self-proclaimed *Herrenvolk* (master folk) welcomed their "repatriation" to Germany in 1939, and supported Hitler in his aims of conquest, subjugation, and genocide.

After the Second World War, the victorious Allies returned Sudeten to Czechoslovakia. The Czechs, feeling that their German Sudeten citizens had proven to be destructive and disloyal, forcibly ejected them into East Germany, expropriated their lands, and turned the land over to loyal ethnic Czechs.

I would have thought that a physician of some intelligence would have possessed sufficient insight to say, "Starting a world war for the second time within a period of less than thirty years, and losing both times, is likely to be provocative, and to be followed by unfavorable consequences for the loser. We brought this on ourselves. We must learn to lie in the bed we have made for ourselves." Instead, he felt victimized and angry. I understood how he felt. I, too, had been displaced, by his like and their allies, but I was not sympathetic to his plight.

In the year 2000, my anger, which had receded over the many years I had spent as a refugee in the United States, was rekindled while we were in Budapest visiting my maternal aunt Erzsebet Meisner. Erzsi had agreed to meet us in Budapest.

Our visit was great; but as we were touring, old images, smells, and sounds assailed me of previous visits to Budapest, of relatives and events in Munkacs, the town of my birth, and other towns I had visited as a boy. The longer we stayed the angrier I became, as I realized that the *Shoah* (Holocaust) in which the Hungarians had played an important part was "old news" to the current generation. Many chose to remain ignorant of it. More aggravating, many who participated got away with it. Completely catching me off guard was the magnitude of the anger I felt. The horror had happened more than a half century ago. Yet I was still angry. Why had I not reached that happy state described as "closure"?

The provocation was too severe, I thought. Perhaps closure for some hurts is impossible.

More than half of my closest relatives had died in the Nazi camps. The survivors were dispersed to Sweden, the United States, Australia, and Israel. Too many murderers had gone on to lead happy, prosperous lives, serene in the knowledge that one or another government or church would protect them against retributive justice. Adding to my anger was the frustration of knowing that the perpetrators were by now either dead or very old, and would remain unpunished, leaving the subsequent generation of haters to conclude that they, too, could get away with venting and acting on their hatreds.

The roiling of my emotions continued even after our return to St. Louis, intruding on other activities that needed my attention. Was I suffering from a greatly delayed post-traumatic stress disorder? Perhaps, but instead of visiting a psychiatrist, I decided that the best way to reduce the disruptive power of my memories was to place them within the larger context of the rest of my life, which has been quite satisfactory, including wonderful moments of gratitude, awe, and ecstasy.

My memory project required that I return to the past in a deliberate attempt to recapture memories I had thought were forgotten, because I had not dwelled on the past. Instead, I had spent most of my energies focused on the future in the pursuit of a career in academic medicine, a consuming occupation, and in helping to raise a family.

The recollections were often painful, but my decision to review the past was reinforced by my children, who wanted to know whence I came and how I became who I am, and by invitations to speak about my experiences of the Shoah, which I accepted as a painful but necessary obligation. My story illustrates the traumas suffered by one Jew at the hands of the Germans and their allies and collaborators during the Shoah. It follows the recuperation of a severely traumatized individual in the benign environs of the United States, with the help of family, friends, and colleagues, and his achievement of a modicum of success and honor in academic medicine, his field of endeavor.

As I began to think, study, and write, another reason accrued—the fear that the Shoah would be minimized or denied, an outcome strongly wished for by many. When people like me have died, the telling of the story of my time will remain with historians. I wish to add my countervailing bits of memory to the existing record. I hope they will deal justly with it.

In the autumn years of my life, having achieved a measure of success, and having read and thought about the issues of the day, I also felt the need to record some of my reflections and conclusions about a variety of subjects. As I was writing, I was constantly reminded of my father's heroism during the Shoah and his continuing influence on my life. I dedicate these memoirs to him with love and respect.

PART I
BEFORE

Munkacs

Memories of my life before the Second World War are pleasant ones. I wish to recall Munkacs, the place of my birth, in some detail, because it fills me with a happy glow. Also, I wish to convey the magnitude of the accommodation required of us as we were degraded from well-to-do, solid middle-class status to a slavish, fear-filled, beast-like existence in the camps; and then our gradual recovery of health and optimism in the United States. But how different was St. Louis from Munkacs!

The Carpathian mountain range in Slovakia runs from the west toward the southeast along the Hungarian border, and then turns south into the Transylvania and Bukovina regions of Romania. Munkacs is near the bend of the Carpathian range as it turns from an east-westerly direction toward the south. It is about twenty kilometers west of a major mountain pass. Munkacs is a Hungarian name. The currently used Ukrainian version is Mukachevo, but I prefer to retain the names of places as I experienced them.

A distant cousin from Columbus, Ohio, is a gifted persistent genealogist. He has traced certain branches of the family back to about 1740. This has prompted me to look at the history of Munkacs. Over the centuries armies have used the passes through the Carpathians to invade the Hungarian plains from the East. The peaks are about 1,500 meters high. Snow-capped mountains were visible from my bedroom window when I awakened in the mornings.

The town sits on the left bank of the Latorca River, a rapidly flowing stream bringing the clear, freezing-cold water, derived from the melting mountain snow down into Munkacs. From there, the water flows generally southward into the Tisza River, on the Hungarian plain, not far from

Tokay where the delicious sweet Hungarian dessert wines are produced. The Tisza flows farther southward into the Danube, which turns east to form the borders between Hungary and the remnants of Yugoslavia (Croatia, Slovenia, Montenegro, Kosovo, and Serbia) and, farther east, between Rumania and Bulgaria, finally emptying into the Black Sea. This region of Central Europe has its places of physical beauty, and many quaint old cultures. It is also a region with a long history of stern repressive autocracies, obscurantist religions, ages-old hatreds, repeated wars, and much killing. Dracula's Transylvania is not far away.

Munkacs possessed many of the amenities of a small central European city of the time: a theater visited by road shows presenting live performances, showcasing local and imported music ensembles, a movie house playing European and American movies, libraries, restaurants, coffeehouses, and pastry shops. The theater, a large, orange-colored stucco building dating from the late nineteenth century, and the movie house, a modern brick structure, were located at the intersection of *Munkacsi Mihaly utca*, a street named after a noted Hungarian painter, and *Fö utca*, Main Street, about one block from our house. Across *Fö utca* to the south was the *Csillag* (Star) Hotel, the best in town, which is still in business, with a popular indoor and outdoor coffeehouse. The taxi stop in front of the hotel was occupied by horse-drawn carriages during most of the year, sleighs in winter, and a few 1920s-1930s vintage automobiles of diverse brands.

The Farkas family, one of whose members would marry my mother's first cousin Charlotte (Sari) Reinhartz, owned a haberdashery on the north side of the street. A kosher restaurant stood nearby, where diners could eat not only during the week but also on Friday nights or Saturdays, provided they paid in advance, as no commercial transactions were permitted on the Sabbath. A kosher patisserie also stood nearby, where my cousin Tuli and his friends would hold eating contests to see who could eat the most *Indianers* (chocolate-covered cake shells filled with chocolate-flavored whipped cream) in one sitting.

Mom went for her pedicures to the *Bata* shoe store on the south side of the street. The store was one of a large chain, owned by a Czech family that later fled Europe to get away from the Nazis. I would sit watching the pedicurist at work, sucking on a gelato cone or piece of candy. *Bata* stores still exist in Europe, South America, and Canada. The broad, paved sidewalks of the *corzo* (a wide street meant for leisurely walking) were a favorite place for strolling. Boys and girls would meet "accidentally," obviating the need for chaperones, among them my cousins Tuli and Shari.

An evening's entertainment for my parents would have consisted of any combination of strolling on the *corzo*, attending the theater, a concert, or a movie, or sitting in the *Csillag* coffeehouse drinking coffee or beer. It was not necessary to consult calendars to make "dates" in advance. One would simply walk along the *corzo* and run into someone companionable. When my parents wished to go out, they needed to walk only one block to be at the center of the city's social life.

◊✖◊

West of *Munkacsi Mihaly utca* at the intersection of *Fö utca* and Jew Street stood two large synagogues across the street from each other. The Grois Beis Medrish, our *shul,* frequented by traditional Jews, was a large stuccoed

13

structure surrounded by a fence of white stucco concrete bricks, topped off with closely spaced metal rods. The *shul* was lit with huge brass candelabra. The Torah scrolls were housed against the eastern *mizrach* wall pointing toward Jerusalem, in the eight-foot-tall elaborately carved and decorated cabinet, the *a'aron kodesh*. Its front was covered with a velvet curtain on which was embroidered the crown and lion of Judah, and an appliqué representation of Moses' stone tablets listing the Ten Commandments. The rabbi and the "better" families sat in the seats up against the eastern wall facing the rest of the worshippers, near the Torah scrolls. We were among them.

In the middle of the synagogue surrounded by benches was the *bimah*, a raised podium, on which sat a large tilted table. The Torah scroll was placed on the table for reading the weekly portion. The *chazzen* (cantor) led the prayers, sometimes with the help of an all-male choir. The congregation chanted along with fervor, while men shook their upper bodies backward and forward from the waist (known as *shukling*).

Men and women were separated in accordance with Jewish tradition dating back to the ancient temples in Jerusalem. The men sat on the main floor, the women upstairs behind screens. The absence of women in the men's section not only permitted the men to observe the religious law, as determined by the rabbis, and to pray without the distraction created by the presence of females, but provided an added benefit—the exchange of gossip, jokes, and bantering.

Children were permitted to run in and out of the *shul* unhindered to play in the yard. It was a lively scene. Decorous, inhibited behavior such as we see in many congregations in the United States would have been judged as lacking in religious fervor.

The "modern" (neologue) synagogue was frequented by the secularists and the "modern orthodox." Another synagogue/study house known as the *Klein Beis Medrish* and the main *mikvah* (ritual bath) stood a block farther south on Jew Street roughly across from each other. Nearby were Jewish butchers and bookstores. In addition to the larger synagogues, small synagogues, *schtiblach* (little rooms), were scattered all over the city, sometimes adjacent to or within private homes.

Despite its amenities, Munkacs retained many aspects of an impoverished primitive Shalom Aleichem-type *shtetl* (small Jewish town). Many homes had no indoor plumbing. Many houses and public buildings were in poor repair, badly in need of new stucco and paint. Only the major streets were paved or had sidewalks. Side streets, dusty in dry weather, turned into mud with rain or snow. Walking from one destination to another nearly always entailed traversing either dusty or muddy areas. To keep the street dirt outside, one removed one's shoes upon entering a house and exchanged them for house slippers, which were widely available, because it was considered risky to walk around in stocking-covered feet. Stockings without shoes were worn only during *shiva* (the initial seven days of mourning for the dead). Wearing socks without shoes was thus considered courting bad luck.

In addition to primitive conditions of the streets and much of the housing, there was the general harshness of daily life. In contrast with the United States where good manners require a lot of smiling to show friendliness and peaceful intent toward one's fellows, not many people smiled in Munkacs. Life was hard. Most people labored long hours at low-paying, physically demanding jobs where supervisors were stern and at times sadistic. The sadism occasionally was accentuated by ethnic differences. The majority was poor, and in marginal health. Various infections and infestations were common, including head lice, intestinal parasites, skin infections, tuberculosis, and typhus. Public health measures were rudimentary by today's standards, and antibiotics were not available. Periodically, school nurses would comb through the hair of students looking for lice. Those harboring "guests" were sent home for such treatment as was available.

People also did not smile much because they did not wish to display their decaying teeth and gums. Many of the adults and even young teenagers smoked cigarettes. Ordinary people rolled their own cigarettes by hand. The affluent could purchase a variety of devices for mechanically "rolling your own." Large numbers of people also smoked pipes, chewed tobacco, or sniffed snuff. Oral hygiene was not commonly practiced, and some people were malnourished. As a consequence, many people had black, crooked, and missing teeth, and unpleasant-smelling breath. Dental preventive and corrective care was available only to those able to afford it. Having an attractive set of teeth and pleasant breath was a sign of affluence. Our parents warned us not to stand too close to strangers in order to avoid their strong oral and body odors and communicable diseases.

Munkacs was not all dust and mud, however. The churches brought some color to the usually gray streets on various saints' days. The Eastern Orthodox Church was a few blocks from our house near the *Kertvaros* (Garden City) section of Munkacs. It was a large, all-wooden structure with several domes. Orthodox Christians would have several parades per year—on various saints' days. People wore colorful costumes, and carried smoking incense, musical bells, intricately jeweled Eastern crosses, and colorful gilded statues and banners depicting the baby Christ or the crucified Christ. Banners also depicted saints in various biblical settings. The Catholics and Calvinists had their own churches and parades. The Jews had their synagogues, and no parades, because public celebrations were thought by the Jewish elders to provoke anti-Semitic, hostile acts by the *goyim* (Gentiles).

Color was also brought into our lives by the seasons. In spring there were the budding flowers and trees and the fresh grass. Storks arrived and nested on the chimneys of farmhouses in the nearby countryside. Lush vegetation abounded. We swam in the Latorca, and hiked into the verdant mountains blanketed with wildflowers. In the fall, the leaves of deciduous trees turned their brilliant colors, not unlike the fall colors of New England. Winters were cold. The snow came early, covered much of the ugliness in brilliant white, and stayed all winter.

Along the banks of the Latorca were the region's two most famous buildings: the fort and the *kuplerei*. The fort was old, located on the right bank of the Latorca, high on a hill, at the northern edge of the town of Oroszveg, the town directly across the river from Munkacs, connected via a bridge. The local garrison of soldiers served as backup for those guarding the border. Also, the troops would parade through the streets during national holidays to remind the population to behave itself.

The *kuplerei* was located on the left bank of the Latorca, within the boundaries of Munkacs, and was visible to the soldiers from the fort—an important advantage for the *kuplerei*. It was a large house with eight chimneys and eight front doors, frequently referred to as the "eight-chimney house" or "eight-door house." Men would line up outside the doors, go inside for a few minutes, and come back outside buttoning their flies. Sundays, when the soldiers of the garrison were off duty, were particularly busy days. When I was about six, my first cousin Tuli told me that women resided in the house and the men were visiting them.

High school (gymnasium) students would congregate outside to see who would emerge. Sometimes they would glimpse one of their "professors." This would lead to taunting and laughter as the teacher would attempt a quick getaway. The eight-chimney house was frequently mentioned among boys and men along with much winking and laughter. The existence of the *kuplerei* reflected the generally held attitude of those days that women were divisible into two types: nice girls who remained "pure" until marriage, and bad girls who slept around either as professionals (prostitutes) or as amateurs. One was expected to marry the former and to satisfy one's "animal needs" with the latter. This animal need was acknowledged as a weakness in the character of men, more or less tolerated, but one did not discuss it in polite company.

On the streets of Munkacs one saw a bewildering variety of people, each wearing apparel meant to differentiate him or her from the others. The Catholic and Eastern Orthodox priests both wore black cassocks reaching to the ground but were distinguishable by their hats, collars, and crosses. Nuns wore white or black habits and a variety of coifs. Peasants of each ethnic group had their own unique native colorful costumes. Laborers wore tattered wrinkled trousers held up by rope belts and suspenders, wrinkled dirty shirts open at the neck, and Russian-style caps with visors. The professional and business people wore modern western European dress. Hassidic Jews wore black morning coats, beards, and *payes* (earlocks). On the streets one could hear Hungarian, Czech, Slovakian, Ruthenian, Polish, Yiddish, and German.

Relationships among the tribes residing in and around Munkacs were limited to the necessities. They transacted whatever business was necessary but did not willingly learn each other's languages, socialize, or intermarry. Each tribe had its own religion and house of worship. In their homes, churches, or synagogues they were taught to regard the others as strangers with repulsive customs, religions, and languages. For example, my mother used to quote a popular Hungarian rhyme: "Speak to me in zesty Hungarian, not in crazy Slovakian." Each regarded the other as victimizers and themselves as noble heroes and simultaneously as victims. The only self-avowed "internationalists" were socialists and communists, and they, too, quickly returned to their tribal loyalties when under pressure, as we saw during both world wars.

Munkacs had a complex history and population mix. For several centuries before the advent of the Republic of Czechoslovakia, successive Hungarian kings, Ottoman sultans, and Austro-Hungarian Hapsburg emperors ruled over the region. There was constant bickering and fighting between the neighboring tribes of Hungarians, Ruthenians (Small Russians), Slovaks, Poles, and Ukrainians. Changes of political boundaries were frequent, leading local comedians to say, "One can be an international traveler without ever leaving Munkacs."

The Hapsburg Empire ruled Munkacs until the end of First World War. Then, the empire's territory was carved into several independent states according to the then altruistic Wilsonian principle of "national self-determination." The aim was to make the world safe for democracy by satisfying the nationalistic yearnings of the various ethnic groups within the old empire. It was assumed that when each group "sat under its own vine," it would be content, and peace would break out among nations.

Unfortunately, policies based on well-meaning, sweeping idealisms but ignorant of local conditions frequently fail when they butt up against concrete reality, and so it was with the treaty painfully cobbled together in Versailles by the victorious Allies with diverse motivations and contradictory postwar aims. Despite the more or less noble efforts of the victors, the varying degrees of ignorance of the leaders and their teams about local issues, and realities on the ground, rendered it impossible to divide the lands of the former Austro-Hungarian Empire to the satisfaction of the various contending groups. National borders that contained solely homogeneous ethnic groups could not be drawn because the ethnic populations were intermingled, especially near border areas.

Therefore, each state in addition to its own ethnic majority also contained appreciable minorities of neighboring ethnic groups. For example, the Czechs and Slovaks were pushed together into a newly created Czechoslovak Republic, along with the several minorities residing along the borders: Sudeten Germans in the west, Ruthenians in the east, and Hungarians in the south. Simultaneously, the "new" Yugoslavia and Rumania each acquired sizable minority populations. The result was that the leadership classes of the majorities felt they were forced to accept less territory than they "needed" or historically "deserved" to accommodate their own major ethnic group. Minorities chafed under majority rule because the majority treated them as second-class citizens, forcing them to send their children to schools teaching the majority's language and culture. Religious differences—Catholic, Russian Orthodox, Calvinist, and Jewish—added to the resentments.

Indeed, even after the borders were drawn, governments continued to encourage feelings of victimization and irredentism at home, and among their ethnic "brothers" living as minorities in the nations next door, keeping resentments boiling. This turned out to be much easier to do than to improve the lives of citizens, which the strutting governors, despite their proud demeanor, did not know how to do. The recent events in Yugoslavia that resulted in its splitting up into component, mutually antagonistic ethnic communities illustrate the ease with which nationalistic attitudes can be aroused. In any case, "national self-determination" turned out to be very much a mixed blessing in the interwar years (1918-1939). It impinged particularly unfavorably upon the

Jews, who received no country of their own. Rather, they remained as hated foreign minorities in every country. My family, of course, carried on its life within these politico-religious crosscurrents. This required some mental and physical fleet-footedness, neither of which we had enough of to escape the oncoming horrors in time.

⸙

Munkacser Jews

It is surprising how fondly Munkacs is remembered by the Jews who had lived there, despite the periodic civic strife, poverty, anti-Semitic prejudice, and persecution they experienced. Even those who left at ages too young to have experienced Munkacs for themselves remember the stories fondly told by their parents. The nostalgia is especially acute for the time under the Czechoslovakian government, because during the twenty years of its existence between the two world wars, the country was a genuine Western-style parliamentary democracy. Its first president, Tomas Masaryk, a sober academic with a large drooping mustache and Van Dyck beard, was highly esteemed. The freely elected multiparty parliament provided proportional representation to the various economic and religious/ethnic interest groups. Religious freedom was the rule, and the state financed the separate educational systems catering to the majority Czechs and Slovaks as well as to the minorities. Political violence was not tolerated. Thus, a critical mass of the electorate felt they were heard and had a stake in the system. Its citizens called the Czechoslovakian Republic of those days "little America."

The Jewish community of Munkacs comprised about half of the total population of twenty-eight thousand. It was organized into a communal structure (*kehillah*) that performed the functions necessary for an observant Jewish religious life. The *kehillah* taxed its members and also received some support from the government of Czechoslovakia to maintain facilities and personnel such as rabbis, *mohels* (men who performed circumcisions), *shochets* (slaughterers of poultry, beef and lambs in a kosher way), synagogues, parochial schools, homes for orphans, *mikvahs*, and cemeteries.

When I was about seven, I found a photo depicting thousands of bearded men wearing big black hats and black coats massed around a coffin, nearly obscuring it. My father told me the photo depicted the funeral of Rabbi Menachem Elazar Schapira, the major Hasidic rabbi of Munkacs, known as the Munkacser rebbe, who had died in 1936. Many dignitaries, Jews as well as Gentiles, came from great distances to pay last respects. Of course most of the mourners were the rebbe's followers, the Hasidim. My father had been his physician, and spoke of the rebbe with great respect.

Although the Enlightenment, and subsequent socialism and Zionism produced major fissures in the Jewish communities of Europe, including Munkacs, the vast majority of Munkacser Jews remained Hasidim, continuing to follow the Munkacser rebbe. Strict traditionalists, they separated themselves from the rest of the world as a matter of doctrine by their distinctive mode of dress. Their adherence to the Halacha (religious law) was punctilious. They ate only kosher food, observed the laws of Shabbat and Jewish holidays, and both men and women regularly immersed themselves in the *mikvah*, separately, of course.

They devoted maximum possible time to the study of Torah, which they considered the literal word of God, given to Moses on Mount Sinai in the presence of about three million Jews as witnesses. To them, the tradition, faithfully passed from generation to generation, retained its pristine validity. Hasidim rejected the biblical scholarship emanating from universities because they felt it to be based on "invalid" methods of textual analyses.

Included in the ban were studies based on the disciplines of "high biblical criticism," history, archeology, and comparative religion. They studied only those practical worldly skills needed to obtain work that paid a living wage, and with rare exceptions discouraged studies of general philosophy or world literature, fearing that they would confuse or "contaminate" the minds of their children.

Only rabbis trained in traditional texts and experienced in the methodologies of interpreting the law were accepted as religious authorities. Only they could provide valid answers to questions regarding the religious aspects (broadly interpreted) of life. Thus, Hasidim looked to their rebbes as authoritative guides not only in religious matters but also in matters of business, marriage, and conflicts with neighbors, relatives, or children. For example, members of my close family regularly consulted the rebbe or his associates on whether or not a chicken, goose, or duck they had purchased was kosher. Conversely, the rebbe's functionaries came regularly to our house to consult my father on medical issues; many stayed to listen to the news of the world on our radio or to use our telephone. Some of the more traditional cousins of my father sought validation of their decisions on business matters and matrimonial prospects for their children. I suspect my father also valued the rebbe's opinions.

Being a Haredi of either the Hassidic or non-Hassidic type was (and still is) a full-time job. Morning prayers lasting thirty to sixty minutes take place six days a week. Morning services on Saturdays last two to three hours. Additional daily services beginning late in the afternoon and running into early evening take thirty to forty-five minutes—all this plus travel time to the synagogue. Annually, there are twelve days of major holidays, several twenty-five-hour fasts, and fifty-two Saturdays that require all-day observance, and over thirty days of minor holidays requiring special actions and prayers. There are strict dietary codes (kosher) and rules on how to dress and even the order in which to cut one's finger- and toenails, as well as how to dispose of the cuttings. The idea is to be absolutely punctilious in observance, which assures that we are constantly aware of God's dominant presence in the world.

The Haredi Jews loved my father because he was one of them by birth, because he made himself available for a chat or a joke, and because he took optimistic, activist approaches to their illnesses. They loved him despite the fact that as a physician, he did not entirely share their philosophy of life and religion, and possessed worldly experience and knowledge they eschewed. My father loved their warm, sly humor, which reflected shrewd and skeptical attitudes about Gentiles—especially as they related to Jews. They also had loving but questioning conversations with God about His insufficient responsiveness to their needs for sustenance, for *nachas* (joy or pride) from the children, and for protection from the depredations by the *goyim*.

The traditional Jews who did not affiliate with any Hassidic rabbinic dynasty were known as Mitnagdim (oppositionists). The word Haredim can be applied to both Hasidim and Mitnagdim. My grandfather, Eliezer Yaakov Schonfeld, was one of the latter. His life and religious practice resembled Hasidim in the strictness of their religious observance, but he carried his questions about religious issues not to a Hassidic rebbe but to the town rabbi or to other generally accepted authorities. As noted, many of his relatives were Hasidim.

The modern Orthodox, while educated in Jewish history, and religion, and observant of the rituals, also valued the "outside" world and pursued careers in business and in the professions. My father and his siblings were modern Orthodox, although they attended the Haredi synagogue. The secularists believed in Jewish culture and peoplehood but were skeptical of religion and lax in observance.

These philosophical/behavioral divisions split families, as well as the Jewish community of Munkacs. In the 1920s the modern Orthodox and the secularists established a Hebrew language gymnasium (middle school and high school), meant to provide an education in Jewish history, philosophy, and religion taught from a secular point of view, as well as the sciences, math, literature, and general history, all taught in Hebrew. The rebbe condemned the effort as secularizing and excommunicated its founders.

The internecine fighting seems a little silly in hindsight. Hitler did not differentiate between the religious and irreligious, between the Zionist, communist, socialist, and capitalist Jews, or between the supporters and opponents of the Hebrew gymnasium. They were all sent to Auschwitz.

Home

My parents were married in August 1931 at the *Bika* Hotel in Debrecen, Hungary. In their wedding picture my father, at twenty-eight years, looks slim, about five-ten, with dark hair combed straight back exposing a large forehead and a handsome straight longish nose, a serious expression on his face. He always carried himself straight without being stiff, giving the impression of someone taller than he actually was. He had an air about him. When entering a room people usually noticed.

My mother was ten years younger, about five-seven, with a fair complexion, light gray eyes, long wavy dark hair, and a strikingly beautiful face and figure. People would turn around to look at her. When my father was about eighty, I asked him to remember his first impressions of his wife. He told me, "When I first saw her I thought she was the most beautiful woman I had ever seen, and I still feel that way." Over the years innumerable people have remarked to me about Mom's beauty, even when she was in her eighties. However, she was never impressed by her own beauty, saying, "I deserve no special credit. I did not work to become this way; I was given it at birth." I suppose this attitude came from her father, who was honest to a fault and not given to offhanded compliments.

Our first home was a rented two-bedroom apartment in the "Stegman yard" on Munkacsi Mihaly Street. The yard was entered through a large metal gate, and contained several contiguous town house-like apartments, whose entrances faced the courtyard. My father's office was in the apartment next door.

My older brother Frédi (Alfred) and I were born in my parents' first home. Fredi was born in June 1933, and I was born in May 1934. We were born in the parental bed with the help of a midwife. Father, who enjoyed doing obstetrics, participated in delivering Fredi, who had to be extracted with obstetrical forceps. Father stood by for my birth, i.e., he worked in his office, but his help was not needed. A third brother, Solomon, was born in November of 1943 in our new house.

The *cheder* (entry-level religious school) I attended was also in the courtyard of our first house. I began learning Hebrew reading and writing and the Chumash, the five books of Moses, when I was four. We read the texts aloud in a singsong and translated them into Yiddish.

A class photograph taken in 1939 has been preserved. It shows Fredi, me, and my thirty other classmates, along with the rabbi-teacher. He would pinch the cheeks of boys who misbehaved and pick them up off the ground this way, making the boys yelp in pain. I found out after the Second World War that I was the only one of my classmates who had survived.

In 1936 my parents built a two-story house two doors away from the Stegman yard, at *Munkacsy Mihaly* Street 10. The house was built of steel-reinforced concrete covered with stucco, sufficiently strong to last for several generations of Schonfelds, but we occupied it for only eight years. I describe it in some detail "for the record" to emphasize that we did not leave such a big, modern, comfortable house voluntarily.

The front of the house abutted the sidewalk. The stucco was cream colored, stippled with small fragments of glass, so that the house glittered in the light of the sun by day and of the streetlights by night. I had the opportunity to appreciate the glitter one evening when I was about six, as I was standing in front of the house having been locked out, awaiting permission to re-enter. My mother had planned to give us a dairy dinner. I preferred the piece of meat sitting on the stove, grabbed it and ate it, ruining her plans. In our kosher house it was impermissible to eat dairy for six hours after eating meat. Mom told my father, who flared up, and swinging his umbrella drove me out of the house. The maid came out to negotiate my reentry. The terms were that I had to beg forgiveness and to kiss my parents' hands. Following that episode I began to call my father Neville Chamberlain, after the British prime minister who always seemed to carry an umbrella.

The front door led to the completely enclosed entry vestibule, at the end of which stairs led up to two doors, one to our home, the second to my father's office suite. The office door facing toward the back of the house opened into a hall. The door to our home opened to the left, into another hallway. An inner door also connected the office and home.

Doors off the residential hallway led to the basement, day room, and kitchen. The dominant feature of the basement was the central hot-water radiator heating system, a rarity in Munkacs, where houses were heated room by room, with wood- or coal-burning tile-covered ovens or stoves.

The day room was entered through double hinged doors containing multifaceted, translucent glass. This room served as the daily dining room and for informal visits with friends. From there one entered the formal living room/dining room combination through a pair of massive sliding wooden doors, stretching from floor to ceiling and containing thick, transparent beveled glass. The living/dining suite occupied the entire front of the house (except for the space occupied by the entrance vestibule). The furniture was made to order, hand carved and heavy. There were stuffed chairs and a coffee table near the windows. The bookcase, which spanned the entire width of the living room, was divided into several sections by stout wooden columns, on which busts of classical authors and philosophers were carved in bas-relief. The desk was huge, sporting an intricately carved Roman chariot pulled by six running horses. The Roman driver stood in the chariot, wielding his whip. The desk chair had a high wooden back, elaborately carved, and the seat was made of intricately designed velvet. The local theater borrowed it whenever it needed a royal throne.

There my parents did their more formal entertaining, sitting down sipping tea or coffee with their guests. Fredi and I were permitted to be present, provided we were quiet. We heard conversation, occasionally punctuated by laughter or sudden exclamations, without necessarily understanding the import of the topics at hand. My father, who was an entertaining storyteller, frequently held forth. At times, during the early 1940s, we heard arguments dealing with Hitler and Germans, and how the Hungarian government was dealing with them. There was also discussion of events on the Eastern front.

The dining room furniture, too, was handmade and equally elaborately carved. Sterling silver and crystal decorations and ceremonial pieces were displayed on the tables and inside cabinets. These included several candelabra for Friday night and the holidays, menorahs for Hanukkah, *kiddush* cups for the Sabbath and holiday blessings over wine, and paraphernalia for the prayer separating the Sabbath or holidays from routine weekdays (known as *havdalah*). These religious artifacts were regularly used on Friday and Saturday nights, and during lunches on Saturdays, after we had returned from synagogue.

The kitchen contained a metal combination oven/stove that burned either wood or coal and was vented to the outside with a metal pipe. There were wooden chopping and cutting blocks, storage cabinets for china and pots and pans, and a small table and chairs for the kids. Off the kitchen was a sunken cool storage room. It contained an icebox filled with meats; butter and farmer cheese; homemade pickles; a small barrel of homemade sauerkraut, goose liver, and *grivenetz* (rendered skin) stored in white goose grease in deep pots; dried mushrooms on strings; fresh and dried fruits; garlic; onions; potatoes; white polished rice; and seasonal vegetables. Mom and her helper held frequent discussions about the menu, and about who would shop at the market and for which items. They were wonderful cooks and we ate very well.

The backyard was visible from the kitchen and from my father's office, but not from the street. It contained a vegetable garden where, among other vegetables, we grew dill, which my mother used to make pickles. There was also a sandbox, a soccer goal, and a round concrete wading pool with a fountain in its center. We would all splash around in it during hot summer days, and I still carry a scar over my left eyebrow placed there by my best friend Tibor, nicknamed Tibi, with a play shovel when we were five and playing in the sandbox. My father stitched the cut in his office as my mother held me. I have often thought, as I recalled this experience, how comforting it must have been for patients to receive their therapies at home in the days when doctors made house calls, a practice now, sadly, nearly defunct.

From the dayroom, carpeted wooden steps led upstairs to a large, well-lit, airy playroom with a wide French double door facing the rear. A large patio opened off the playroom, half of which was under roof and half open to the sky. Its floor formed the roof of my father's office suite. My bother Fredi, my friend Tibi, and I would play in the enclosed playroom in cold or rainy weather and on the patio or in the backyard when it was clear and warm. We played table football (soccer), Ping-Pong, or rode our tricycles, livening up the house with our chatter.

Three bedrooms opened from the upstairs playroom. The two facing the front of the house, directly above the living-dining room, had a bathroom between them. I still remember standing in front of the toilet bowl when I was two or three, being told by my mother that I was a big boy now and it was time to get rid of my pacifier *(tzutzl)*. With a feeling of pride at having reached the "big boy" status I threw the *tzutzl* into the toilet and flushed it away.

Fredi and I occupied the northern bedroom, and my parents occupied the southern bedroom. Doors and windows from both front bedrooms opened onto the front balcony. The third bedroom facing the north side of the house was the guest bedroom. Hanging on its wall was a still life, painted in oil by my father when he was in gymnasium, depicting fruit sitting on a table covered by an elaborately colored cloth. He was very good at drawing, painting, and lettering, gifts he never pursued in a serious way. He was too busy being a doctor.

In addition to our house, my parents owned an apartment house on *Kossuth Lajos utca* as rental property. (My school was on the same street.) It was apparently a mixed blessing. While it generated them some income, it was also the source of much aggravation. The tenants were loud and constantly demanding repairs and services.

The worldwide economic depression, which crippled the world economy in the 1930s, was not a topic of conversation. If it was, I did not hear it or understand. We lived in a beautiful, modern, well-furnished house in a desirable spot one block from the center of the city. We did not lack for shelter, food, or clothing.

As I describe my life in Munkacs, I remember the distinct feeling that I belonged to the privileged class. My custom-made clothes fit better than my classmates', and I lived in a larger and more modern house. My father's occupation and his habit of working very hard kept us in that social class throughout the time I was under his care. My parents reminded us to be grateful for what we had, and only when times became very bad did I realize how fragile my previous existence had been. Since then, my feeling has been one of profound gratitude for what America stands for, coupled with a feeling of uncertainty about the inherent historical fragility of political arrangements, and the evanescence of material goods.

Thursdays were "beggar days" in Munkacs. All day the poor came to the front door, where they were given coins. They thanked and blessed us before leaving. One man received special treatment. He was a grizzled, gray-haired, disheveled man, with one eye partially closed, who walked with a shuffle and spoke in a hoarse growl. In contrast with the others he was permitted to enter the house and given a shot of slivovitz, to which he added two drops of water from the kitchen sink and downed in one swallow. He bestowed extensive blessings and walked out. I suspect he must have been a relative.

On Friday afternoons we carried the *cholent* (a combination of meat, beans, and potatoes in an earthen pot), and *kugel* (made of flavored, ground potatoes in a flat pan) across the street to Itzik the baker's, a childhood friend of my father's, in whose ovens the delicacies baked overnight.

As we walked to the *Grois Bes Medrish*, along with scores of others, walking to the *shuls* of their choice, the streets would be dark, filled with the long black coats and black felt or fur-trimmed hats *(shtreimlach)* of the men. By Munkacs standards we were traditional but not punctilious in our orthodoxy. We attended synagogue most, but not all, Friday nights, Saturdays, and holidays, and we did keep a kosher house.

After *shul*, we picked up the *cholent* and *kugl* and ate them for lunch, followed by a nap. People used to say that after such a meal it was not surprising that Jews took a nap. What was surprising is that they were able to get up.

My friend Tibor Schonfeld's family lived next door on our right. Tibi was my age but smaller than I. The Schonfelds owned a bicycle sales and repair shop located around the corner from the Csillag Hotel, next door to my Uncle Henrik's store and across the street from City Hall—a standout landmark because of its clock tower. Fredi, Tibor, and I were always either at his house or mine playing Ping-Pong, soccer, riding tricycles, and in winter throwing snowballs at passersby from behind the safety of the large brown wooden gates of his house. In the fall we would play a game resembling marbles, using either walnuts or hazelnuts.

We entered Tibor's house through huge brown wooden gates that opened into a garden. In spring and summer the garden was filled with blooming flowers and lilac bushes. His immediate family and paternal grandparents lived in adjacent, connected townhouses both facing into the yard. The grandfather's house had a porch, enclosed with double French-style outward opening windows. It had a wonderful roof that could be opened with a system of pulleys from inside. The roof was opened every year for the seven days of Succoth, a fall holiday commemorating the residence of our ancestors in tents in the Sinai desert.

We, of course, had our own *succah*, (temporary shelter), but ours was made of wood siding, covered with freshly cut reeds, and decorated with fresh fruits hanging from the roof and pictures of Jerusalem tacked onto the walls. It was put up on the patio directly outside our kitchen. People visited each others' *succahs*, so a spirit of competition erupted annually. Everyone took a lot of trouble to decorate.

We ate most of our meals during those seven days in the *succah*, unless it was raining hard. Integral to each meal were the blessings over food and the singing of songs appropriate for the holiday. The Haredi men regularly slept in their succoth, in fair weather or foul. I must admit even at that young age I could not understand how a cold pouring fall rain was supposed to help us to commemorate the actions of our ancestors as they sat or slept in the desert of the Sinai Peninsula over three thousand years ago.

Passover (Pesach) was another major holiday. Women and their maids undertook major house cleaning every spring just before Passover to rid Jewish houses of any leavened bread or related products. Floors were thoroughly scrubbed, including a careful inspection of all corners. Rugs were hung on ropes and beaten with bamboo sticks specially fashioned for the purpose, and all bedding including mattresses was stripped, beaten to get the dust out, and aired out.

Tibi's grandfather, who kept his hundreds of books in the enclosed porch with the wonderful roof, would bring each one outside into his yard, placed them on benches and tables, opened them, and dusted them inside and out. He put washed bricks or stones on the books to keep them from being blown away by the strong seasonal winds, but he was unable to keep the pages from fluttering in the wind, providing me with an indelible memory of the pre-Passover season in Munkacs. Although our house, too, underwent a thorough cleaning, we spent most of our Passovers with my Gottesmann (maternal) grandparents in Hungary.

Although my life was generally pleasant, it was occasionally interrupted by frightening conversations I overheard between my parents. Behind our property was a small house, accessed by a narrow road lying between my house and Tibor's. In it lived a Jewish family, along with some relatives. On day in 1943, the relatives were taken away. I saw them driving away in a wagon, with whichever possessions the wagon could carry, accompanied by Hungarian gendarmes. Later, I overheard my parents saying that these people were Polish Jews hoping to find refuge with their Hungarian relatives. Someone must have betrayed them to the Hungarian authorities, who in turn had delivered them to the Germans. Further, my parents recited the rumor that the Germans were killing Jews in Poland. This made me very uneasy, but my parents said not to worry. This would not happen to us.

I put it to the back of my mind, to be reminded of it soon enough.

The neighbors on our left were the two Geiger sisters and their husbands and children. The younger sister was a pathologist and "parlor communist," a designation applied to "socially conscious" members of the intelligentsia sympathetic with the humane ideals of socialism or communism. Parlor communists did not build or defend barricades, but in Munkacs they did make the argument to traditional Jews, such as my father, that communism would wipe out all antagonisms between peoples when victorious communism replaced fascist dictatorships with "democratic people's republics." The older Geiger sister was a housewife. My parents had cordial neighborly relations with both sisters.

North of us along the Latorca River lay Kertvaros, the villa section of Munkacs where individual houses were surrounded by gardens. Near the river was a pretty park where we would walk with my parents and play. Mr. Laci, a pharmacist, and his wife, friends of my parents, lived in one of the villas. He was well read, elderly, short, rotund, and gentle. Mrs. Laci was flamboyant, fat, and ostentatiously "cultured." Their son Sandor Laci, who actually ran the pharmacy, was a well-known bon vivant and "*shiksa kriecher*"—a Yiddish expression of opprobrium applied mostly by Jewish women to Jewish men who chased after Gentile women—as many and as often as possible. My major interest in the Lacis was related to the cakes and cookies we were offered in their house.

A drug representative was also a friend. He would visit us frequently, ostensibly to see my father but in reality to pay court to my beautiful mother. Whenever he showed up at my father's office, Dad would say, "Go visit with my wife and kids." During the course of several excursions, he taught me to swim in the Latorca during the summer of 1941. My father had owned a kayak and before he became too busy with his medical practice frequently kayaked on the quieter, wider stretches of the river near Kertvaros. Our friend took me to the same area for my swimming lessons. The water was clear and bracingly cold as we waded and eventually jumped in. When I became a better swimmer, we ventured into areas where the current was more rapid. At times we had to wait to swim because cows were in the river a few hundred yards upstream from us. They would enter to cool off and drink the water. We waited for a few minutes after they left in order to avoid their droppings. As we waited my instructor would point to various places in the mountains he had visited, recounting his adventures. No external noise interfered, except for the distant mooing of the cows, the rush of water, and the chirping of birds. If this sounds idyllic, it's because it was.

Father's Medical Practice

My father was a general practitioner and saw his patients in the office that faced the large backyard at the rear of the house. It consisted of the patient waiting room, the combination examining/procedure rooms, and the water closet. He treated people of all ages, both genders, and all ethnic groups, speaking with them in their native languages: Yiddish, Czech, Russian, Hungarian, and German.

Since he had no nurse or receptionist, he fetched his patients from the waiting room to the exam room where he tended their needs, when necessary performing minor surgery such as sewing of wounds, lancing abscesses, or placing casts on fractures. His own Roentgen apparatus permitted him to diagnose pneumonia, enlarged heart, and fractures with some exactness. At times he would call Mom in to help him. He apparently was not taught about the dangers of X-irradiation, because in his later years the skin on his hands became ulcerated and had difficulty healing.

Few people had telephones, so patients would simply show up at the house at any time of the day or night, routinely interrupting our meals. I often heard my father upbraiding patients for waiting until the middle of the night to visit him when they had been sick all day. Still, he admitted them to his office and took care of them. My memory of those years is of big-bellied young women, snot-nosed babies and toddlers, and bent-over old people visiting the office. They would pay in cash, chickens, geese, or services. Poor people did not pay. In fact, Dad gave them money to pay for medications.

He delivered babies in patients' homes with the help of a midwife and made house calls to those who were too old or infirm to come to the office. He used a variety of modes of transportation: his bicycle, auto, or horse-drawn *fiakers* (taxis). As was the usual practice in Europe, when hospitalization was necessary, my father turned his patients over to "house physicians" (today known as "hospitalists") for in-hospital care. Upon discharge, the patients returned to his office.

Father traveled the countryside quite often and sometimes took me along. At those times he was performing as the public health officer for the rural district northeast of Munkacs, encompassing several villages in the mountains. He would visit each village monthly to inspect food producers, consult with public health nurses, and take care of patients.

Some of my fondest memories consist of walking across green mountain meadows full of wildflowers, passing grazing cows and goats, some with bells around their necks, carefully placing our feet so as to avoid their excreta. The air was cool even in summer and smelled fresh, scented by pine trees.

Ice-cold clear brooks and streams flowed in abundance. I came to know the frogs, lizards, and fish living in or near them. They were the first subjects of my lessons in biology. In summers we would sit in the streams, using the boulders as lounging chairs, letting the cooling water wash over us. We rode around the area in my father's two-horse carriage, later his Fiat sedan, and still later his red Skoda sports convertible, or on a farmer's horse- or ox-drawn wagon, taking in the scenery.

Another lesson in biology: as the "honored doctor's" son I was taken on little tours. One was to watch the stud servicing skittish mares with manual aid from the farmer. I was also invited to watch the slaughtering and butchering of beef, veal, and fowl. The farmers would stun the cattle by hitting them between the horns with a large hammer, as a colleague steadied their heads. Then the hind limbs would be bound and the animal would be hoisted up, head down. Someone would come along with a large sharp knife and slit the animal's throat, leading to gushing of blood and flailing. The animal would be still after a minute, when it was then butchered with great skill and rapidity.

Years later, when we were living in the United States, many people asked my father why he had not left Europe before the war. His answer was, "I would not have left in the 1930s for the job of president of the United States." Life was too good. In fact when I was a child, the considerable amount of admiration for America was mixed with a little bit of contempt among the successful and well-to-do among the people I knew. They felt that America drew the unsuccessful, the unfit, and the persecuted. Though crediting it for its wealth and personal liberties, better-off Europeans considered it to be a country ruled by greedy, crudely materialistic, marginally civilized nouveau riche businessmen, citing "America's business is business."

My Lineage

The Schonfeld Family. The Schonfelds were lively, sufficiently different from each other to produce some sharp disagreements, but intensely loyal and helpful. I enumerate relatives of three family lines.

Dad was a utilitarian when it came to religious belief. Although he understood the principles of evolution, he always said that he preferred to consider himself a descendant of our biblical forefathers Abraham, Isaac, and Jacob, rather than of apes, because this enabled him to be proud of his ancestry. I accept his claim of deriving from our patriarchs, in the spiritual sense, without insisting on its biological veracity since I have been able to trace my own roots back only five generations. (We have a relative who claims to have traced some branches of the family to 1740.) The earliest family stories date back to my paternal great-great-grandfather Schonfeld whose original family name was Mendelovich, which he dropped, taking his wife's name of Schonfeld in response to an edict from the Emperor of Austria-Hungary demanding that his subjects take German sounding surnames. He settled in Mezolaborc near Munkacs. His son, my great-grandfather Naftali after whom I am named, sold Jewish religious texts for a living, going from town to town in his horse-drawn wagon. The family lore is that he was murdered on one of his selling trips.

My great-grandfather Naftali's son, my grandfather Eliezer Yaakov Schonfeld, was born in Munkacs in the 1870s. He was a Haredi with long *payes* and a beard, and dressed in a knee-length black coat. He smoked cigars. I would see him at his home and in ours, and at the *Klein Beth Hamedrish,* the small study house on Jew Street where he spent most of his days studying in the hall filled with classical Jewish texts, taking a break for prayers three times a day. My fleeting impressions of him are of a kindly face, the smell of tobacco, stained teeth, a beard and mustache, a benign touch, and a hairy kiss.

Men at study sat on wooden chairs at tables, or stood at wooden lecterns (*shtenders*). They usually studied in pairs or groups of three and declaimed the Babylonian Talmud written in Aramaic, in a singsong, discussing the finer points in Yiddish. My grandfather would also visit the *mikvah* across the street on Friday afternoons before Shabbes or holidays. The ritual bath's two large, round basins, one containing hot water and the other cold, each had a capacity of about twenty men. Men would sit and gossip, at the same time achieving physical and ritual purity.

My grandfather apparently was not a financial success, destroying in my mind the anti-Semitic claim that all Jews were rich. He went to New York in 1904 for a few months to earn some money, where he worked in a cigar factory rolling cigars and remitting the money home, which was used to buy a store that set the family on its way to a better financial position. Unfortunately for his descendants, he returned to Munkacs. Apparently America was too secular for him, and the Lower East Side of New York, probably too poor.

My grandmother Hudya Gitel Schonfeld was born a Welber. The Welbers were a large, relatively prosperous family spread throughout our region. A few years ago a genealogist cousin residing in Ohio sent me a Welber pedigree he had assembled over several years of intensive research into our genealogy. The document contained over one thousand names.

My father used to tell the following Welber story every time he had a new audience. In the nineteenth century (and even today among the very observant), marriages were arranged by marriage brokers (*shadchanim*). They would make certain that marriages occurred only between families of like social/financial status and degree of piety. The only exception permitted was for a poor but exceptionally bright student of the Talmud to marry into a wealthy family so he could pursue his studies, with the financial help of his father-in-law, without needing to be preoccupied either with money or unfilled sexual needs. The bride and groom would meet only a few days or weeks before the wedding ceremony. Sometimes they did not meet at all until they were led to the *chuppah,* wedding canopy.

Great-grandfather Welber had arranged for the marriage of one of his handsome, studious, observant teenage sons to the daughter of his well-to-do friend. Neither he nor my great-grandmother met the prospective bride, nor did the intended groom.

On the wedding day, before the ceremony, the men would witness the signing of the wedding contract (*ketubah*) in one room. Simultaneously, female friends and relatives visited with the bride in another room. Great-grandmother went to visit the bride and found her to be very plain and considerably older than her son. She took her husband aside and complained bitterly, "I went to look at our bride. What have you done to my beautiful son?" He answered her, "Who told you to look? Had I looked at you before our wedding, I would not have married you."

Because of Eliezer Yaakov Schonfeld's limited earnings, Hudya Gitel was forced into supplementing the family's income. This was common at that time, as unworldly Haredi men, poorly educated for anything except menial employment and preferring spiritual matters over secular careers, earned very little. She opened a dry goods store, and later, in about 1930, she and my uncle Henryk bought a store that sold school and office supplies and books, both wholesale and retail. Within a short time it became the biggest such store in the region and supplied textbooks and writing materials to the schools in the whole area. As a result it brought some measure of fiscal comfort to the family.

Hudya was a driving, ambitious woman, pushing her children to succeed in the worldly sense. My father at the age of four told his mother, "When I grow up I am going to be a doctor and buy you a fur coat," which I suppose tells us about some of his motivation as a physician and of his love for his mother. My grandmother strongly supported him in his aim, both morally and financially, and he was very grateful. As an indication of his great affection and respect for his mother, he visited her daily and sought her advice, which he almost always followed in even small matters. For example, my father always wore his hats with the brims turned up, even in the United States. Mom and I tried to have him turn the front part of the brim down for a more jaunty appearance but he refused, saying that his mother always told him wearing the brim up was more elegant. He never changed his mind.

As my grandfather grew older he developed pleural effusions, probably due to tobacco-induced lung cancer. My father or a colleague would regularly tap Grandfather's effusions. When my grandmother became an insulin-requiring diabetic, Dad administered her insulin daily until he taught her granddaughters—my cousins Esther and Heszi, Mechl's daughters who lived next door to Grandmother—to do it. My grandmother died in January 1941 and my grandfather died in June 1939. They had produced five sons and a daughter.

My father's oldest bother Saul left Munkacs in 1913 at the age of sixteen to seek better opportunities and to avoid serving in the Austro-Hungarian army. He very likely would have been drafted because he was a tall, strapping, strong, muscular young man—ideal cannon fodder. Saul wound up in St. Louis because some relatives from the Welber side had already settled there. He anglicized his name to Schoenfeld.

Because he had no education beyond the eighth grade and no particular skills, he struggled for his initial few years as a physical laborer, and even fought as a boxer for money.

Eventually, he went into the automobile and truck tire business and did well enough to invest in rental housing. For several years he was prosperous. He married Lottie, a vivacious lady who loved to tell off-color jokes, even to me when I was in my early teens, and had two children, Flora and Sanford. The economic depression of the 1930s sent Saul back into poverty for several years. But he managed to pick himself up and wound up owning a huge store named Sanford's General Merchandise, where he and his son bought and sold new and used electric motors, fans, lamps, and other home appliances, tools, and all sorts of "junk."

Saul regularly sent pictures and mail to Munkacs but visited only once, by himself, in 1931. As a high school graduation present, he sent his daughter Flora to Munkacs in 1937 to visit the family. Among many others, Flora met my uncle Alex Gottesmann (my mother's brother). They began a correspondence, and she returned to Europe in 1939 and married him. Flora and Alex wisely left for St. Louis in 1940, after the Anschluss of Austria, the annexation of Sudeten by Germany and Munkacs by Hungary. Poland, too, had been invaded. It was past time for anyone who could to get out. We had waited too long and were stuck.

The second-oldest brother Mihaly (Mechl) had a short dark beard, a limp from a childhood injury, and a sense of humor. He used to tell me, *"Mein nomen is Mechl, kish mir in toches lechl"* (My name is Mechl, kiss my ass). Mechl tried his hand at various businesses—watch repair, gasoline station—but was not very successful. His brothers helped. He had two daughters, Esther and Helga. Helga wound up in New Jersey, Esther in Israel. Their parents died in the gas chambers of Auschwitz.

Henryk (Hugo) was the third Schonfeld son. He and Aunt Jolan had two sons and a daughter. Eugen (Naphtali or Tuli for short) and Beinish (Benjamin) were nine and five years older than I—too far apart in age for us to be close playmates, although Tuli would frequently have Shabbes lunch with us. Esther was one month older than I. We were close friends.

My Schonfeld grandparents, Mechl and his family, and Hugo and his family, lived about a five-minute walk from us in two houses facing into the same courtyard near the open-air food and clothing market. The market held on Thursdays was filled with hundreds of squatting farm women selling fruits, vegetables, live poultry, and sometimes clothes. A wooden fence surrounded the Schonfelds' property, and Esther and I would run around her house and yard playing "hide and seek." On one occasion we trespassed next door into an old abandoned outdoor bowling alley located between her courtyard and a tavern frequented by the farmers and customers of the market. There were many places to hide. Unfortunately, some of the men from the tavern used the abandoned alley as an outdoor toilet, and we blundered into some smelly places, a reflection of the primitive state of plumbing and personal hygiene in much of Munkacs.

Jolan, Esther, and Beinish died in Auschwitz. Hugo and Tuli survived. Hugo stayed in Munkacs for the rest of his life. Tuli immigrated to the United States, changed his name to Eugen Schoenfeld, and carved out a successful career for himself as a professor of sociology and head of the department at Georgia State University in Atlanta. He had four children and is now a great-grandfather. We are in frequent touch by telephone and e-mail. He has written his memoirs and had them published as *My Reconstructed Life* by Kennesaw University Press.

My father was the fourth son. He lost one son in Auschwitz in 1944, my baby brother Solomon. Alfred, my senior, died with nephritis in 1942.

Nathan (Nandor), my father's youngestbrother, married twice while in Munkacs. The first marriage, to a wealthy young woman from a "good family," was forced upon him by my ambitious, social-climbing grandmother, with the aid of my father, who shared her ambition to elevate the family's wealth and social standing. It ended in divorce. Nathan then married Irene, whom he had wanted in the first place. He and Irene had two boys and lived happily in a nice apartment about a ten-minute walk from us. He had a "culturally advanced" bookstore, which he kept open only a few hours per day, that carried the latest titles from all over Europe and the United States, catering to the intelligentsia. Nathan was a bright autodidact, with an alert, inquisitive mind, but he was not as ambitious as the rest of the family. He fancied himself to be an intellectual, and in fact he was, based on my own many conversations with him. The family thought him lazy.

Nathan survived and immigrated to St. Louis, but his wife and children perished in Auschwitz. In St. Louis, he dated a bright woman who owned a book and music record store. (She introduced me to classical music by way of Prokofiev and Stravinsky.) He wanted to marry her but was talked out of it by his brothers Saul and my father. The woman had no family of which they could be proud, and she had little money. Instead, he married into a large American-Jewish family of Hungarian origin, went into the grocery business, worked very hard, and became financially comfortable.

Unfortunately, there were no offspring, which he regretted very much.

My father's youngest sibling was his sister Lujza, a dark-eyed vivacious woman who lived in Szöllös, about one hour from Munkacs with her husband Jenö, a banker, and two daughters. We saw Lujza only two or three times a year, when they drove to Munkacs for some of the holidays. Lujza perished with her children; only Jenö survived. He spent the rest of his life in Budapest.

I shared my name, Naftali Schonfeld, with two other relatives. One was my first cousin Tuli, and the second was my father's first cousin, a tall, energetic, heavy-set forty-year-old man with a short beard. He used to visit us about once a week, speaking mostly with my father, but always stopping to say hello to my mother and asking me how I was doing. Despite his cheerful mien, he always looked busy and somewhat harried. My father told me he was in the lumber business, hauling logs and boards in his horse-drawn wagon. This did not yield him sufficient income to support his large family. Without having it spelled out, I gathered he left his visits with us with some of my father's money in his pockets. I observed Dad's openhandedness throughout his life. In this he was always supported by my mother.

The Gottesmann Family. Grandfather Solomon Gottesmann was born in approximately 1882 in Tarpa, a small town near the city of Beregszaz (Berehovo), about thirty kilometers from Munkacs. He was one of five: two sisters, Betty (Sonnenwirth) and Rezsi (Reinhartz), and two brothers, Kalman, the rabbi of Nagyleta (now Létavértes), and Izidor, a businessman in Debrecen. Solomon trained to be a rabbi but never used his degree. Instead he became a successful lumber merchant in a small town in Hungary. A veteran of the First World War, having fought for Austria-Hungary for four years, he warned my mother in the early1930s that the rest of the twentieth century would follow the same course as the first third. It would be filled with financial insecurity and instability, wars, wholesale killings, and terror. This pessimistic outlook, amply confirmed by events, affected my mother's attitude for the rest of her life.

Grandfather Gottesmann met my grandmother Irene Sonnenwirth in Nagyvarad (now Oradea Mare, Romania) where he was sent for advanced religious training that led to his ordination as a rabbi. They met at the Sonnenwirth dinner table.

Householders who could afford it used to feed rabbinic students. The students would eat dinner at several different houses each week, and each house had its own designated day (*essen täg*). Solomon was about twenty-two and Irene about eighteen. In old photographs, Grandfather Solomon appears as a handsome, tall and slender young man with dark hair, a jaunty mustache, a small pointed beard, and piercing light-colored eyes. He retained his good looks until he died. He was measured, soft-spoken and had a wide ranging intellectual curiosity. Despite his being a *yeshiva* student he studied music, philosophy, history, and current events on his own. He owned an old-fashioned hand-wound record player on which he played some of the early discs of Italian operas. Irene was beautiful, sharp, and vivacious, with long curly light hair and a shapely, full body.

They were initially not deemed a "suitable" match by *her* parents, because her father was prosperous while Solomon's family was poor. There was to be no marriage until he proved that he was a man to be respected, one that could provide for his bride. After his rabbinical ordination, Grandfather moved to Nagyleta (where his brother was the village rabbi) and went into business with an older man who owned an established lumberyard. He kept in touch with Irene over a three-year interval by mail. My mother read some of the letters and recounted their poetic, romantic tones. Eventually the senior Sonnenwirths gave their blessings, and in 1908 Irene moved from Nagyvarad, a metropolis with a population of one hundred thousand, indoor plumbing, trams, coffeehouses, opera, theater, and elegant synagogues, to backwater Nagyleta, populated by ten thousand souls, only a few Jewish families, unpaved streets, and no indoor plumbing, at least not until the early 1940s. The main street was paved only in the late 1930s.

They were very devoted to each other. This was clear to me even when I was four or five from observing how they approached and spoke to another. Their three children, Sandor (Alexander, Alex) or Sanyi, Ilona (Helena), and Erzsebet (Erzsi) were born between 1910 and 1915.

Grandfather provided good service and ready credit without interest to the customers of his lumberyard, the Hungarian farmers in the area. My mother and Uncle Sanyi would recall the great respect paid him by the local officials and "intelligentsia," the village notary, the priests, doctors, lawyers, and schoolteachers. These people almost uniformly held most Jews in contempt but would address my grandfather formally, with deference, and frequently sought his advice on a variety of issues. My mother recalls that when Jewish children walked on the street the peasant children would frequently taunt them and throw stones, but when Grandfather came by they would say, "Quiet, here comes Mr. Gottesmann."

Sanyi studied at a Jewish gymnasium in Debrecen, and pitched in at the lumberyard during vacations. The school taught both Jewish and general subjects. In the 1930s he entered the law faculty of the University of Debrecen and graduated with a law degree just before the beginning of the war. He was a very good-looking young man with an eye for the ladies. He told me stories of exploits in the swimming pool in Debrecen during his university days that convinced me that sexually aggressive women existed before women's liberation and the birth control pill. He, of course, did nothing to discourage their attentions.

Erzsi, who was a lovely, vivacious, bright woman who loved to laugh, was married to Meisner Tibor, a lawyer. They resided in Derecske, a town about twenty kilometers south of Debrecen. He reminded me a little of Lawrence Olivier both in looks and in the elegant, precise, histrionic elocution he used. He came from a large well-to-do family, and was ferociously intelligent, quick on his feet, arrogant, and very successful in his profession. Although Tibor was clearly the dominant partner, at least in public, and constantly demanded his wife's attention, the marriage was a happy one. They had no children.

My great uncle Izidor Gottesmann and his wife Etelka (Aunt Ethel) were both small, shy, and soft-spoken, without children. We often visited them in Debrecen on our way to or from Nagyleta. Sometimes we slept in their soft beds under huge fluffy duvets. Etelka would prepare scrambled eggs for dinner. My father was accustomed to eating very quickly, I suppose because he had experienced hunger as a child and because he never knew when his meal would be interrupted by patients, so he rarely paid attention to the food in front of him—a pity, because my mother was a really superb cook. On one occasion my father ate one of Etelka's plates of scrambled eggs. At the end of the meal he felt very full, and an hour later he vomited. When he asked her how many eggs she had prepared, she said twelve! Izidor and Etelka were gassed in Auschwitz.

The other Gottesmann relatives in Nagyleta consisted of my great-grandmother Gitel Gottesmann, a gaunt, bent woman who wore a wig (*shaitel*). Many years before I met her, she lost her husband in Tarpa and moved to Nagyleta to be near to her son Kalman and his wife Eszti, the beautiful daughter of the rabbi of Vertes, the town just down the road. I suppose Kalman wound up in Nagyleta through the good offices of his father-in-law.

Kalman and Eszti had four children (my mother's first cousins): Shimon (Shimi), Moshe, Rozsi, and Ilonka. They lived in the center of the village in a multifamily house, which opened onto a courtyard. Kalman died at a young age, and Grandfather assumed the moral and financial support of his sister-in-law, nephews, and nieces until they were able to fend for themselves. Shimi worked in my grandfather's lumberyard. Moshe, when I knew him, was a handsome thirtyish man with a small black beard, who had inherited the post of rabbi of Nagyleta from his father. He and his wife had several young children. Shimi and Moshe and his family were gassed in Auschwitz.

Ilonka was a good-looking, tall, slender young woman living at home. There were rumors that there was a boyfriend somewhere, but we never met him. We saw the cousins frequently while visiting my grandparents. We saw Rozsi Nagy rarely as she lived in Budapest with her husband and two children. After the War, Ilonka wound up marrying Kalman Vogelhut and lived out her life happily in Stockholm. She died with breast cancer, without children. Rozsi stayed in Budapest, and her daughter and son now live in Sweden, where I saw them about twenty years ago.

We had several cousins named Reinhartz in Munkacs. The relationship was through the Gottesmann side. Aunt Rezsi Gottesmann, a sister of my grandfather Solomon Gottesmann, was married to Lipot Reinhartz of Munkacs. Betty Gottesmann, another sister of Grandpa Gottesmann, was married to Moritz Sonnenwirth, my mother's uncle residing in Nagyvarad. Rezsi and her sister Betty arranged the introduction of my parents to each other.

Lipot Reinhartz owned a tavern/restaurant that my parents would visit. The adults would sit at a table and talk, eat, and drink, while I sat under the table playing. After a while someone would bring me a tiny glass of beer.

The Reinhartzes had five children: Alex, Lilly, Sari, Hershi, and Hindu. They were a lively family with strongly held pro-Zionist opinions. Hershi, the oldest, left Munkacs in the mid-1930s along with several Zionist friends. They sneaked into British Palestine in the face of British limitations on Jewish immigration. They traveled to Istambul by train and hiked through Turkey and Syria into Palestine. Hindu and Alex left for Palestine in the late 1930s. Lilly married Hugo Pollack.

As Lilly and Hugo saw the threatening clouds of war, they decided to immigrate to Chicago where Hugo had several cousins. He preceded Lilly because his travel documents were in order. The arrangements for Lilly took a longer time, and she left Munkacs literally hours before the Hungarians arrived. My father cajoled and bribed a Czech police officer acquaintance to sign the necessary papers permitting her to board the last train leaving for Prague just before the Hungarians moved into Munkacs and closed the border. The Pollacks first settled in Calumet City, Indiana, a poor working-class town. In the early 1950s they moved to Los Angeles. They had two children, both still living in the Los Angeles area.

Sari (Charlotte) Reinhartz was one of my favorite cousins, petite and pretty. She was at our house often and played with me. She became engaged to Fred (Fishi) Farkas in the early 1940s. Fishi is short and chubby and is a gifted natural comedian. He loves puns, plays on words, funny couplets, and practical jokes. A typical trick follows: I am taking a nap on the couch. A gentle tap on my shoulder awakens me and Fishi, leaning over me, asks softly, "Hey Guszti, Guszti, if someone wants to wake you, should I let him?" After the war and many vicissitudes I will recount later, they were married and eventually moved to Los Angeles, where they had one son and prospered.

The Sonnenwirth Family. Great-grandfather Sonnenwirth, Irene Gottesmann's father, owned a goose feather supply business in Nagyvarad. He bought goose feathers from farmers, owned the shop that cleaned them, sorted them by grades and sold them to pillow and duvet makers. Apparently his catchments area was large and the business was quite successful. My maternal grandmother Irene had three brothers and two sisters.

The Sonnenwirth great-grandparents did not agree on how the children should be raised. He wanted the boys to have traditional yeshiva training and the girls to become religious, dutiful housewives. She insisted on a modern education, and when he refused to pay for it, she opened her own grocery store and used its proceeds to pay for the children's secular education. Aaron, the oldest son, eventually ran the grocery with his mother. He and his family perished in Auschwitz.

Noszi Sonnenwirth became a radiologist. He trained at the Sorbonne in Paris where he met his wife, also a physician. She was a parlor communist and he eventually adopted her political views. They settled in Kolozsvar (now Cluj, Romania) where they raised a family. Noszi and his wife died in Auschwitz.

Lajos Sonnenwirth settled in Debrecen, where he had a daughter and eventually divorced his wife. He practiced law in Debrecen and was an outspoken socialist. He and Noszi did not speak with each other for about twenty-five years, allegedly because of their doctrinal differences. Lajos died an ugly death at the hands of the Hungarians who beat him and literally cut him to pieces. I did not see this happen, but the event haunts my imagination.

The third son Moritz (Maurice) Sonnenwirth became a successful wholesaler of cloth and apparel in Nagyvarad. Moritz was married twice, the first time to a fashionable rich woman who rode horses for amusement, a distinctly unusual activity for Jews at that time, especially in that part of the world. The marriage was annulled. His second marriage was to Betty Gottesmann, my grandfather's sister. Moritz and Betty had a daughter who was tragically killed at the age of eight by a tram directly in front of their apartment, and Alex, also known as *kiss* (pronounced "kish") Sanyi (small Sanyi). Alex eventually made a successful career as a professor of microbiology and pathology at the Washington University School of Medicine in St. Louis. His parents died in Auschwitz.

Irene Sonnenwirth's sisters all made "good marriages." Szerén married a Kálmán, a successful businessman in Temesvar. They had two sons and a daughter: Andre, now a physician in Brooklyn; Chaim Kedar, the general counsel for Bezek, the Israeli Telecom Company; and Hedvig Schonfeld (no relation to our Schonfeld family), a mother and grandmother of several offspring, who lived in Tel Aviv. The parents were gassed in Auschwitz.

Rozsi, my grandmother's youngest sister married a handsome physician named Jozsef Berger, a card player, raconteur, gourmet, and ladies' man. They had no children. Both of them perished in Auschwitz.

Although our family suffered many losses, those of us who survived consider ourselves lucky. Polish, Czech, and German Jewish families suffered much greater proportionate losses.

Golden Days in Nagyleta

Our summer vacations and Passover visits with the Gottesmann grandparents in Nagyleta comprised the most pleasant experiences of my foreshortened childhood. When my father traveled with us, he would drive his car. Before 1939, we were held up at the international borders between Czechoslovakia and Hungary. This turned a three-hour trip into a five or six-hour trip. Lazy, truculent Hungarian officials exuding hostility to "foreign" visitors would slowly check our passports, visas, and luggage. Finally, reluctantly, as if Hungary was a paradise they were reluctant to share with the less worthy, we were permitted to enter.

In 1937 my father was driving his newly purchased Fiat sedan, which had a manual shift. Flora, who was visiting from St. Louis, was traveling with us. My father's "workaholic" schedule had not provided him with sufficient time to learn how to shift the new car into reverse. Whenever the car needed to be backed up, it was pushed with the help of onlookers, until Dad found a mechanic who was able to teach him how to shift into reverse. Very few cars were seen on the roads in that part of Europe in the 1930s. We were objects of curiosity whenever we stopped in villages. People would gather around, stare, touch the car, and comment.

When Dad could not travel with us, we went to Debrecen by train, where we transferred to the local spur to Nagyleta. At times we would spend the night in Debrecen at Etelka and Izidor's house and eat eggs.

Upon our arrival in Nagyleta by train, Jozsi, the handyman, would pick us up in my grandfather's horse-drawn carriage. The house and lumberyard were located at the edge of the village, five hundred meters from the railroad station, across a large open field called the "Csinos." Frédi and I would sit with Jozsi and he would let us hold the reins and "drive" the carriage home.

To the right of Grandfather's property was the village of Vertes with its farms. To the left, several hundred yards away, was a flour mill far enough away to be inaudible. Beyond the mill was the village of Nagyleta. The area around the lumberyard was quiet. Every day we heard the crowing of roosters, the cooing of pigeons, the cackling of geese, and the quacking of ducks. Cows would be driven to and from pasture in the mornings and evenings along the road in front of the property. We heard mooing, cowbells, the crack of whips, and the barking of herder dogs. No more than five motorized vehicles passed the lumberyard on any given day.

Farm wagons entered and exited the lumberyard through a gate and parked in the courtyard, which the house faced. The front door led into a small vestibule, then the kitchen, and beyond were the dining and living rooms. The three bedrooms opened off the living room. Next to the house was an herb garden, and on the other side the outdoor toilet. In 1940 my grandparents moved into the village into a more modern house with indoor plumbing, but kept the lumberyard until it was confiscated by the government. Across the courtyard was the office in a one-story building two steps off the ground. It contained high desks, stools, and along the wall deep wooden bins for nails, hinges, and tools. Grandfather had but to open the front door of his house and walk perhaps a hundred feet to his office.

The horse stables; coops for chickens, ducks, and geese; and a tool shed were one hundred feet to the left as one faced the front door of the house. One hundred feet to the right was a large, ornate pigeon coop on a wooden pole about eight feet off the ground, made by Jozsi, housing several hundred pigeons. The water well was about twenty-five feet from the pigeon coop. It had a roof from which a rope and pulley were suspended. We lowered buckets attached to the rope and drew up cold water that, after heating, was used for bathing, laundry, and for the animals. The water for drinking came from elsewhere.

The lumberyard stretched for about 150 meters behind the office. Several, four-meter-tall roofed structures were filled with stacks of boards. They had open sides for easy access. A resinous smell emanating from the boards permeated the atmosphere. Two men cut the boards to the desired lengths with handheld saws. The courtyard was a busy place during the week as farmers and other customers crowded it with their horse-drawn wagons to pick up the materials needed for their building projects.

Grandma had hired help with her work. Still, she was always busy growing fruits and vegetables, feeding the fowl, collecting eggs, arranging with the shochet for the slaughter of fowl, and cooking and baking. Only occasionally would she need to buy any food produced off the premises. She cooked and baked several times per week and canned her own food for winter. Grandma was a fabulous cook in the Hungarian style—paprikas chicken, duck, or goose pecsenye, lecso, and my favorite before I knew about cholesterol, goose grease and tepertő (*grivenetz*) on bread baked in her own outdoor oven, liberally sprinkled with paprika. She also baked fabulous rolls and challah, cheese pockets, chocolate coffeecake rolls, *kindli* (rolled dough with either a walnut or poppy seed filling), and *vajas pogácsa*, a uniquely flavored butter biscuit. My mother used to cook and bake just like Grandma, and she taught my wife, Miriam, and our daughter Julia.

Laundry was done by hand and dried on rope lines in the yard or in front of the stove. House cleaning, too, was done by hand without the aid of electrical devices, such as vacuum cleaners and the like. Rugs were draped on rope lines and beaten with bamboo beaters to rid them of dirt and dust.

Although our visits added greatly to her work, Grandma was always pleased to see us. On our part, we enjoyed the visits very much. She was tolerant of our chasing the fowl around the yard, and was not upset by the attendant cackling and flying feathers. At times the geese would stand their ground and hiss and make threatening gestures. Once Grandma gave me five freshly hatched fuzzy cheeping ducklings, which I loved to death by handling them too often. Occasionally, we would help Grandma with some of her chores, like collecting eggs or feeding chickens.

The most pleasant memory of my grandmother is of her loving presence, and her smile and laughter as she contemplated us, and I will never forget one of my grandfather's admonitions after I had done something unsafe around a wagon that got Jozsi, their handyman, upset. He told me, "Guszti, you are like a young colt, full of energy and mischief. That's good, but eventually colts have to be trained to become careful and responsible." He did not frighten me, but what he said caused me to think.

My mother's cousin Shimi Gottesmann was in his thirties when I knew him. He was an unworldly bachelor who lived and worked in the lumberyard. He sold lumber and studied the Talmud, at which he excelled. He and Grandfather studied together nearly every day. Shimi usually sported a "five o'clock shadow," as he shaved only on Fridays, for Shabbes, using a depilatory cream and wooden blade he carved for himself. (Orthodox Jews do not permit razors to touch their faces. That is why so many have beards.) He shaved outdoors because the depilatory had an awful smell.

Frédi and I viewed him as a playmate. He would run around the yard with us. Sometimes we dragged him by the arm while he put on a pretense of protesting. He showed us where we could safely climb and hide in the stacks of boards.

Shimi finally married in 1943, happily it seems. However, he enjoyed married bliss only for a year, because in 1944 he and his wife were taken to Auschwitz. They did not return.

Every few days we went to the train station in the wooden wagon with Shimi and Jozsi to pick up lumber. We also visited the horses in their barn and took a hand in brushing them, shoveling hay and straw with a wooden pitchfork and manure with a shovel. Jozsi would put us on the horses and lead us around the yard.

In the evenings we listened to classical music or opera either on the radio or on Grandpa's old-fashioned manually-wound Victrola-type record player. My mother or Grandma washed us every evening as we stood in a blue-white heavy porcelain basin, using the matching porcelain pitcher. Then she told us some stories and put us to sleep. When we arose in the mornings, she washed our faces and hands. On Thursdays, the maids heated water on the kitchen stove and we bathed sitting in a metal tub in the kitchen.

On Friday Grandma, my mother, and the maids made extensive preparations for the Sabbath, cleaning, and cooking. They set the Sabbath table with a shining white tablecloth, the finest plates, and sterling silver utensils. A bottle of wine and the home-baked challah, draped with a satin cover on which the prayer for bread was written in Hebrew, was placed in front of Grandpa's chair. The women lit candles forty minutes before sunset and asked God to bless us. The adults recited and sang the Friday evening prayers. Grandfather then sat in his chair at the head of the table and blessed us with the priestly blessing, his hands covering our heads. We sat at the table, and all of us sang "Shalom Aleichem" (a song welcoming the peace of Sabbath). Then, we stood and

Grandpa sang the Kiddush, consisting of a few verses from the Bible describing the origins of the Sabbath at creation, and including the prayer over wine. All then washed hands. After returning to the table, Grandpa said the prayer over the challah, cut it into small pieces, and passed them around to everyone. Thus, sitting around the festive table, the meal began. We ate Grandma's delicious food, interspersing Sabbath songs (*zmirot*). At the completion of the meal, we sang the prayer of thanks for the meal (benching), and adjourned for washing and bed.

On most Saturday mornings we dressed in our best clothes and walked to the synagogue in the center of the village. Along the way, the male inhabitants of the village would raise their hats and the women would curtsy in honor of Mr. Gottesmann. In the synagogue, the men would treat Grandpa with great courtesy because his nephew was the rabbi. We sat next to him in the seats of honor on the eastern wall.

When we returned home, there was a Sabbath lunch, frequently consisting of homemade *cholent* and *kugl* baked in Grandma's oven in the yard. On Saturday afternoons we napped and before sundown had *Shalosh suddoth*, the third meal. On Saturday night as dusk appeared, Grandma and Mom said a Yiddish prayer asking the God of Abraham, Isaac, and Jacob to bless their families during the coming week. After three stars became visible, Grandfather said Havdalah, the prayer declaring the end of the holy Sabbath and separating it from rest of the secular days of the week. He then smoked his first cigarette in over twenty-five hours.

After I grew up and took up smoking, I was in awe of Grandfather's self-discipline. He was a chain-smoker, always using a cigarette holder, but he emptied his pockets of everything, including cigarettes and matches, on late Friday afternoons and did not smoke again until after Havdalah, twenty-five hours later.

◦❧◦

Passovers drew a big crowd to Nagyleta. Preparations were much more elaborate than for a routine Shabbes, because the *chametz* (food forbidden during Passover) had to be searched out and sold or destroyed, requiring extensive housecleaning. In addition to us, members of the Sonnenwirth clan came from Nagyvarad. Erzsi and Tibor would come from Derecske. Everyone stayed at my grandparents' house, filling all the beds and couches. There was much coming and going. Tibor Meisner had a penetrating voice, and I could hear him declaiming his opinions on Hitler, the economy, and America in every room of the house. He and Erzsi were very playful with each other, laughing, talking baby talk, and kissing frequently. My father told his stories of the Hasidim of Munkacs.

One Pesach evening, when Alex Sonnenwirth was out of the house, Betty and Moritz Sonnenwirth discussed their son's love life with the family. Alex, an advanced gymnasium student at that time, was seeing a young woman deemed utterly unsuitable for him by his parents, as she came from a low-class family and was forthcoming in ways respectable young women were not expected to be in those days. I was asleep when this discussion began, but I was awakened by Betty's shouting to the assembled family that should Alex bring the hussy home, she, Betty, would take a shit-filled broom and sweep her out of her house.

At other times, there were serious-sounding discussions about Hitler, the Anschluss of Austria, the dividing up of Czechoslovakia, and the Germans' mistreatment of the Jews in Poland. Beyond the somber mood imparted, the full import of these discussions escaped me. I certainly saw no immediate relevance to my own life.

PART II
DURING

The Darkening

Our peaceful, pleasant life in Munkacs was abruptly disrupted one morning in late 1939, by a loud noise. Dust rapidly filled the house. We ran upstairs and found that a large part of the wall of the guest bedroom had collapsed into the playroom. There was also a large hole in the rear wall of the room. Our parents told us that a cannonball had been fired by the Czech army, angry at having to vacate Munkacs in favor of the hated Hungarians, and that it had inadvertently hit the house. They assured us there would be no more shooting. The wall and hole were soon repaired, but our life had changed irretrievably and forever.

I shudder at the memory and all it portended. I have heard it said repeatedly that our ignorance of the future is a blessing. How true! I do not know what my parents would have done had they been able to predict the events of the next few years. Some of their friends committed suicide.

The turnover of Carpatho-Ukraine and Transylvania to the Hungarians resulted from the land-for-peace deal Britain's appeasing prime minister Neville Chamberlain had arranged with Hitler during their meeting in Munich in 1938, resulting in the dismemberment of Czechoslovakia. For the Czechs this was a gross betrayal by the League of Nations and most specifically by Great Britain. It still reeks not only of betrayal but also of the arrogance of one country being in a position to permit the dismembering of another, breaking its word to an ally to do so. For the Hungarians, Munich represented "restitution" of land they considered their own, as they had never accepted their defeat during the First World War. In 1918, the Axis could not believe that the decadent democracies were capable of inflicting such a defeat, and blamed the loss to a "backstabbing" betrayal by the Jews.

(I never learned the details of how the alleged betrayal was carried out nor how such great powers could be brought low by a tiny, unarmed, peace-loving minority. But millennia of anti-Semitism carefully nurtured by the churches of Europe had prepared the minds of Europeans to accept any accusations, however illogical or unlikely, leveled against Jews.) In any case, after their loss of the First World War, Carpatho-Ukraine was taken from Austria-Hungary and incorporated into Czechoslovakia.

Having burned with unrequited irredentist fever for twenty years, the Hungarians wasted no time in reclaiming "their" territories. In 1939, strutting Magyar troops appeared on the street, and the proud Magyar ruling classes that had chafed under Czech rule took over government offices, gleefully booting out the Czechs. Suddenly, without consultation or consent, we were "blessed" with being Hungarians. Knowing of the pro-German sympathies of the Hungarians, we referred to the takeover as the "dark liberation." Soon, my father was jailed in Kohner castle for having made an antiwar speech a few weeks before at a peace rally in our football stadium, while we were still part of Czechoslovakia. The authorities also revoked his license to practice medicine.

Anti-Semitic speeches, slogans, and epithets voiced in public became acceptable public discourse. Hungarian officials were arrogant, particularly with Jews. They made it clear we were living in new times, that we should disabuse ourselves of the notion that in what was now Hungary again we were equal citizens with the ethnic Magyars.

Nuremberg-type laws restricting Jews in all sorts of ways were enacted. Quotas severely liming the number of Jews in universities were put in place until gradually no Jewish students were admitted. Among them was my cousin Alex

Sonnenwirth, who was refused admission despite an outstanding academic record in gymnasium. Licenses to practice professions were restricted. My father's problems were one example. Limitations were placed on ownership of property and businesses. Whereas intermarriage between Jews and Magyars had been frequent among the liberal classes in Budapest, any romantic liaisons between Jews and Christians now became illegal. All of this was done voluntarily, without pressure from the Germans.

Bribery and corruption became for us the modus operandi in government offices. My mother bought my father's way out of Kohner castle by paying a large bribe to an official in Budapest. Still, it took six weeks to get him out, and more bribing for a restoration of his license. I still wonder how my mother, a girl raised in a small town, with only a high school education, was able at the age of twenty-seven to face the big shots in Budapest.

I started first grade in the Munkacs Jewish day school in the fall of 1940. The ten- to fifteen-minute walks back and forth to school were at times exhilarating and at times intimidating. Hungarians boys on their way to or from their schools would taunt us and throw rocks at us, calling us "dirty Jew, stinking Jew, Jew-pig." We would sometimes throw rocks back; at other times we ran, depending on the relative strengths of the two sides on any given day. There were few dull days of walking in peace.

The lower school, housed in a modern three-story smooth concrete structure, had used Hebrew as the teaching language under the Czechs, but the Hungarians insisted on their own language. Thus, I was denied learning Hebrew in the same intensive fashion as Tuli in earlier times.

I have generally pleasant memories of the school. My mother tells me the teachers liked me but complained about my tendency to laugh and tell jokes in class. They told her I was a "cut up" because I had extra time on my hands, since I finished doing what was required before many of my classmates. At the age of eight, I fell in love with my classmate Gita, the beautiful daughter of the lovely Mrs. and Dr. Steinberger, a dentist, friends of my parents. Naturally, I never spoke more than a few words to her.

Omens of Worse Things to Come

Frédi and I were roommates for his whole life. We bathed, ate, went to school, and played together. Although he was older by eleven months, he was weaker and smaller. He took more and longer naps and could not perform some of the physically demanding activities Tibor and I were able to do, such as tree climbing, fence straddling, jumping over puddles, or jumping off steps onto the ground. Nevertheless, he was a constant presence at my side and I protected him from other children.

I sensed nothing wrong until one day in 1940 when my mother explained that Frédi had to be taken to Budapest for an examination by a professor, and she wanted me to come along. I remember Mother and Frédi coming out of the professor's office with the professor accompanying them. All were very somber, and speaking in low tones, words I had difficulty hearing much less understanding. The news turned out to be bad. He had nephritis. Nothing could be done. This was decades before renal dialysis or transplantation became viable options. We took Frédi back to Munkacs. He gradually faded, becoming weaker, losing weight, and finally spending most of his time in bed. He died on January 20, 1942.

In accordance with tradition, pallbearers carried his coffin through the streets to the graveyard, with the crowd of mourners walking behind. At the gravesite, after my father said the Kaddish prayer, he draped his torso over the coffin, which was lying on the ground, and delivered a keening, wailing apology for any insult or harm he may have done, begging Frédi to forgive us and to intercede for us in heaven. Then the coffin, made of untreated boards, was lowered into the ground and the mourners threw dirt into the grave. I watched the whole procedure as if from a great height, numb, not understanding the full import of his death for me or Mom and Dad. I do not remember whether or not I wept.

At various times in my long life I have thought how great it would be to have my brother at my side—at our various graduations, whenever I did well or poorly, when I had complaints against one parent or another, at my wedding, at the births of my children, and at their life events. How nice it would have been to have Frédi to share with me the aging of my parents and the responsibility of caring for them. In short, I have never stopped missing him, and regard with some envy my friends who are fortunate to have siblings. Mom and Dad never stopped mourning for him. Some of her zest for life left my mother after Frédi's death. For years, I would note at times she would sit quietly by herself, taking sobbing, deep breaths.

In early January 1943, Grandfather Gottesmann had a stroke. He was taken from Nagyleta to the Jewish hospital in Nagyvarad where we visited him. He was lying in bed, pale, partially paralyzed, hardly able to speak. After a few days, he realized he would not survive and asked to be taken back to Nagyleta, to die at home. My father and Noszi hired a taxi on January 12 and sat Grandfather between them for the trip. About one hour outside of Nagyleta my grandfather died sitting in the taxi. Dad and Noszi propped him up to keep him from falling over, in order to keep the driver ignorant, fearing he would involve the police, which would result in interminable delays. Sometimes even bribes would not speed things up.

Grandpa was buried in the small cemetery in Nagyleta, next to his brother Rabbi Kalman and his mother Gitl. He was sixty-one. As I mentioned, he foresaw that the twentieth century would be full of strife, and told my mother, "I do not envy those who will live after me, because life will be difficult." Years later, Mom expressed gratitude that he died when he did and missed the full brunt of the Shoah in Hungary, a country to which he was loyal and for which he had fought during the First World War. She felt he would have collapsed. His disposition was too refined to endure such suffering.

When I recall my grandfather's loyalty to Hungary, the accusations leveled against Jews of being disloyal citizens angers me still. There was very little basis for this in fact, and I have often wondered why Jews continued to express so little hostility toward the Hungarians, even in private, until it was too late to flee, i.e., when it became clear that the Jews were doomed. Only then did most wise up. Still, even after the Shoah tens of thousands of them decided to remain there as citizens. A few idiots even expressed the desire to help the Hungarians to build socialism in Hungary!

The War Draws Near

As the tide of war turned against the Axis following the Russian victories at Moscow and Stalingrad (now Volgograd), the Red Army began its major westward push that over nearly two years of hard, bloody fighting costing millions of lives brought it to Berlin. The Germans demanded of their reluctant Hungarian allies that they throw more and more men onto the Russian front. We saw increasingly longer lines of Hungarian soldiers marching and riding into the mountains, along with their equipment. Jewish men of fighting age, irrespective of marital or parental status, were also drafted, not into the army but as slaves into work battalions (*munkatábor*), and sent to the Eastern front.

Jewish men returning from the front reported that they were being used for digging trenches, hauling material, and serving as human shields for the Hungarian troops. Positioned in between the "real" Hungarian army and the Russians, the Jews were the first to be hit by whatever was incoming. We were asking ourselves what had happened to the Hungarian heroes of old who prided themselves on their physical bravery and readiness to sacrifice their lives for their Magyar homeland. We concluded that the history books and history teachers probably had lied.

In contrast to World War I, where many Jews distinguished themselves by their bravery and disproportionately died in battle, the Jewish men were not eager to participate in World War II. Was this treason by the "perfidious" Jews, or betrayal of Jewish loyalty by the government? Were the Jews supposed to serve and sacrifice for a government whose policy it was to treat them as vermin? Even under a dictatorship a government and its subjects have a reciprocal obligation to each other. In the absence of any reciprocity, a government deserves no loyalty or obedience from its subjects.

My father did his bit to sabotage the Hungarian army. I happened to be in his office one day, and saw him treat a large deep ulceration on a man's left leg. I asked him what it was. Surprisingly, he explained that he had placed the wound to keep the man from being taken into the work battalion. He used a chemical that caused large, ugly, deep, slow-healing ulcers, and then treated the ulcers. He did this with a number of men. At the same time, he certified the men as being unfit for service. Fortunately, in those relatively early days, before the Germans invaded, this was accepted, and the men were reprieved at least for a while. Dad, of course, swore me to secrecy, and I must have appreciated the gravity of what I had been told because I mentioned the episode to no one.

In the spring of 1943, my father was drafted to serve as physician to the Hungarian army and the population of a mountain village near Munkacs called Csontos (now Kostryna). He disappeared for one to two weeks at a time. When he reappeared, he was preoccupied, harried, disheveled, unshaved, and dirty. We visited Csontos once. I was nine, and enjoyed the break in the mountains, unable to appreciate the full import of what was going on.

On one of his furloughs, my father gave me an injection that was meant to prevent epidemic typhus. It must have worked, because I never contracted typhus. However, a few weeks later he came home with a high fever that almost killed him. Subsequently he told me he had contracted the disease.

He had not taken the preventive medicine because he was able to obtain only one dose, and had given me the injection meant for him. This sort of thing happened repeatedly. How could I not love him and feel beholden to him for my very life?

In what can only be considered an act of blind optimism my mother gave birth to Solomon (Shlomo), my youngest brother, in November 1943 at our house. I have no idea what my parents were thinking, and never had the chutzpah to ask. The brith ceremony was a somber affair. Grandma Irene, who was living with us, took on the role of nurse.

One day in mid-1943 a short, stocky high-ranking Hungarian officer of severe, serious mien, appeared at our house with his orderly. He ordered us to provide him with our living/dining room as living quarters. Suddenly, Hungarian officers were in and out of the house, and we lost the use of most of our downstairs rooms. This officer was always curt, all business. After about three months, the orderly suddenly packed his bags, and they left—abruptly, with hardly a "thank you."

As Hungarian anti-Jewish acts multiplied and stories of German cruelty filtered in, we prayed for a rapid Allied victory, especially on the eastern front, and hungered for truthful news, which the Hungarian radio and newspapers did not provide. Only propaganda favorable to the Axis was broadcast, and it was illegal to listen to foreign news broadcasts.

My father simply ignored this injunction. He listened to the BBC news on our Telefunken radio with shortwave capability. He would listen at night huddled over the radio, tuned to a low volume, with the doors and windows closed. Often, relatives and trusted friends would drop by to listen. We used large map of Europe on the wall near the radio to follow the course of the war.

We greeted with great relief and satisfaction the halting by the Russian army of the rapid German advances at Moscow, Leningrad, and Stalingrad, and the subsequent reversal of movement as the Russians drove the Germans westward, back toward Berlin. We hoped they would reach us in time to spare us from more trouble. But the Russians were too slow, and Hungary's ruler, Regent Admiral Miklos Horthy, failed in his inept, belated attempts to extricate Hungary from the war.

The German Army in Munkacs

The Hungarian parliament and government had been divided in its response to the ascent of Hitler to power. The landed gentry, industrialists, and the army leadership were highly nationalistic and had never given up on their claims to the lands lost in World War I. They favored an alliance with Germany because they thought an alliance would help them to achieve their goals of "recovering Hungarian land" at a small cost in men and material, thinking the Germans would take most of the risks and do the bulk of the fighting, while the Hungarians would quietly benefit. The indigenous Hungarian Arrow-cross (Nyilas) Nazi party led by Ferenc Szálasi, of course, strongly supported the alliance. On the other hand, the Social Democrats, Socialists, and the Small Holder Party opposed any alliance. They wished to remain neutral.

None of the parties wished to side with the Western democracies, apparently because they correctly viewed Britain's Chamberlain-led government and the French as weak and unreliable against any potential German reprisals. The United States was in full-blown isolationism. Germany, of course, wanted Hungary as an ally, and applied both persuasion and coercion.

In the late 1930s, with Admiral Horthy's support, the government made its decision to ally itself with Germany. Early in the war when things looked good for the Axis and few Hungarian soldiers were dying, Horthy was a hero. That quickly changed when, as a result of their catastrophic losses on the eastern front, the Germans began to coerce more and more Hungarian involvement. By 1944, it was clear to all that the Axis were losing the War. Horthy gradually lost the confidence of the Germans. Rumors abounded that he was trying to make a separate peace with the Allies. For whatever reasons, the Germans decided to invade Hungary.

Elements of the German army entered Munkacs on an overcast morning in March 1944. Long columns of heavily armed infantry marched past our house, accompanied by loaded personnel carriers, tanks, and artillery. It took them more than forty minutes to pass our house. Both the Wehrmacht and SS were present. SS officers wore hats with visors, long black-leather coats belted at the waist, long boots, and pistols. The death's-head symbol was pinned to their hats and the lapels of their coats. Armbands on their coats displayed the swastika. The officers carried riding whips. This was not a friendly parade by a visiting ally. They marched with their arms at the ready, determined, menacing expressions on their faces. If the troops were meant to intimidate, they certainly succeeded. Suddenly, uniformed German soldiers seemed to be everywhere in the city. I did not know what all this portended, but I knew it was not good.

Apparently, by October 1944, the Germans had had enough of Horthy and replaced him with the rabid Hungarian Nazi Ferenc Szálasi at the head of the puppet government. By that time we had long been in the concentration camps. So Horthy gets some of the credit for our deportation.

Within a few days of the invasion the Jews of Munkacs were forced to wear yellow armbands and stars of David on our chests, curfews were imposed, and any remaining Jewish stores were closed and confiscated. After two to three weeks, Hungarian gendarmes herded the Jews from all over town into our neighborhood, which became the ghetto. Nine families in addition to our own were moved into our house, creating chaos and overflowing toilets. No one knew exactly what to expect, but there was no running away from the situation. People felt trapped. Parents could not protect their children from the ominous menacing future. It is fair to say there was much panic, manifested by much unfocussed hyperkinetic speech and activity, and even much praying— all to no avail.

At about that time my parents gave a pillowcase full of money to a maid of ours in return for her taking baby Solomon to her home to care for him until the situation became settled. She took the money, but never returned for Solomon.

Fortunately, we were spared the worst of the ghetto experience. My father was drafted to serve as physician to the village of Barkaszo (now Barkasove) about an hour from Munkacs, by horse and wagon. Grandmother Irene, my mother, my brother Solomon, and I were permitted to go with him.

In Barkaszo, we moved into the house of two elderly unmarried sisters, where my mother and Grandma tried to keep a kosher kitchen, while my father practiced medicine. The village was quiet and pleasant, and as usual we saw little of my father. He was busy. The two sisters were helpful and correct. My mother and Grandma became very inventive with the cuisine, because there was no kosher food to be had. The Jews of Barkaszo had been herded into the ghetto.

Two memories stand out. First, my mother and Grandma made delicious meat-free "hamburgers" using hardboiled eggs, bread and vegetables, which they called "false hamburgers." Second, I overheard a nighttime conversation between my parents about the terrible conditions in the Munkacs ghetto and the suicide of the Steinberger family. When the gendarmes had arrived to take them into the ghetto, Dr. Steinberger killed Gita, his wife, and himself with injections of poison. They were not the only ones to do so. My parents were discussing whether they should do the same thing. I piped up and said that I wanted to live. Mom tells me that stopped any further considerations of suicide. She also said that the desire to see the outcome of the coming "adventure" kept her alive later, in the camps.

During the few weeks we stayed in Barkaszo, the Hungarian gendarmes, *not* the German soldiers, herded the Jews of Munkacs from the ghetto into a brick factory at the edge of town. We heard that during the move, people who were slow were beaten and a few were shot, among them Tibor's grandfather, the owner of the *succah* with the marvelous roof.

I permanently lost track of my friend Tibi, and later heard he and his family perished in Auschwitz.

In mid-May 1944 a couple of weeks past my tenth birthday, two gendarmes, resplendent in their feathered hats with capes covering their shoulders and armed with rifles, ordered us to pack. They were going to take us to Munkacs for "a few days." We did not believe them, but we had no choice except to comply. They had the guns. My mother begged our landladies to take Solomon and care for him until we returned. They refused. The gendarmes ordered us into a horse-drawn freight wagon. In a short time we were in the brick factory, reunited with our extended family.

The brick factory occupied several acres. Bricks were stored in a number of large storage sheds. In normal times bricks were shipped out by train, and several sets of railroad tracks had been laid for that purpose. The Jews of Munkacs were living between the bricks on dirt floors covered with straw. Families spread blankets on the straw and carried on with daily life cheek-to-jowl. We had little to eat.

For the first time in my life I ate non-kosher food. My parents urged me to eat the ham they had brought from Barkaszo, and I did. The fact that a bolt of lightning did not strike me as a result told me, for the first time, that God either forgave me, did not care about me, or that the rabbis had been telling me untruths. In fairness I should add that when life is at stake, the eating of non-kosher food is permitted by the rabbis.

After a few days, the gendarmes told us my father was needed back in Barkaszo and loaded us on a wagon. However, it was to be only his immediate family. Grandma had to stay behind. Mom pleaded, cried, and carried on, to no avail. Grandma reassured us she would be fine with the rest of the family, and encouraged us to leave without her. We returned to Barkaszo. This episode had an enormous effect on my mother. She talked about it in sorrow and bitterness until her death, emphasizing the terror engendered in her by the separation, and the cruelty of the Hungarian gendarmes who enforced the separation.

Two days later, without explanation, the gendarmes were back in Barkaszo. On the same horse-drawn wagon they returned us to the brick factory for the final time, reuniting us with Grandma. It is a tribute to the determined, fanatical anti-Semitism of those in power that they denied themselves and their fellow Hungarians the services of a gifted, caring physician in order to kill a few more Jews.

In hindsight, it is surprising that the rough treatment by the gendarmes, the menacing pointing of rifles, and the repeated dislocations evoked no sense of panic in me. I did not cry. I merely went along quietly. The sheltering presence of my parents provides a partial explanation. But at some point, I do not know when, I must also have become emotionally numbed.

Deportation to Auschwitz-Birkenau

Cattle cars stuffed full of people were leaving the brick factory daily. The gendarmes told us we were being taken on a one-day voyage to work camps in the center of Hungary. We found this lie reassuring, because it was better than the rumor that turned out to be real, that we would be sent to Poland to be killed. When our turn came, fifty of us carrying a few pieces of hand luggage and a little food were pushed into a cattle car, one of many cars comprising the train. The doors were locked. At the first stop a few hours later, German guards replaced the Hungarians. We knew then that the

Hungarian gendarmes had lied to us. We were not going into Hungary, but we still did not know our destination.

We spent three days in that crowded cattle car. The toilet facility consisted of one bucket. It was almost always overflowing onto the floor, so we were standing, walking and sitting in each other's excrement. Quite a change from the meticulously clean house my mother kept at 10 Munkacsi Mihaly Street. Of course there were no provisions for privacy or for washing any part of one's body, even our hands. We made a few short stops; the doors were opened and the bucket emptied, but the floors were not cleaned and no one was permitted to descend. People could not sit or lie down unless someone else stood up. Given the filth on the floor it was preferable to stand, but eventually one had to rest one's feet. As we lowered ourselves into the muck, our hands became soiled and pants filthy. We were given no food or drink.

From the time the Germans invaded Hungary in March 1944 until the train stopped for the final time on about May 26, we had gradually been converted from civilized prosperous individuals—living in what had for centuries been proudly proclaimed as the progressive, civilized, Christian Europe that had felt entitled to impose itself, to civilize, and to convert the barbarous heathens of the world to the loving religion of Christianity and the wonders of Western civilization—to a stinking, cowering mass. We were deliberately brought to this state by people who had been taught for millennia that Jews were the Antichrist, disease-carrying vermin, devils, bloodsuckers, capitalists, and simultaneously communists. It must have felt familiar and natural to denigrate, calumniate, rob, torture, and kill the Jews. It had all been done before, albeit on a smaller scale. Hitler and his thugs merely validated, confirmed, and strengthened long-held attitudes and provided the modern industrial-scale tools to act in a major way.

Some people in the transport were lucky; they died during the trip and were spared the subsequent fate of the rest. By the time we arrived at our destination, my nervous system must have adapted because I moved without emotion and probably remained that way for most of the following year.

SS troops armed with automatic guns and holding onto ferocious-looking German shepherds ordered us off the train onto a concrete platform, yelling, *"Macht schnell! Macht schnell!"* (Move it! Move it!) All belongings of any worth were to be left behind on the platform upon pain of death. We were permitted to carry only our clothes. My mother threw away her diamonds, which she had hidden in a tube of toothpaste. I discarded my stamp collection.

We proceeded toward the front of the train toward a line of SS officers. The soldiers were shouting, "If you are strong and can walk a few kilometers, go to the left. If you cannot, go to the right and trucks will take you." My mother was carrying my baby brother Solomon, Grandma was walking beside her, and I followed. My father ran ahead. In few minutes he was back. We do not understand how he made it back to us, since everyone was forced to move only in one direction, forward. He told me to say, if asked, that I was sixteen years old. He told my mother to say she was a nurse. He took Solomon from my mother and gave him to Grandma.

When we reached the line of officers, my father volunteered to the officer in charge—who later, in the camp, was identified for us as the "great medical experimentalist" Dr. Mengele, whose activities later stimulated the physicians' trials at Nuremberg, and later the Helsinki Declarations on human experimentation—that my age was sixteen and my mother was a nurse. Mengele told Grandma and Solomon to go right and the rest of us to go left. That was the last time we saw Grandma and Solomon. She was fifty-six years old. He was seven months old. Others who "went by truck" were Aunt Jolan, her children Esther and Beinish, Aunt Irene and her two children, and Mechl and his wife.

After that, they separated men from women, and my mother went off with the cousins. For the next year we did not know whether she was alive or dead.

The camp was surrounded by double rows of barbed wire fencing, which we were told was electrified. At frequent intervals along the fence were watchtowers containing mounted machine guns, manned by SS guards. The air stank of burning flesh. The sights of the fire and smoke and the smell were constantly with us. It made for a potent sensory experience. As we entered the camp, veteran inmates told us that we were in Auschwitz-Birkenau.

Prisoners supervised by SS guards told us to strip, then took our clothes, shaved our heads, and gave us button-down jackets and pants made of blue-striped gray material. They also told us that we would never again see the relatives who had gone "by truck," because they were probably being gassed and burned as we spoke. I simply could not absorb the news.

The prisoner uniform represented my first pair of long pants. In Europe at that time boys of my age wore short pants with long socks or knickers. The purchase of the first pair of long pants was considered a rite of passage toward adulthood, an event to be celebrated. I "celebrated" this rite in Auschwitz by giving up my childhood naiveté.

Along with wearing the long pants came the never-to-be-forgotten knowledge seared into my brain of what human beings w ere capable of doing to each other. Was that the knowledge that God did not want Adam and Eve to learn? Or did He not want them to know what evil He was capable of tolerating or actively inflicting? Is God capable of being ashamed of Himself?

A unique identifying number and colored triangular symbol were sewn on the left breast pocket of each jacket. My recollection is that my number was 90140. The colors of the symbols represented the crime for which one was incarcerated. For example, murderers wore green triangles. Jews wore two triangles that formed the Star of David, for the "congenital disease" or "crime" of being Jewish.

We lived in wooden barracks filled with three-tiered bunks, each level covered with straw. Ten persons slept on each tier. My father and I, my uncles Henrik and Nathan, and my cousin Tuli stayed together. We ate watery soup with a little grass floating in it—we called it grass soup—and coarse dark German bread (which I cannot stand to eat to this day). I wish I could remember what we spoke about, but I cannot, except that I heard constant preoccupation with food, with when the war would be over, and who would survive long enough to be liberated.

The toilets in an adjacent building were long open trenches with wooden boards serving as seats. Many left their seats with soiled pants from dysentery. Lye was tossed into the trenches, and the stench of excrement, lye, and burning flesh in the crematoria made for a potent and unforgettable olfactory mixture.

Our jobs consisted of digging holes in the ground in front of the barracks, shoveling the soil into triangular mini-railroad dump cars, pushing the cars perhaps twenty yards away on a narrow gauge rail, and dumping out their contents. We then refilled the cars with soil and reversed the process until the holes were refilled. This make-work was taken seriously. *Kapos* (prisoner trustees/supervisors) beat slow workers with truncheons made of rubber hoses filled with metal rods, resulting in maiming and killing. The German guards chose kapos from among the bullies and murderers.

Inmates died daily from starvation, disease, or beatings by guards or kapos. Some prisoners deliberately ran to the fence, where they were electrocuted and shot. One day an angry kapo took a swing at the man next to me with a shovel, hit him in the neck. The man fell and was carried away. On another day the same kapo took a swing at my head. Fortunately, I ducked in time and ran.

Every day, bodies of those who had died were loaded onto the little railcars and taken to an area at the back of the toilet building, separated from the rest of the building by a six-foot-high wall made of loosely fitted wooden boards. I would frequently peek through the wall, transfixed by the dozens of naked, pale, thin male bodies stacked like cordwood.

Much later, when I was in medical school, our instructors of anatomy would complain about the scarcity of cadavers for our anatomic studies. German medical schools in the 1930s and 1940s did not suffer similar shortages. They merely had to place orders for various anatomic specimens with the appropriate concentration camp authorities to obtain prime Jewish bodies and organs. Some of the bodies I saw behind the wall may have been among those shipped off to teach German doctors-to-be human anatomy. Some of these specimens were preserved for the benefit of German medicine, and used for many years after the war. The Jews were a gift that kept on giving.

The Warsaw Ghetto

After about two weeks in Auschwitz we were loaded into cattle cars and some time later arrived in another camp. Our fellow prisoners told us we had arrived at the destroyed Warsaw ghetto. I, of course, did not know what that meant, but I soon learned from relatives and other inmates, and much later from study.

A few months before our arrival to the Warsaw ghetto, tens of thousands of Polish Jews had already died of typhoid, tuberculosis, other diseases, and starvation, and hundreds of thousands had been shipped off to Treblinka to be killed. Only fifty thousand remained. A group of fighters led by Mordechai Anilewitch decided that if they were fated to die anyway, they would die fighting, taking with them as many German soldiers as possible. They fought the vaunted German army that had brought the *Blitzkrieg* to Poland and France with a few rifles, pistols, and Molotov cocktails. In response, the German army, using tanks, airplanes, artillery, and infantry, systematically burned down the ghetto and killed its inhabitants. But it took them several weeks, and they lost significant numbers of men and war machines in the process. It took the Germans longer to capture the Warsaw ghetto than it took them to subdue the French army, the largest in Europe.

The Germans created our camp for the specific purpose of salvaging the remains of the ghetto buildings for any reusable materials, e.g., bricks and metal beams to be used for building repairs in Germany. So, instead of attending school with my classmates, I participated in on-the-job training, marching out to the salvage site with my fellow inmates, where my specific job was to remove mortar from bricks with a trowel and pile the bricks into neat piles. I sometimes did not see my father for several hours during the day, even though he worked at a nearby site. Others loaded the bricks onto freight cars. The trains went to Germany. One could say that the Germans stole not only the wealth of Poland but even the rubble of the buildings that they had destroyed. I wonder what Beethoven and Goethe would have thought.

The population of the camp consisted of Jews from Poland, Greece, and in particular, Salonika, Czechoslovakia, and Hungary. There were also non-Jewish political prisoners, murderers, and homosexuals. We lived in barracks not unlike the ones we had come to know in Auschwitz.

Every morning before going off to work and every evening after returning from work my father and I, along with my uncles and cousin Tuli, lined up for *appel* (roll call). The meticulous Germans were eager to account for everyone. Indeed, *appel* exemplified the ruthless, punctilious attention to detail with which the Germans carried out their murderous enterprise. Breakfast consisted of tea and black bread. We sometimes had lunch, more often not. In the late afternoon we marched "home" to line up for *appel* again. We then had dinner of grass soup, black bread with a pat of margarine, and tea, eaten in the barracks. The black bread sometimes tasted strongly of straw and sawdust, the tea was brewed of who knows what, and the soup was thin, darkly colored with floating grass and rarely small bits of blutwurst in it. Before going to bed, we picked the lice out of our clothes as best as we could, and then fell into our bunks.

The identification and killing of lice is a fine art. You have to know that lice like to live in the folds of the body in areas like the neck, the crotch, and armpits. They camp out in the seams of clothes and are difficult to find, but their presence is strongly suggested by the unpleasant itching they engender. The combination of dirty bodies, hands, and fingernails along with scratching of itching injured skin can lead to unpleasant and at times dangerous skin infections. Killing lice requires putting them on one thumbnail and crushing them between two thumbnails. The crushing produced a little snapping sound and a little squirt of blood, my blood, onto my thumbnail. (When we learned in medical school about louse-borne diseases, I knew all about "practical lousology.")

Kapos and soldier-guards ruled the camp. Instant obedience was expected. Cursing (*verfluchtete Jude*—damned Jews, *schweinhund*—pig-dog) and beatings with the hoses were constant. I was frightened, tired, and hungry most of the time.

At that point my father did not function as a physician. He worked along with others in the salvage operation. However, he did speak up to the kapos and guards in defense of the sick or infirm. On more than one occasion he received "formal" punishments for it, ten lashes across the back with the hose, in front of amassed inmates, designed for maximum effect on him and the onlookers. Frankly, I do not know how he survived those beatings; many did not.

On the Road from Warsaw to Kutno and Dachau

Rumors about the progress of the war along the Russian front were widely circulated and intensely discussed. In August 1944 we heard that the Russians were near Warsaw. Some said, "You'll see, we'll soon be liberated by the Russians." Instead, the Germans told us we were being "evacuated." That those wishing to be transported by truck should go to one area of the camp, and those willing to hike, to another. We were grateful to the Germans for their unoriginality. They repeated the same story they had told us before they sent us off to Auschwitz. Since we knew well what was meant by "truck transport," the members of our family decided to hike. We packed our metal soup bowls, spoons, and a few rags and set off flanked by armed SS men. The "wandering Jews" were off again. Within a few minutes we heard machine-gun fire behind us. Our distrust of the Germans had been vindicated.

Approximately two thousand prisoners hiked with "encouragement" from the guards placed at intervals of a few yards on both sides of our column. Although it was hot, we were given little food and no water. We took this as signs that that this evacuation was not being carried out for our own benefit, i.e., to be "saved" from the "brutal" Russians; rather it was an attempt by the Germans to hide or delay the discovery of their brutal and murderous acts insofar as possible, and to save their slaves for another day for any work they might still be able to perform.

On the afternoon of the second day we reached the banks of a river tired, dusty, dehydrated, with filthy, blistered feet. The guards beat or shot at those who attempted to approach the river. They, of course, took all the water they wanted, and taunted us as they washed their hands and faces, drank, rinsed their mouths, and poured water onto the ground, laughing in our faces. My father begged a soldier to let him get me some water. In reply, the soldier cursed him and hit the left upper front side of his chest with the butt of his rifle, knocking him onto the ground. My father screamed as he fell. I was determined to be brave, not to show any pain to the Germans, should they afflict me with pain. Fortunately, they did not test my resolve.

We commenced the march. Those falling behind were shot. Toward dusk we reached a large field where we would rest for the night. The field was very crowded and noisy. People milled around trying to find friends and relatives lost during the day. At twilight, news filtered back to us that Greek Jews had started digging in the ground with sticks and their metal soup bowls and had found water one-foot down. Soon there were holes all over the field and people were able to obtain at least a few sips of muddy liquid. The Germans, livid with anger, lashed out with whips, hoses, and rifle butts attempting to keep people from digging and from drinking, to no avail. There were simply too many thirsty people to be contained.

Some prisoners considered the finding of water to be a miracle from God. I wondered why He had brought us to this field in the first place.

On the third day it rained, bringing relief. We marched for a few more hours to a railway siding near the town of Kutno, still in Poland, where the guards loaded us into cattle cars. Some time later, we were unloaded at a large camp called Dachau.

My father told me that of the two thousand people setting off from the Warsaw ghetto, half died or were killed on the march.

Dachau

Dachau was the venerable death camp near Munich where many of the early opponents of Hitler were imprisoned and martyred, including many of his own countrymen. It reminded me of Auschwitz, with its electrified fences, guard towers, SS guards, dogs, and crematorium. Here, too, the chimney belched smoke redolent of burning flesh. After disembarkation, we were told we were going to be marched to showers.

As we were marching, I felt a sense of accomplishment at having survived an ordeal, sort of what a soldier might have felt after surviving the Battle of the Bulge, except we did not have the satisfaction of shooting back at our enemies. We discussed the likelihood that we were in fact being led to gas-spewing pseudo-showers. Most of our group, confident of the Germans' efficient methods of management, were convinced the Germans, this time, were telling us the truth—not because we felt that they had suddenly turned soft; rather, we felt they were too thrifty to have brought us all the way from Warsaw just to burn us in Dachau. They could have killed us in Warsaw or on the road. At that point it did not matter much to me what the end point of the walk would be. I had already proved my mettle to myself.

After ridding ourselves of the grime, we were powdered with anti-louse powder and given clean uniforms. This treatment gave rise to a rumor that the end of the war must be near. The Germans were treating us unexpectedly well because they wanted us to testify favorably on their behalf to the victorious allies. Unfortunately, the war still had nearly eight months to run, and after a few days of "rest and recreation" in Dachau, we were shipped, again by "cattle-class" train to the Waldlager Muhldorf a few hours away.

Waldlager Muhldorf

The Waldlager (forest camp), although very primitive, was a spa in comparison to the concentration camps in which we had previously subsisted, and I was frankly glad to be there, away from the big concrete-covered places with the evil-smelling chimneys and lime pits. Crazy, was it not? It was relatively small, set in a deep green quiet forest, surrounded only by a single barbed wire fence. However, SS guards with dogs, guard towers with machine guns, and kapos with hoses were still very much present.

When we first arrived in late summer 1944, we were housed in round pressboard huts with peaked roofs painted green as camouflage against aerial bombing, with circular entrances and earthen, straw-covered floors. Each hut held about ten persons who slept with their heads toward the periphery and their feet toward the center. The huts were lined up in rows, and outhouses (holes in the ground sur-rounded by a fence) were spaced throughout.

As the winter approached, we built winter quarters in the forest adjacent to the summer camp. The prisoners laid out rectangular areas on the ground about fifteen feet wide and sixty feet long. A trench was dug down the middle of the long side to a depth of about six feet and a width of three. This served as the central aisle. On each side of the aisle shelves were excavated, six feet wide and four feet deep, which served as bunks. Roofs were constructed of wooden beams and boards. Walls were made of bricks we fashioned out of straw and mud, reminiscent of our bondage in Egypt. The bunks were covered with straw. The entrance was covered with a blanket. To go to bed one had to go down the aisle, find one's spot, turn left or right, and crawl up onto the shelf, under a blanket teeming with lice and other vermin—nevertheless a welcome respite away from the kapos and guards, and sometimes an escape into comforting dreams.

There was one large central kitchen from which food was carried to various areas of the camp for distribution. The guards lived in more plush barracks within sight of the camp across the road outside the fence. The commandant lived in a small villa among his troops.

Sick prisoners and trauma victims were brought to the *Revier* or dispensary, a building that contained a waiting area, cubicles for outpatient examinations and procedures, and a small inpatient ward housing a few double bunk beds. The medications consisted of aspirin and acetaminophen. There were no anesthetics, sterilizers, or antimicrobials. The surgical instruments consisted of scalpels, scissors, and hemostats. Bandages were made of crepe paper. The Revier was the domain of my father and a Hungarian Jewish surgeon, Dr. Bence.

❦

The task of the prisoners under the supervision of Organizations Todt, which used us as slave labor, and the SS was to construct an underground airplane factory in the forest.

At dawn, after a breakfast of "tea" and bread, the men would line up for *appel* and march to the worksite, a mile or so from the camp. There, they would form lines and carry twenty-five-kilogram bags of cement up earthen embankments to cement mixers. Along the way stood guards with rifles and kapos with hoses to encourage a certain pace and rhythm of work. "Slackers" were dealt with severely, frequently dying from the beatings received. After about twelve hours the prisoners returned exhausted, with bruises where they had been beaten and with blistered, bloody, filthy feet. There were no days off and no paydays. Many died of exhaustion and malnutrition. Others simply gave up, and were consigned to the gas chambers in Dachau at the monthly "*Selektions*," during which my father urged me to hide.

Periodically, to add to the general misery, usually after all had returned from work, one of the SS sergeant guards, a short man of about forty-five years with a violent temper and a loud raspy voice, felt the need to assert his authority over a prisoner, usually in sight of other prisoners for maximum effect. Dressed in shiny black boots, a death's-head on his visor cap, with his Lugar pistol drawn, he would chase a poor, malnourished, terror-stricken inmate with soiled trousers around the camp, screaming about some imagined infraction and threatening to shoot the *schweinhund Jude* in front of all of us. I never saw him actually shoot anyone, but all scattered when he appeared.

My initial job was peeling potatoes at the camp kitchen. This was a truly great job since it was relatively easy, kept me out of the weather, and even more important enabled me to steal potatoes to feed the family. Fellow inmates taught me to place the potatoes in my pant legs and bind the pants above my ankles with string, converting them into knickers that held several potatoes on each side without arousing the suspicion of guards or kapos. We baked the potatoes and had "feasts." Occasionally, we received a few grams of wurst. It was my job to fry the wurst in a pan for my father and me. The first time I did, I discovered that the wurst had shrunk to less than half its original size. My father explained that the water content of the wurst must have been extraordinarily high. He frequently shared his portion of food with me, saying he had already eaten or that he was not hungry.

I must have impressed someone in the kitchen because I was promoted to be a part-time washer of the commandant's dishes, including his drinking glasses. I was ten and a half at the time and no one instructed me on how the job was to be performed. The guards permitted me to leave the camp, cross the road, and work in the backyard of the commandant. He had nice crystal glasses, which I would wash in a soapy bowl, rinse in clear water, dry and return to the orderly, who struck me as being nice. One day I piled too many glasses on top of each other, the pile turned over and two glasses broke. No one, including the orderly, said anything, which was a great relief since my life was in their hands. Instead, the next day I was returned to my potatoes full time.

The commandant was a white-haired, soft-spoken, dignified Wehrmacht officer in his sixties. He had been a gymnasium principal in civilian life. I never saw him threaten anyone, or even raise his voice in anger.

After the liberation of the camp, my father found out that he had been ordered to douse camp with gasoline, burn it down, and kill the inmates with machine gun fire. Apparently, other commandants had carried out such orders, leaving the liberators to find burned-out camps and heaps of partially burned, murdered inmates. He did not obey, and so through the disobedience of one man, we were permitted to live. Later, the United States Army questioned my father and other inmates about the behaviors of the Germans during our imprisonment. My father and others testified favorably about the commandant, and he wrote a letter on the old

German's behalf. As a result he was permitted to return to his home soon after the end of the war.

This story reminded me of the Biblical story of Sodom and Gomorra, cities full of evil behaviors, which God wished to destroy. Our patriarch Abraham pleaded with God to save the cities, if even as few as ten righteous men were to be found in them, and God agreed. Unfortunately, there were no righteous men to be found, and God destroyed the cities and their inhabitants.

In *our* story my father played the noble role of Abraham, while the Germans, Sodom and Gomorrah, and the Americans were the all-powerful gods. Although there was never any risk that the Americans would destroy Germany and the Germans, my father's act did demonstrate an Abraham-like nobility, above and beyond what may have been expected of inmates who had so recently been subjected to record levels of barbarity. Clearly, my father and the inmates who testified demonstrated a degree of humanity that distinguished between degrees of evil. Their act also demonstrated an ability to forgive those who showed even minimum decency.

After a few weeks in Muhldorf, my father was able to bring me into the Revier as an assistant/orderly. He wanted to keep a close eye on me because there was a group of homosexuals in the camp. Several were kapos who preyed on young men. One day, one of the Greek prisoners with a black mustache called me over and told me I was a handsome boy, and kissed me on the mouth. He told me if I were to become his friend he would give me lots of food. I had no idea what he was doing, but reported it to my father. He warned me sternly to stay away from this man and his friends, to stay out of sight when they were around. I took his advice. When they waved to me from a distance, I did not wave back. Instead, I ran in the opposite direction. After a while they quit waving.

The Revier provided my father with the opportunity of saving many lives, including those of our relatives. The precarious physical and mental conditions of the prisoners induced by starvation, illness, work without pause, beatings, and injuries could be alleviated by as little as a couple of days of rest. My father used the beds for just such purposes. A few days would suffice to begin the healing of traumatized feet and limbs, the abatement of diarrhea, and the improvement of respiratory infections. Many suffered from multiple infected skin ulcers on their legs probably due to a combination of trauma and impaired immune defenses due to malnutrition. Little could be done for them by way of specific therapy, but bed rest and the cleansing and binding of wounds even in crepe paper helped to tide some people over. Of course many died. My uncles were frequent patients. Cousin Tuli complained that he was given less frequent rest cures than his father and uncles. My father countered that he was young, strong, and healthy, and could work more than the others.

One day a sixteen-year-old Dutch-Jewish boy entered the Revier with shaking chills, fever, and a red, swollen left buttock. The diagnosis of peri-rectal abscess was made. My father told me that the homosexual kapos had done this, that he had been their plaything. Clearly the wolves had been put in charge of the sheep. Dr. Bence decided to operate despite the primitive conditions. The surgery was performed on the bottom tier of a two-tier bunk bed. There was no anesthesia. Some men held the boy still. My father assisted the surgeon and I held the light, sitting on the top bunk. I also wiped the sweat from the brows of the operating team. It is difficult to forget the moaning of the boy, the sight of the deep surgical wound, and the putrid smell of the pus. Amazingly, the boy survived the camp.

The more typical patients admitted to the Revier were severely emaciated men, with sunken cheeks and eyes; arms and legs devoid of muscle; loose skin hanging from the chest, abdomen, and long bones. As a result of the near-absence of subcutaneous fat and muscles, the ribs, femoral condyles at the knee, and the hip and ankle joint were accentuated; abdomens were concave, with the pelvic bones easily visible. Superimposed on malnutrition were the bouts of dysentery circulating around the camp, which further weakened our patients, resulting in soiled pants that were impossible to wash. There were many lesions scattered over the patients' lower extremities, due to work-related trauma or beatings by the guards or kapos, worsened by nutritional deficiency that impaired healing. Invariably these lesions were infected by the dysentery, which ran down the legs and soiled the pants.

Our poor patients walked with a slow shuffling gait and appeared short of breath. The expression on their faces was one of profound depression. They hardly spoke, and when they did, the voices were raspy and hardly audible. They told us they were ready, even eager to die. That they had "had enough." It was impossible to guess their ages. They could have been twenty-five or sixty-five years old, and the camp was filled with people like them.

The malnutrition was due to the conscious policy of the Germans. They fed us starvation diets, exploiting us as slaves, until we died. There was a seemingly unending supply of Jews and others available for slave labor, hence no need to conserve their fitness or even minimum health. The Germans used us and threw us away with less consideration than we give to discarding a used paper cup.

Where were the Christian churches who feel they have much to teach the rest of the world about love, and accuse the Jews of following a harsh unforgiving creed? Is this the world their Messiah has brought us?

My father had the emaciated men placed in bed, cleansed their bodies and their wounds, and covered their wounds with bandages made of crepe paper. Vitamins, nutritional supplements, antibiotic powders, crèmes, or clean (much less sterile) cloth bandages were not available. My father tried to obtain more grass soup than usual for such men, and perhaps an extra ration of sawdust-covered black bread. He also encouraged \such patients to persist. "Can you hear the American bombers flying overhead? Soon we will be liberated." To accomplish any of this for his patients my father had an ongoing discussion with his SS supervisor. When the supervisor had a good day he would agree to allow the patient to be kept in bed for two to three days.

Imagine a daily stream of such men and you have an idea of my father's medical practice. One would not have thought it, but these simple, even primitive measures, saved lives.

Much, much later, about a year after I married Miriam, she told me of an occurrence while she was testing a man's hearing at the Columbia-Presbyterian Hospital's Speech and Hearing Clinic in New York. He was about my father's age and spoke with an accent that sounded familiar to Miriam, because it resembled my father's. The patient looked at her name tag, which bore her recently acquired surname of

Schonfeld. He asked whether she knew a Dr. Schonfeld from Munkacs. It turned out that the man had been at Muhldorf with us, and that my father had saved his life by bringing him into the Revier for a few days of rest. I have heard similar "Dr. Schonfeld stories" many years after the fact, from others. I found my father a hard act to follow both as a physician and a *mensch.*

It has been interesting to contemplate my father's actions in the camps in comparison with the activities of people like Dr. Mengele and his colleagues in Auschwitz. It is also an interesting statistic that about fifty percent of German physicians joined the Nazi party in the early 1930s, out of choice, it appears, not compulsion. This represented a gross betrayal of even the minimum standards of the medical profession. The conclusion I draw from my father's actions is that persons like him and Dr. Bence helped salvage the good name of our profession under awful circumstances.

⚭

As the months in the various camps passed, I had become a regular worker at several jobs in several camps, going to work like an adult, acquiring the "work ethic" of necessity, along with my adult long blue and gray striped pants—all of this between the ages of ten and eleven years.

Despite the working, the misery, and the dying there were prisoners who were able to provide enjoyable lighter moments, which I consider awe-inspiring, under the circumstances. People told stories of home, jokes, and best of all sang Yiddish songs. There was one short, muscular Polish Jew of about thirty-five, who had been in various camps in

Poland and Germany for four years and nevertheless retained his humor. How he managed to survive is an unanswerable question. He had a very pleasant baritone voice and provided us with songs such as "Oif Dem Pripitchik," "Mein Shtetele Belz," "Rozinkes mit Mandlen," and "The Song of the Partizans." My father, who had a great voice and loved to sing, sometimes joined in.

I became reasonably fluent in German, certainly fluent enough to understand *schweinhund* and *verfluchtete Jude*, and enjoyed hearing the song "Lili Marlene" sung in German. I also drew comfort from my father's presence, and from frequent dreams of food and of my mother hugging and kissing me. Of course I also had nightmares. In one, a German soldier is running toward me with a bayonet pointed toward my chest. Just before he reaches me I awaken, terrorized and in a sweat. This nightmare lasted for several years after the camp. I would wake up startled, wondering where I was. It was comforting to realize I was in my own bed in East St. Louis, Illinois. Gradually over some years those dreams left me.

General George Patton's American Soldiers Liberate Us

With the passage of the war as German casualties multiplied, the German army came to rely increasingly on boys and older men to fight the war. In the spring of 1945 we noticed that fifty-plus-year-old men, in Wehrmacht uniforms were gradually replacing the younger SS guards. On average, the older men were not as gratuitously cruel as the younger men had been. We overheard them making light of Hitler's promises that Germany would win the war with new weapons that were to appear at any moment. The guards would rhyme, "*Wir alte apfen, sind die neue waffen.*" (We old apes are the new weapons.) Their joke fueled our hope that we might be nearing the end of our incarceration.

As spring progressed we also saw and heard increasing numbers of American bomber formations flying overhead. Occasionally we heard some muffled explosions. Rumors kept flying around the camp that the American army was approaching. Indeed, the presence of the bombers and the aging of the guards were taken as evidence of the freedom to come. Still, some prisoners doubted we would be permitted to survive. They were convinced the Germans would rather kill us than see us free. By that point, based on the aging of the guards, the rumors of Allied progress on all fronts, and what we took to be the Americans' bombing nearby, I was pretty confident that we would survive to be freed.

On the last day of April 1945, the guards began to disappear, but enough of them remained at their guns to keep us inside the fence. Then on May 2nd the rest of the German guards disappeared. At about eleven a.m. we saw a lone soldier wearing an American-style helmet, a khaki uniform, and laced boots walking on the road leading to the camp. He was alert, walking bent at the waist, holding a tommy gun at waist level, scanning from side to side. A few yards behind him followed a couple of other soldiers. Behind them two tanks were moving slowly. A few men opened the gates and moved into the road in front of the camp. My cousin Tuli addressed them in English, and they answered, definitively identifying themselves as Americans by their accents. The tanks and soldiers entered. It was six days shy of my eleventh birthday.

We mobbed them. The tank hatches opened and the soldiers started throwing candy and C-rations at us. I picked up a C-ration. It was shaped like a brick with a waxy outer covering. I thought it was a large piece of chocolate and started to eat it, but I could not bite into it. One of the soldiers showed me how to open it and I found a can of spam, crackers, five cigarettes, and toilet paper. I rapidly devoured the food.

In a few minutes the Americans had rounded up a few of the guards. The prisoners started to beat them. But, our liberators wrested them away from us and placed them on top of the tanks, to protect them from us. It was clear to me on that day, for the first but not the last time, that although the Americans were sympathetic to our plight, they did not feel what we felt.

A few years later when we were already in America, the U.S. government announced that the Germans were becoming our allies in the Cold War against the communists. The scene of the German guards standing on the tanks flashed back into my mind. The tank scene also reappeared during the various Arab-Israeli wars when the U.S. government helped Israel, but always forced it to stop and retire just short of a decisive victory over the Arabs; perhaps the victories, had they been permitted to be decisive, might have driven some of the Arabs to the peace table. One cannot know, but the Americans could have permitted the experiment to be performed at least once, just to see what effect an unequivocal victory by Israel would have accomplished for peace in the Middle East.

A few days after liberation we were moved a short distance in American Army trucks to a large beautiful convent located on a hill above the Inn River. Its previous inhabitants had consisted of disabled and retarded Germans, cared for by Catholic nuns. The nuns told us that these unfortunates had been euthanized in accordance with Nazi dictates. How ironic! The murders of the German inmates by Germans provided us with the housing where we began our recuperation.

The big white three- or four-story structure, decorated with metal trim and two towers topped by cupolas, possessed a spacious pebble-covered courtyard surrounded by several acres of green grounds. The food was good and plentiful, the beds were clean, and no one threatened us or beat us. American military trucks and ambulances and German cars were in and out every day, hauling food, linens, and people. We spent six weeks recuperating, eating, sleeping and walking around the grounds. American soldiers, doctors, German nuns, and other staff helped us to return to better health.

Our happiness was marred, however, by deaths of fellow former inmates. Saddest were the deaths that occurred within a few days of liberation due to dysentery. The starvation-induced atrophy of gastrointestinal tracts rendered these people unable to handle the foods presented to them. People also died in auto accidents. If God was responsible, He had a fine sense of irony, killing people who had managed to survive the torments and deprivations of the camps before they could enjoy the fruits of their survival; but in the minds of believers He was credited with saving lives and not blamed for deaths.

Some of the men, who had been without a woman for one or more years, befriended the German *frauleins* for sex. Interesting that within a very few weeks after the war that had meant to exterminate the Jews, the *frauleins* were now compliant. My father entered into short-term relations with one of them. He even introduced me to her, and asked me,

"Doesn't she look just like your mother?" I have never held this against him. On the contrary, in hindsight I was pleased he had enough life and energy left to pursue sex. Nor did I ever discuss this with anyone except Tuli, who confirmed the existence of the relationship.

One day a young German man with a car offered to take a couple of young ex-prisoners, including me, to visit a nearby lake. My father approved, so I accepted the invitation although I was uneasy because I was not convinced that this German man could be trusted. He took us in a tiny car. The roads were so full of potholes and the springs on his car so bad that my stomach was queasy most of the way. The trip took two or more hours, but it was worthwhile. The "see," set in a green hilly countryside, was calm, dark blue, and large enough that its distant shore was invisible. Snow-capped mountains were visible in the background some distance away. After staring at the scene for a while, the realization hit me that I was in an area without any surrounding fences for the first time in over a year. Was my mother still alive? Who else survived? Where would life steer us next?

PART III
AFTER

Back to Czechoslovakia

In mid-June 1945 we climbed into U.S. military Dodge trucks, this time without any encouragement from rifle butts, rubber hoses, or curses, and U.S. Army personnel drove us to Pilsen, Czechoslovakia. They had to leave us there because by mutual agreement among Roosevelt, Churchill, and Stalin in Yalta, the farthest point of eastward penetration permitted to the U.S. Army was Pilsen, which therefore became the jumping-off point for those liberated from the camps in the West who wished to return to Central or Eastern Europe. From Pilsen, my father and I took the train to Prague.

In Prague Dad found out that the Russian army was occupying Munkacs. As soon as he learned that, he decided not to return there, despite the agreement the family had made that those surviving the camps would meet in Munkacs. The Munkacser Jews used to call the Russians and Ukrainians "Ivan shtinkes" because both groups were strongly anti-Semitic. It was this anti-Semitism that drove over two million Jews to immigrate to the United States, and more to South Africa, Australia, South America, and elsewhere around the turn of the twentieth century. We had no reason to assume these anti-Semitic attitudes ingrained over millennia had changed.

As an added incentive for staying in the West, we discovered that many Ukrainian men, early in the war, had joined the Nazis in fighting against the Russians. The Ukrainians had a centuries-long grudge against the Russians whom they resented for depriving them of political independence, Ukrainian culture, and their Catholicism. As if that did not suffice, the Communists took away their farms. In the 1930s, under Stalin's policy of agricultural collectivization, Ukrainian landed peasants (dubbed *kulaks* by the communists) were driven from their lands. This policy, mercilessly applied, produced widespread famine. Millions of Ukrainians died.

In 1941 the Ukrainians welcomed the Nazis as liberators, and tens of thousands of Ukrainian men volunteered to join the Ukrainian Nazi Army under the leadership of their own General Vlassov. This army fought alongside the Germans on the eastern front. They also served as guards in death camps. Among Jews, the Ukrainian Nazi troops had the reputation of being even more sadistic than the German SS.

The disincentives for returning to Munkacs are illustrated by two stories about Russian soldiers circulated widely immediately after the war: they apparently liked wristwatches, because they confiscated them, saying, *"Davey chasi"* (Give me your watch.). Watches in the 1940s had to be manually wound every day. The soldiers did not know that, and discarded the watches that had stopped running. So, Soviet soldiers were commonly seen at the end of the war with several watches running up their wrists and forearms.

The other story is that those from primitive villages, of which there were many, did not know about flush toilets and mistook them for sinks. Soviet soldiers washed themselves, their laundry, or other objects in toilet bowls. When they flushed the toilets thinking they were merely filling the bowl with more water, their soaps and other toiletries disappeared. Believing that someone from the floor below was robbing them they would shoot into the bowls. I cannot guarantee the authenticity of these stories, but they were widely circulated and believed.

There was a maxim about Stalin in wide circulation right after the war to the effect that although he fought a good fight against the Germans, he made two big mistakes. First, he showed Europe to the Red Army, thereby opening his soldiers' eyes to the disparities between primitive Russia and advanced Western Europe; and second, he showed the Red Army to Europe, exposing its primitiveness and brutality to Europeans. The effect was that his soldiers became disillusioned with the false propaganda extolling the bounties of communism in Russia. Indeed many veterans of the European war were imprisoned upon returning from Europe to keep them from telling the truth of what they had found in the West. Another effect was to convince the Europeans that they did not wish to live under communism.

My father was convinced that were he to return to Munkacs, he would soon be inundated with patients. He dreaded the prospect of becoming trapped into restarting his practice, under Communist rule with Ukrainians and Russians in charge. The Nazis in a sense had given him the opportunity to start a new life, elsewhere, although he did not quite put it that way. Why should we return there? His choice has turned out to be wise. The people of that region and the Schonfeld family have learned to live very well without each other.

My father knew Prague well. He had spent six years at the Charles University medical school and had graduated in 1928. He decided that we would remain in Prague while he explored opportunities with acquaintances. Awaiting the results of his "networking," we wandered around the city, which had survived the war intact because it had been surrendered to the Germans in 1939. The city occupies both banks of the Vltava (Moldau) river, and there are many attractive bridges, but the Charles Bridge stands out. It is about five hundred years old, impressively decorated. Stone statues of saints and churchmen are spaced every few yards. Jesus Christ is nailed to a cross. Above his head is written *Kadosh, Kadosh, Kadosh,* (Holy, Holy, Holy) in gilded Hebrew letters.

Prague's Jewish population dates back at least eight hundred years. The old Jewish quarter was the home of the famous mystic Rabbi Loew in the seventeenth century, who legend has it created the Golem by pronouncing God's ineffable name over a piece of clay he had fashioned into the shape of a man. The fearless, indestructible Golem protected the Jews against the depredations of their Christian neighbors. At one point the Golem went out of control and Rabbi Loew withdrew the spirit that kept him alive, turning him back into a lump of clay. Legend says the clay can still be found in the attic of the old synagogue.

During the war, the Germans, in anticipation of successfully eradicating the Jewish people, decided to construct a Museum of an Extinct People in Prague. They "collected" Jewish ceremonial artifacts from all over conquered Europe. Thousands of artifacts such as Torah scrolls, Torah medallions, kiddush cups, candelabra, and Seder plates are stored in the synagogues of the old Jewish quarter. Currently, many of these items are on display in the old Jewish quarter, along with a memorial tablet listing the names of the many thousands of Czech Jews who died in the Shoah. A sample of about 150 of these ceremonial objects was assembled into a traveling show known as "The Precious Legacy" that toured several United States museums in the 1980s.

Prague, since the fall of the Berlin Wall in 1989, has become a major tourist attraction. The old Jewish quarter is a strong tourist draw. Similar old Jewish tourist sites have been developed all over Europe. This just goes to illustrate that Jews have been useful beings to the Europeans. In addition to the many cultural, scientific, medical, economic, and artistic contributions they made before the war, as citizens of their countries, the Germans, wasting nothing but the squeal, found uses for parts of their dead bodies such as their gold teeth, hair, skin, and even body fat. After the war, with much of Europe *Judenrein*, desecrated, desolate, orphaned synagogues, fragments of paraphernalia, and memories remained. The synagogues have been restored, in many cases with Jewish money, and have become marketable destinations in the flourishing tourist trade. Here is another example of the Jews being "a gift that keeps on giving." Ironic is it not?

This truth does not diminish the significance of these sites for Shoah survivors and their offspring, and for young Jews who wish to learn about the Shoah and honor its victims. I imagine some small proportion of the non-Jewish population also visit these sites for their own reasons. I have resisted pointing out the irony connected with these Jewish sites to my grandchildren. I do not wish to rob them of their youthful innocence too early in life. It can wait until they are adults.

My father and I went to see the Altneuschul, the old cemetery nearby, and the tower clock with Hebrew letters on its face. We also spent some time at the YMCA where survivors gathered to exchange information on their relatives and friends. We witnessed and participated in several emotional reunions as well as tearful responses to bad news. Several people who had just come in from Munkacs told us that Mom had survived. I was dubious.

Within a few days of our arrival in Prague, my father secured a job, at a tuberculosis sanatorium thirty kilometers south of Prague at Nova Ves pod Pleši. (Apparently, the old network from his medical school days was still in place.)

Before the advent of antibiotic therapy, the most effective antitubercular treatment consisted of a minimum of several months of rest in a calm place where clean fresh air, mild exercise, and wholesome food were available. A limited number of surgical procedures involving the lungs or chest wall were performed, as indicated by the patient's condition. Tuberculosis sanatoria were built all over the world. As soon as he secured the job, Dad sent messages to Mom asking her to join us, and then he and I left by train for Pleš.

Reunion in Pleš and My Mother's Story

As I mentioned previously, my mother had been separated from my brother Solomon, whom she had been nursing. When she arrived at the women's camp in Auschwitz, it was several hours since she had seen her infant son and her lactating breasts were full and painful. She asked one of the veteran inmates when her son and mother would arrive. She told my mother, "See that smoke? That's where your mother and son are. You will never see them again. Get used to it, otherwise you will go crazy and die." Mom remembers being crazy for a while. She felt that she was responsible for sending both Solomon and her mother to their deaths. At the same time, she suffered from her swollen, painful milk-filled breasts that could not be relieved. Yet, she was determined to survive to see how the camp story would end.

After some weeks, the surviving women of the family group traveled by cattle-car train to Stutfhof, another notorious concentration camp in northern Poland. Eventually, they wound up in a work camp in northern Poland. Mom became one of the cooks in the kitchen that fed the SS troops. These women were treated relatively well. They were encouraged to be careful of their personal hygiene, to bathe regularly and to wear clean clothes. Obviously, the SS did this for their own benefit. It was also helpful to the prisoners that one of them, Mrs. G from Munkacs, was sleeping with the sergeant in charge. Mrs. G's actions could have been used to brand her a collaborator with the enemy. My mother had many unkind things to say about that "bitch" who carried herself like a "queen" in the camp "while others were dying." At the same time, Mrs. G exercised her influence to help the other women in the kitchen to survive. Such were the morally ambiguous behaviours evoked in the camps. My mother was also in a favored position. Albeit at considerable risk, she was able to steal food for the cousins.

In January 1945 as the Red Army drew near, the camp was evacuated with the aim of driving the prisoners westward. Seven Jewish women, including the cooks, the cousins, along with their SS guards, separated themselves from the rest of the evacuees. The women persuaded the guards to let them go. In a few days they found their way to the Hela peninsula dear Gdansk, where they passed themselves off as Hungarian Christian refugees and lived on Hela for several weeks.

The Germans and their allies by early 1945 saw the front in northern Poland crumbling under the onslaught of the Red Army. The question became to whom would they surrender, the American or the Russian Army? They much preferred surrendering to Americans because they correctly surmised that the Americans would likely treat them with more consideration than the Red Army. (Of course we admired the Red Army for the way it treated the Germans, believing that the Reds and the Germans deserved each other.) Thus, they tried to escape westward toward Germany, toward the American front. Part of the evacuation was by sea. Early in the spring of 1945, the Germans loaded my mother and her group onto a westward bound ship. The women preferred to be liberated as soon as possible, by the oncoming Russians if necessary, but they had to play along or risk being discovered and killed.

Along with hundreds of others they were deep down in the hold of a ship ready to depart from Hela when Russian airplanes bombed the ship and set it on fire. There was a mad scramble to ascend to the deck in order to disembark. My mother had just gotten over a case of typhus and was very weak. She escaped only with the help of the cousins. They stayed in Hela until May 1945, when the Red Army finally liberated them.

Initially the Russians wanted to imprison them as enemy aliens, despite their protestations that they were Jews. After much pleading, a Russian-Jewish army officer was sent to test them. The women spoke to him in Yiddish. They were then permitted to depart for Munkacs. Over several weeks, they traveled southward by a series of trains through chaotic postwar Poland, toward what they had called home, wondering whom and what they would find.

My mother found our house occupied by a nursery school. So, she went to live with the cousins and spent most of every day at the train station, searching among the arrivals for us.

At the same time we, unaware of her fate, were recovering at the convent near Munich. Survivors arriving at the Munkacs station reported seeing us, but we did not appear. She was prepared to believe that Dad had survived but was very skeptical of reports that I had survived, since very few of my age had. Indeed, many of the "witnesses," in trying to evoke some hope, reported seeing us in places we had not been.

After she had been in Munkacs for some weeks, one of the Munkacser people we had met in Prague arrived. In his thirties, he had been one of the many thousands of members of the Hungarian forced labor battalions that had been captured by the Russians and placed in POW camps. In 1943, the Russians permitted the Czechoslovak government-in-exile in London to form a volunteer Czech Army Corps consisting of Czechoslovak citizen volunteers who were in the USSR. Our Munkacser messenger had volunteered and fought against the Germans alongside the Red Army. The man told my mother that he had just seen my father and me a few days ago in Prague. Mother did not believe him. He then showed her the piece of paper on which my father had written the address where we could be reached. My mother recognized the handwriting and for the first time since her return to Munkacs believed that both my father and I indeed had survived.

Soon my mother and Sari Reinhartz took a series of trains to Budapest where they stopped to visit their cousin Rozsi Nagy, and then traveled on to Prague. Fishi met the train and confirmed our survival. My mother and Sari then took a train to Pleš. Sari related to us a few years ago that, as the train approached the station, my mother saw me and tearfully told Sari, "I am a mother again."

My father had organized a horse and open carriage to take us back to the sanatorium. We rode through the village holding each other and crying, as pedestrians stared at us.

Post-War Inventory of the Family

Sometime after our reunion Mom and Dad traced the fates of the relatives from Munkacs and Nagyleta. Half had survived. The survivors all returned to Munkacs initially, but all except Henryk moved away, either to Israel, Sweden, or the United States.

Tuli's ambitions extended beyond Munkacs, so he came to Prague, where he enrolled in medical school (see his memoirs: Eugen Schoenfeld, *My Reconstructed Life*, Kennesaw University Press). Barely supporting himself with janitorial and lab technician jobs around the medical school, he soon realized there was no future for him in Europe and decided to migrate to America. He heard from friends who had returned to Germany that life was easier there, and the likelihood of receiving an entry visa to the United States was also greater. He decided to try his luck, sneaking across the border with a friend and a group of orphaned children he had agreed to take to a displaced persons camp in Germany. Because he was bright, nervy, and fluent in English, he was able to obtain a job with UNRRA (United Nations Relief and Rehabilitation Administration) working in the displaced persons camps. He became a big shot administrator, with his own car and driver. He arrived to the United States in 1948.

Henryk had agreed to follow his son Tuli, but he delayed his departure because he had found his business intact. For several months after the war, international borders were uncontrolled and people moved freely between countries. Henryk believed he had plenty of time to accumulate some money. He opened his store and, unfortunately for his relationship with his son, the money started coming in. The time he spent in Munkacs provided the opportunity for Henryk and Dr. Geiger, our neighbor pathologist who had lost her husband and family, to start seeing each other. She had no wish to go the United States, stating that she wished to stay to help "build socialism." Henryk became conflicted about leaving.

Finally, late in 1945 he decided to leave. Unfortunately, he had waited too long. By then the borders were closed. Nevertheless, it was still possible to escape, if one was willing to take the attendant risk. For a fee "guides" were available to arrange illegal crossings by bribing border guards to look the other way.

Henryk hired a guide who was either inept or duplicitous. He was caught at the border attempting to cross into Czechoslovakia. His luggage and money were confiscated and he wound up serving six months in prison. Later his store was "nationalized," and he became a poorly compensated employee in what used to be his own store. Eventually, Dr. Geiger and Henryk were married, and both remained in Munkacs. Henryk died in the 1980s and was buried in Munkacs.

Dr. Geiger survived her husband by several years. In her late seventies she decided that she had had her fill of communism (I suppose the cognitive dissonance between "parlor" communism and "real life" communism became intolerable) and she moved to Beer Sheva in Israel, to live out the rest of her days with relatives. She was not the only person disillusioned by communism. It just took her much longer than most, proving what Jews had known for a long time—that not every Jewish doctor is smart.

Tuli felt abandoned by his father, and their relationship was never repaired, despite two visits by Henryk and his wife to the United States.

Nathan (Nandor), bereft of his family, decided to come to America with us and reached St. Louis a few months after us.

Alex Sonnenwirth returned to Oradea (Nagyvarad) from the camps to find that his parents had perished. The girl-friend to whom his mother Betty objected so vehemently also returned. Alex was thrilled to have found someone, but she had picked up a new boyfriend who had amassed some money on the black market. Alex had nothing. She chose the other man. Alex became deeply depressed.

He eventually went to Germany where he attended medical school in Marburg for two years and found a new love, who healed him. Another survivor was also courting the lady and they literally fought for her. Alex won. Still, the friendship among the three survived. Ironically, she and the other man obtained visas to the United States before Alex, who gallantly urged her to grab the opportunity of going to America. He had no idea how long it would take for him to obtain his visa and she risked her own chances if she waited. She departed with his rival whom, she eventually married.

Alex and Tuli both succeeded in winning Hillel Foundation scholarships that supported their immigration to the United States.

Rozsi, the other sister, survived the war in Budapest with her two children, but her husband, who had been drafted into a forced labor battalion, perished on the Russian front. Rozsi stayed in Budapest after the war and raised her two children under difficult circumstances. My parents sent money and clothes from America. In 1956 during the Hungarian revolution, the son escaped to his Aunt Ilonka in Stockholm.

He eventually became a professor of Romance languages in Uppsala. He has been married twice, to two Swedish women, and still lives in Sweden. His sister moved to Stockholm a few years later with her Hungarian Jewish husband-to-be. They married, had a child, and are living in Stockholm.

Sari Reinhartz and Fishi Farkas married in Prague in 1945 and migrated to the United States in 1948. Sari's siblings all survived, Lilly in the United States, and the rest by having gone to British Palestine.

I have asked myself, "Should those who have survived thank God for His mercy, or should they resent His complicity in the killing and wounding of so many?" Is it possible to do both? Perhaps one should do neither, and instead give all the credit to Hitler, his millions of supporters, and the passive bystanders.

Fresh Air in Pleš

The tuberculosis sanatorium at Nova Ves pod Pleši was built on the crest of a high forest-covered hill called Pleš. It consisted of about twenty buildings, set in meticulously maintained grass-covered grounds surrounded by a fence. The village of Nova Ves was spread out below, and a curving paved road led up from the village to a set of imposing metal gates built into stucco-covered brick columns. One needed permission to enter. The gatehouse sat on the left just inside the gates and served as residence to the Dolan family, whose son Jiři became my friend. Mr. Dolan, a pleasant, soft-spoken heavy smoker then in his forties, served as the physician/director's driver, pickup and deliveryman, and gatekeeper.

About one hundred adult patients of both sexes were housed in several one-story buildings. Accommodations were spacious. Each patient had a separate room with one door opening onto an inside corridor and another opening onto an outside veranda that surrounded the building. Some patients brought their own furnishings.

The patients spent several hours daily, year-round, lying on chaise lounges on the verandas and strolling around the grounds. One patient stands out, an attractive, tall, elegant woman in her forties who befriended my parents and me. She visited us frequently and I had the sense that she spoke an elegant Czech. I spoke no Czech, but she encouraged me to speak and corrected my mistakes. My father taught me about tuberculosis and even drew some pictures of healthy and diseased lungs, which I later discovered greatly resembled the drawings of medical texts in clarity. He told me of patients with cavitary disease (which fortunately our friend did not have. We did not socialize with cavitary patients because they were contagious.) Dad treated them by injecting air into their plural cavities under X-ray fluoroscopic guidance, to collapse their cavities, which helped in healing.

The sanatorium employed a large staff of nurses, aides, dieticians, cooks, administrators, and maintenance staff. The three staff physicians and their families shared a two-story multifamily dwelling. My parents and I shared the second floor with Dr. Uchitil and his mother. Each family had bedrooms opening off a large central vestibule with a skylight, which also served as the living room/dining hall. A shared kitchen was available but seldom used, as physicians and their families ate food specifically prepared for them in the house.

The director, Svatopluk Basar, then in his fifties, was a tall, huge man, who carried the honorific title of MUDr, which designated a faculty appointment as "docent" at the medical faculty in Prague. He lived in a large house on the premises with his wife, and had a large black sedan available to him, driven by Mr. Dolan. My father treated him with elaborate courtesy and respect. They maintained a frequent correspondence until Dr. Basar's death in the early 1980s.

Nova Ves was a picturesque village of perhaps two thousand people built on hilly terrain. Most of the houses were single story one-family two- to three-room residences with thick stucco walls, deep-set double-hinged windows, and thatched roofs. The curved main street contained several small, individually owned stores, a church with a steeple, and a tavern that served beer on tap. The church bells rang every quarter hour and could be heard throughout the village and its surrounding fields, even distantly in the sanatorium.

Most of the people in the village were farmers. Their animals and implements were housed in fenced-in areas near their homes. Their lands surrounded the village. The men left their homes early, worked the land all day, and slowly walked home dusty and bowed with fatigue. In late afternoons, wives and children carrying pitchers or buckets would form long lines visible from Pleš outside the tavern. Their containers would be filled with beer and carried home for dinner. The pace of life was slow. People took time to stop for a chat, and most of the road traffic consisted of bicycles, while conveyances were drawn by oxen or moved by people power. Occasionally, an automobile would pass through the village, or a Dodge truck marked with Red Army insignia ferrying Soviet soldiers, or Mr. Dolan on his motorcycle.

A few weeks after she arrived to Pleš, my mother became terribly ill with lower abdominal pain and fever. Dr. Basar arranged for her to be seen by a surgeon in Prague. She underwent surgery but was not doing well due a persistent infection. She appeared again to me to resemble a concentration camp inmate, and I was wondering whether I was going to lose her. After a few days in hospital, my father somehow obtained penicillin, which saved her life.

Sari and Fishi Farkas came to visit her in hospital daily. One afternoon they took me to a Russian movie about the wartime sufferings of the Russians at the hands of the Germans. The scene in which a German tank knowingly drove over a Russian baby is still vivid in my mind. When I returned, Mom was very hurt. She accused me of being unfeeling for having gone to a movie while she was so sick. I was very hurt that she would think of me as uncaring.

Many years later Mom told me she had suffered from an infected ectopic pregnancy. The surgeon must have done a hysterectomy because she was unable to conceive thereafter—very sad because she and Dad wanted more children after the war.

During that summer, I saw Jiři several times a week. We would run around the grounds and the forest, and it was through him that I came to know the purposes of the various buildings. He had to coax me to enter the forest because I was not sure whether any German soldiers were hiding in it. Indeed, we found many unspent bullets in the forest. We also saw several intact grenades, which led me to expect German soldiers to pop out from behind the trees. He reassured me all was safe, but just for fun, Jiři removed the bullet from its casing and dumped out most of the gunpowder. He then forced the bullet back into its casing, followed by a little gunpowder, touched a lighted match to the opening and threw the bullet a few feet away. The lighted bullet twirled around and made a hissing noise, and sometimes produced a satisfyingly frightening loud bang. It took several repetitions of this trick for me to feel comfortable doing it.

Jiři was very adept at making whistles from peach pits and slingshots from Y-shaped branches of trees, pieces of rubber cut into bands, oval pieces of leather, and string. He was a very accurate shooter. Fortunately for me, he was a patient teacher and I soon learned to make my own whistles and slingshots, and to knock squirrels out of trees. This education occurred in sign language and in Czech.

During the summer of 1946, it rained frequently and we experienced dramatic, but fortunately usually only short-lasting thunderstorms. High up on Pleš lightning frequently hit the ground, trees, or the lightning rod of our house, producing a hissing noise and an "electrical" smell. The ferocity of the storms initially startled all of us until we realized that within a few hours of a rain the forest smelled fresh and was full of mushrooms.

Mrs. Uchitil, expert at distinguishing the edible from poisonous mushrooms, and mushrooms from bullets lying on the floor of the forest, would go mushroom picking. She frequently invited me to accompany her. We each took a small woven basket and walked into the forest, where we would see both poisonous and edible mushrooms in abundance, growing up from between fallen half-rotten leaves. Some of the largest, most colorful were inedible. In an hour we would return with baskets full of several species of fresh mushrooms, which Mom would fix with onions, gravy and potatoes. The mushrooms were welcome additions to what otherwise tended to be monotonous cuisine (for which we were nevertheless grateful).

We ate a lot of *knedliki* and *zeli* (Czech national dumplings and cabbage), potatoes fixed in various ways, breads, and soups. Meat and fish were difficult to come by. Occasionally Mr. Dolan would bring us a live fish, which we kept in the bathtub until cooking. These were significant occasions. A couple of times we took the fish into Prague to the Farkas apartment. We ballooned up on the relative plenitude of high-carbohydrate food.

❧

I had almost completed four grades in Munkacs. By the time school started in September I was able to carry on a rudimentary conversation in Czech. Therefore, I was placed into fifth grade along with Jiři in Mňisek, a village two kilometers from Pleš, on the other side of the forest. Jiři and I walked together most days. Fairly often Russian soldiers would give us a lift in the backs of their Dodge trucks. They would be friendly, boisterous, and gentle as they lifted us into or lowered us down from their trucks. Very little cargo was being ferried, and I never learned the purposes of their trips, except perhaps to impress the Czechs with their presence.

It was good to be back in school, where I was well treated. I find it amazing that I was able to pick up the Czech language and at the same time to learn topics such as arithmetic, simple science, and history after only a couple of months. I understood and absorbed sufficient amounts of material so that at midyear I was promoted to the sixth grade, bringing me up to the grade I would have attained had I not missed the 1944-45 school year.

Only one incident marred my time in Mňisek. A few weeks after arriving in school a boy classmate said something I did not fully understand but I heard the word "*Zhid*," the pejorative for Jew. I interpreted what he said as hostile, and turned away from him. He then repeated a phrase containing "*Zhid.*" I had had enough of denigration. My resentment overflowed. I was ready to hurt and to kill. I removed the inkwell from its hole in the desk, and poured the ink on his head. I then began pummeling him with my fists and kicking him. I do not know how long or how severely I would have beaten that boy, but the teacher stepped in, separated us, and took the boy out of the room. I was not disciplined in school, heard no more about the episode, and saw no more of that boy. My parents did not praise me, but neither did they berate me.

As I became increasingly fluent in Czech my father asked for my help in spelling and pronunciation. Perhaps he was subtly testing my knowledge. He requests for help certainly encouraged me to try harder.

During our year at Pleš, my father was offered several opportunities to practice in Sudeten. The offers usually included a house, a car, and a generous salary. Although our St. Louis relatives were working on our immigration papers to the United States, my father was very tempted to stay because the transition for him would have been minimal. He already had a Czech medical license and was fluent in Czech and German. My mother was very determined in opposition. She refused even to consider remaining in Europe, saying she did not wish to live among "murderers" in a "huge graveyard."

Toward the spring of 1946 ominous signs of an impending major political change appeared. We were introduced to the Russian Cyrillic alphabet and warned by clearly unhappy teachers that during the summer we would have to attend a course in the Russian language.

Political campaigning began. The hammer and sickle symbols of the Communist Party were pasted all over the village. The village urchin, a small twelve-year-old boy out-fitted in rags and with a lit cigarette constantly in his lips, was one of the "operatives" for the party. He draped an enor-mous Communist political banner over the side of the Pleš hill facing the village of Nova Ves. Political signs of other parties were much more modest and were torn down dur-ing the night. Red Army trucks made increasing numbers of trips through the village. The communists were clearly deter-mined to win. No one complained about the unfairness of the campaign and the not so subtle intimidation, as people correctly surmised that they could do nothing in the face of the overwhelming might of the Red Army and the absence of support from the West.

My father, seeing which way the wind was blowing, became eager to leave, too. With both parents in agreement, we were going to turn our backs on Europe, making a clean break with the past and a leap into the unknown, following in the foot-steps of millions of European Jews who had sought refuge in the United States over the past two centuries. At the end of the war it seemed as if Europe had finally succeeded in rid-ding itself of its Jews, whom they had always regarded as an undesirable foreign body to be rejected, much as a body rejects a transplanted organ foreign to it. We in turn, tired of being rejected, were pleased to leave the Europeans to stew in their own juices. I embraced the new start and tried not to dwell on the unpleasant past. I did succeed to a surprising extent, despite the host of everyday events that would remind me almost daily of where I had been and what I had experienced.

PART IV
LEAVING EUROPE

The USA or Palestine?

Many survivors chose to go to what was then known as the League of Nations' British Mandate of Palestine. How did that choice come about? For centuries Jews had accepted their low status and suffering as the will of God, encouraged by their rabbis who taught that God would someday send a Messiah to end their troubles, and all would return to Zion. By the late nineteenth and early twentieth centuries, the more active ones, impatient to wait any longer than the nearly two thousand years they had already waited, sought other options.

Some of the well-placed Jews had hoped the goodwill of kings would continue to see them through. Those hopes were dashed by the First World War with the fall of the monarchies. Hopes were also placed on conversion to Christianity, the ascent of socialism, liberal democracy, or communism. Each of these options was, at least initially, attractive to some segment of the Jewish people. However, ultimately they all failed to ameliorate their condition.

As to conversion, many pure-blooded "real" Christians still taunted the tainted "new" Christians and continued to ostracize them. Hitler accepted one Jewish grandparent as sufficient to "taint" one as a Jew. Socialists followed their national leaders into the bloody First World War, and the liberal democracies appeased Hitler. Liberal France folded in six weeks and its Petain government collaborated in the transport of French Jews to the death camps. England took a courageous stance, finally, when it became clear there was no option to opposing Hitler, and then Churchill was brought into power. Unfortunately Britain took in a small number of refugees relative to the need and closed the doors to Palestine, in effect trapping the Jews in Hitler's Europe. The communists turned out to be brutal dictators and, despite their professed internationalism, strong anti-Semites.

To say the least, Europe greatly disappointed. After nineteen hundred years of toying with the Jews as a cat does with a mouse, Europe in the twentieth century finally decided, along with Hitler, that there was simply no room for Jews in Europe and proceeded to help Hitler in making Europe *Judenrein* (clean of Jews). Much controversy exists as to how much help was extended and by whom, but the bottom line is that with the rare exceptions of persons such as the "Righteous Gentiles," no one rose in any of the countries to oppose Hitler's actions against the Jews. The well-planned, finely engineered, and coordinated job of extermination proceeded essentially unhindered. (In fact, European countries were supine in even their own liberation. Although after the war they all trotted out their own liberator equivalents of Charles de Gaulle, in fact indigenous European forces made trivial contributions to the liberation of Europe. It was largely through the fortitude and efforts of the USSR, the British Empire, and the United States that Europe was liberated.)

While most of their brethren were casting about for a European solution to the "Jewish Problem," many sought solutions beyond the borders of Europe. Most found safety and opportunities for themselves and their families in the United States. Smaller numbers went to Canada, South America, South Africa, or Australia. A relatively few who wished to ensure not only their own safety but also to create a place of refuge for their people left for the land of Israel, then called Palestine. They called themselves Zionists. Through a truly Herculean effort they managed to establish a homeland that was ready to receive the survivors of the Shoah.

Initially, the Allies wanted the survivors "repatriated" to their countries of origin. It soon became clear, however, that the survivors did not wish to be "repatriated." They had had enough of the hospitality of Europe, and their countrymen did not want them back. The few Jews who returned to Poland, for example, found former Christian neighbors occupying their houses, businesses, and lands. These new owners wanted to know why the Jews had come back, why Hitler had not "finished the job." Returnees were sometimes killed. No country was ready to take all of the survivors except for the Zionists, and so they went and built Israel largely through their own efforts, with financial help from German reparations and aid from the United States, despite the best efforts of the Arabs to wipe them out.

We left for the United States because that is where our closest relatives were residing. In 1946, the British were blockading Palestine, attempting strenuously to keep the Jews out. They captured many ships attempting to run their blockade, and took the passengers to camps in Cyprus. The survivors of the Nazi camps found themselves locked behind barbed wire again, courtesy of the British. We were in the fortunate position to be spared that fate.

Arriving In the United States

When we arrived it was with some apprehension, but also with the fervent hope that we could start life anew in a country largely free of the sort of blatant, murderous anti-Semitism we had experienced in Europe. Soon after our liberation my father had written to Flora and Sanyi Gottesmann and Saul Schoenfeld, reporting on our survival and detailing the fate of the rest of the family. They immediately began to work on our immigrant entry visa. Flora later told us that obtaining visas for us had been expensive, difficult, and time-consuming.

Perhaps this should not have surprised us. We gradually came to know that in the mid to late 1930s when Hitler was already persecuting the Jews and many of them sought to escape from Europe, the United States government had chosen not to accept any refugees, except for a handful of eminent scientists and artists, e.g., Albert Einstein and Marc Chagall. The story of the ship *St. Louis* illustrates the attitude. In 1939, the *St. Louis,* carrying over nine hundred European refugees, sailed from Europe first to the port of Havana, Cuba, where, after two weeks of negotiations, she was refused landing rights. The ship then sailed to Miami, Florida. There, too, it was refused landing rights. People who had been living in the United States were refused permission even to visit their relatives on board. After several weeks, the *St. Louis* was forced to sail back to Europe, where many of its passengers eventually perished in the Shoah.

One would have hoped that the white Anglo-Saxon Protestant (WASP) elite class, who right after the war comprised the majority of the foreign policy establishment in the U.S. Department of State and in the Immigration and Naturalization Service, would have experienced a bit of shame and regret, and would have expedited the entry of Shoah survivors. But the bureaucracy's forehead was made of brass; it felt no shame or regret and continued to move at its usual leisurely pace while survivors, many of them living in displaced persons camps in Germany, were waiting to move on with their lives.

Flora, Sanyi, and Saul were required to guarantee that they would support us after our arrival in the United States, lest we become burdens on publicly financed institutions. The INS required proof of sufficient net financial worth to make the guarantees credible. Testimonials were required from banks, business suppliers, and Dunn and Bradstreet. The bureaucratic maneuverings in the United States took nearly a year. Fortunately, the Czechs placed no impediments to our leaving.

My complaints about the State Department and INS are not meant to imply that the refugees and survivors were owed an entrance into the United States. After all, the United States did not persecute and kill any Jews; and few, if any, countries were helpful to strangers, particularly to Jews. The world was (and still is) a hard place for the poor and powerless. Still, when judged against its self-image as a haven for the persecuted, which the political classes have sought to project to the world (based on the large immigrations of the past), one would have expected perhaps a little more of the United States than it actually did in the 1930s and 1940s when the need was even more acute than in earlier times. Despite all that, we are grateful for the refuge we found here and the opportunity for a better life.

We departed from Prague by train in June 1946 and stayed in Paris for six days, where I was in charge of picking up the baguettes at the bakery around the corner. I did not know then, of course, that I would be back to Paris many times in the later years as a consultant to a French pharmaceutical company. At LaBourget airport we boarded a TWA four-engine propeller-powered Constellation and flew to New York with intermediate fueling stops in

Shannon, Ireland, and Gander, Newfoundland. The plane was clean and comfortable. Attractive, attentive flight attendants served what seemed to us to be gourmet food. We landed at Idlewild (now Kennedy) Airport in New York on June 26, 1946—apprehensive about the future, but glad to be out of Europe.

The Gottesmanns met us. I found New York huge, noisy, busy, and disorienting. One day, while I visited relatives in Brooklyn, an ambulance came by, its siren blaring. It produced the same sort of noise made by the air-raid sirens in Europe. I asked, "Has the war started again?" and urgently suggested we seek an air-raid shelter.

After a few days, we boarded the train to St. Louis. Saul, Lottie, Sanford, and Lillian Schoenfeld met us at Union Station. We drove to 5744 Cates Avenue at Goodfellow Boulevard, the Gottesmann family home where we would live for our first two years in the United States. We had survived the Shoah and reached our place of refuge. What now?

Fig 1. My cheder class, 1939. I am directly in front of the rabbi. Fredi is to my right, his face partially hidden.

Fig 2. Fredi next to my father; and I next to my mother, in Munkacs, Kertvaros, 1940.

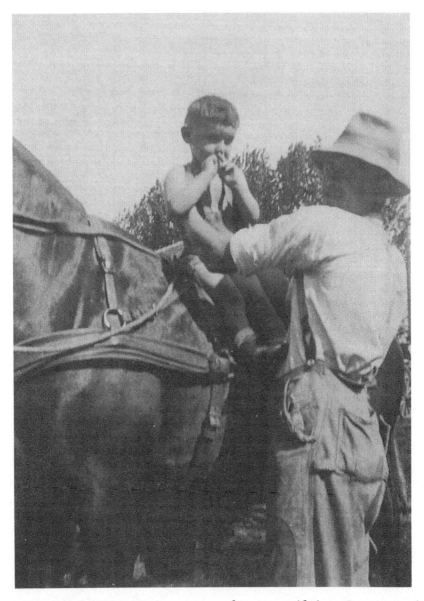

Fig 3. Jozsi holding Fredi on one of my grandfather Gottesmann's horses, Nagyleta 1936.

Fig 4. The hole in our guest bedroom caused by a Czechoslovak cannonball, Munkacs 1939.

Fig 5. Gustav Schonfeld posing in a prisoner jacket six weeks after liberation, 1945.

Fig 6. My father within a day of our liberation in May 1945, taken by a sergeant in the US Army whose name is lost to us.

Fig 7. Partially completed airplane assembly plant, Muhldorf 1945. Taken by 2nd Lieutenant Joseph Tucker of St. Louis, US Army Air Corps.

PART V

Starting Over Again from the Beginning

In hindsight, I must have determined soon after our arrival that I would do my best to ignore our recent experiences in Europe, and to concentrate on becoming "Americanized." It was an easy choice, which was reinforced by my parents and relatives, because it was easier not to be too obviously different from everyone else. People would ask my parents how it had been in the camps. When they started to describe the conditions and the losses of relatives, most people interrupted them and told them they should forget the past and start anew—try to fit in—not an easy piece of advice to follow when you are in your thirties and forties and have suffered grievous losses. My parents were hurt, and they determined not to speak of the past except with other camp survivors who trickled into St. Louis in subsequent years, and who understood. I picked up the same message, shut up about the past, and became an American. Nevertheless, despite my determination to fit in, I am certain that my attitudes and actions were influenced by what I had seen, heard, and felt between 1939 and 1945. In fact, not a day has passed since our liberation that the camps have not entered my mind, albeit sometimes only fleetingly.

The Gottesmanns resided in a three-story, single-family stone house with a round, uncovered front porch six stairs up from the street level. The kitchen and living and dining rooms were downstairs, four bedrooms were on the second floor with an attic on the third. That block of Cates Avenue was full of one-family homes, most built of brick. In the 1940s, solid middle-class Jewish families occupied most of the houses. The lawns were neatly tended and contained mature trees. Trees also lined the sidewalks.

A few days after our arrival the St. Louis newspapers carried our photograph and story, providing us with instant recognition as "the refugees" in the neighborhood, and within the circle of acquaintances of the Schoenfeld and Gottesmann families.

Gerald Goldberg, who lived at 5740 Cates in one of the several four- to six-family apartment houses located at either end of the block, became my first friend. Bob Diamond, who lived in an apartment at the eastern end of our block, became my second friend. Gerry and Bob were my age and taught me the names of baseball teams and baseball players, how to play catch with a glove, how to ride a bicycle, and a few curse words in English. Gerry also taught me the names and model years of automobiles as they drove by on Goodfellow Boulevard. Bob, who was a jazz clarinetist, taught me about the jazz greats while we listened to his 78 rpm records. I have lost track of Bob, but I still hear occasionally from Gerry, who joined the Navy after high school, changed his last name to Sanford, and maintained a long career as a scriptwriter and producer in Hollywood. My cousins Larry and Helene were toddlers with whom I was too old to play, but when I did, I teased them mercilessly with scary grimaces. I was never asked to babysit.

In the fall of 1946 I was enrolled in the seventh grade of the Dozier School. English was still difficult. Neither the teacher nor the pupils were particularly sympathetic. The Gottesmanns saw me struggling and petitioned the school board to permit me to transfer to Hamilton School, which had a much larger population of Jewish kids and teachers.

It was good move. The administrators and teachers welcomed me warmly. By that time my English was much improved and that helped. In short order I became a patrol boy (street crossing guard) with a white sash across my chest and waist and a badge pinned to my chest. I was also the operator of the mimeograph copying machine for my class, which gained me frequent authorized absences from the classroom to go to the copier in the principal's office. Each morning and afternoon I was one of the kids who raised and lowered the American flag in front of the school. Soon everyone knew me.

I also attended the Miriam Hebrew School, along with several of my Hamilton schoolmates. Tiny Mr. Melman did his best to prepare us for our bar mitzvah. He drilled us to read our individual parts of the portion of the week from the Torah and to read the week's Haftorah, both with their appropriate blessings and cantillations. He wrote me a typical bar mitzvah speech, which I was meant to deliver in English.

The big day came in May 1947. The *shul,* located on the second floor of the synagogue building on DeBaliviere Blvd., was filled to capacity. I was the first refugee kid from the war to be bar mitzvahed there, adding to my apprehension. I performed the Hebrew part without stumbling. But a few sentences into my English speech, I froze, unable to proceed. Poor Mr. Melman tried to unobtrusively prompt me from his seat, to no avail. It was necessary for him to walk over and whisper his prompt into my ear before I could proceed.

Uncle Sanyi Gottesmann had adopted the American ethic of having kids earn their own pocket money. He arranged an after-school job for me at Shenberg's supermarket on DeBaleviere, stocking shelves and sweeping floors. I shared the work with another boy a few years older than I. The making of money was good, and the work was undemanding. I lasted for several weeks until one day my colleague neglected to sweep his aisle. The boss told me to sweep it. I replied that I had already swept my aisle and that it was not fair for him to be asking me to do someone else's work. A few days later I was told that they were laying me off. I was very upset, but there was no recourse. After that, I went to work in my Uncle Nathan's store where I not only stocked shelves and swept floors but also packed bags at the checkout counter. In later years, Uncle Sanyi hired me in his wholesale costume jewelry office, where I pulled merchandise from shelves, packed it, and delivered the packages to the post office. Thus, I was kept off the streets and out of trouble.

Dad Establishes Himself, and Takes Us along

My father had the hardest job. He had to find a way to make a living for his family. There was some discussion as to what he should do. My uncle Gottesmann had graduated from law school in Hungary, but to become a lawyer in the United States he would have had to repeat law school. No one was prepared to support him in doing that, so he became a businessman, starting off as a door-to-door salesman of ladies' stockings and later adding costume jewelry. He eventually worked himself up to being a successful wholesaler of costume jewelry. For my father there was never any question that he would continue as a physician, despite the intervening difficulties. He simply refused to consider anything else.

Graduates of foreign medical schools, in addition to doing an internship, were required to take state board medical licensing examinations in each state in which they wished to practice. Illinois permitted noncitizens to take the licensing examination, whereas Missouri required United States citizenship, which took a minimum of five years to obtain, before one was permitted to sit for the exam. Dad was eager to become financially independent at the earliest possible moment. He decided he would take the Illinois exam, which implied we would be living in Illinois across the Mississippi River from St. Louis.

My father became an intern at the Jewish Hospital of St. Louis in the summer of 1946, at the age of forty-three. He struggled to learn English and concomitantly to pick up the American ways of practicing medicine. He was on call for thirty-six hours and off for twelve, for the princely sum of thirty-five dollars per month plus room and board. He found some of his colleagues to be sympathetic and helpful. Others were arrogant. It was difficult for him to take orders from twenty-seven-year-old residents, especially from those he felt knew less than he did. One of the "nice ones" was Sam Schechter, who was kind and helpful. Sam practiced in Clayton, Missouri, for over forty years. When he was well into his eighties he approached me and told me he was establishing a professorial chair in internal medicine at Washington University School of Medicine, and he wished me to be its first occupant. Thus, Sam was good to the father and also to the son.

The hospital is about two miles from Cates Avenue, and the bus fare was ten cents each way. In order to save the money, my father walked most of the time. On his way he routinely passed Temple Israel, which was housed in an imposing Romanesque building with huge stone columns along its front portico. It had a few Hebrew letters carved on its pediment. My father saw the Hebrew letters, and on Saturdays he heard male and female choral singing and organ music emanating from the building. Not associating mixed gender choruses and organ music with Judaism, Dad was not sure what sort of church this represented. The Gottesmanns explained the Reform Jewish ritual.

Dad sat for the Illinois licensing exam for foreign graduates in late 1947, the first possible time after our arrival, but failed the English part. He then decided to take a job requiring only a temporary medical license as a resident physician at Christian Welfare Hospital in East St. Louis, the city in Illinois closest to St. Louis, Missouri. He reasoned that during that year he would study for the medicine board exam and gain more proficiency in the English language. At the same time he would come to know the city, colleagues, and potential patients, and scout out locations for his office and home. By the summer of 1948, a little over two years after our arrival, my father was fully licensed to practice medicine, and had provisional privileges to admit patients to the three local area community hospitals on the east side of the Mississippi. I have seen several other foreign graduates struggle to establish themselves in the United States, and I believe my father set a record among non-English speakers for the rapidity with which he established himself. This was not a surprise for those of us who knew him. His favorite phrase when it came to achieving was "I can break iron."

Father remained on temporary hospital admitting privileges for several years, a source of embarrassment and chagrin. Permanent admitting privileges came only with membership in the St. Clair County Medical Society, the local affiliate of the American Medical Association. Membership in the society required *unanimous* approval by the membership committee. In effect it gave a single physician on the membership committee veto power over any hospital staff appointments, an invitation to abuse of power, which was exercised in the case of my father over several years. He was accepted only after one of the members in particular rotated off the committee. This arrangement between hospitals and medical societies used to be common. Eventually it was judged to be a "restraint of trade" and was declared illegal.

We moved into a large old house at 610 Washington Place. To the north of us was the First Christian Science Church housed in a Greco-Roman building, a quiet respectable neighbor. In contrast, we had an example of *Tobacco Road* to the south of us, a redneck family of five people, several of whom were alcoholics. They parked several beat-up cars in front of their house and in their driveway, within a few feet of our house, and filled their backyard with discarded old refrigerators, stoves, and junked machinery and equipment. These neighbors provided us with noisy country music on the radio, drunken yelling, screaming, and the sounds of slapping several times per week. Police cars were frequent visitors, but there was never any gunplay.

My father had his office in the living and dining rooms of the house. We lived in the rest. His practice succeeded quickly, possibly in part because he was able to speak with many of his patients, who were members of immigrant families from Central or Eastern Europe, in their native languages. Also, he made house calls and was available days, nights, and seven days per week in the office and home. He took on the responsibility for their well-being and imbued them with optimism that they would get better, all for only five dollars per visit.

Mr. Hartstein's grocery was around the corner to the north. Mr. Hartstein was a short, truculent, Jewish immigrant of long standing. He favored us with stories on how "greenies" had screwed up in the United States, and provided us free advice on how to get along in our new country, specifically in East St. Louis. In contrast, his wife and son were very kind. As Mr. Hartstein aged, and as he saw my father succeeding, he mellowed and his tone of voice softened.

The Knights of Columbus were one block to the south in their grand building. I did not know what to make of the Knights as I had not known that private non-governmental organizations with their own financial and moral power could exist in a society. In Hungary, the government had a monopoly on such powers. It took me a while to become convinced that the Knights were, in fact, not part of the U.S. government's armed services.

After a few months my father became sufficiently busy to rent a "real" office on the second floor of a small office building, next door to Dr. Hundley who became our dentist, at 40th and Waverly avenues near Washington Park. My father's practice continued to flourish. In the 1950s when a small office building next door came on the market, he bought it. Soon thereafter, the family moved to 1527 North 43rd Street, six blocks from the office, away from the drunken neighbors to a clean, quiet, working-class, all-Caucasian neighborhood, a five-minute walk from the office. In those days everything was segregated by race including neighborhoods, schools, and hospitals. Segregation as government policy did not appear to me to be just, but it was definitely not strange. We Jews had also been segregated, and worse.

My father kept a selection of medicines in his office for those who could not afford to buy them. This upset some pharmacists, who claimed it was unfair competition. They enlisted their physician friends in successfully opposing my father's acceptance into the St. Clair County Medical Society, which aggravated him very much. Nevertheless, after several years, with the help of newly acquired allies and over the opposition of a few foes, he was accepted. Finally, with this membership came full privileges at the local hospitals, and he felt he was a full member of the profession.

My father was a beloved physician. Some of his patients became lifelong loyal friends. Joe, a small businessman, credited my father with helping him to overcome his alcoholism. Joe let his wife run the business, while he hung around the office, running errands and fixing things for us. He was a good handyman.

Joe also taught me to drive. My father initially attempted to teach me in his sporty 1948 black Chevrolet Fleetline hatchback, but his efforts were unsuccessful. He had little time, and what he had was after dark. His presence in the seat next to me was intimidating and I made errors. Once I turned a corner too quickly and scraped a car on the side. My father agitatedly told me to get the hell out of there, and I drove off in a hurry.

It was soon thereafter that Joe volunteered to teach me to drive, using his 1941 Plymouth, which had its gear shift mounted on the post of the steering wheel. We drove during daylight, and he was calm, spoke slowly, and kept me relaxed. He initially took me to huge empty lots. I soon became comfortable driving his car and then gradually moved on to streets. When my father was convinced that I knew how to drive, I became the driver on our family outings. However,

I could not use his car for movies or dates because he was always on call for his patients.

Many patients came from St. Louis. Some were quite well to do. One of his patients, the owner of a regional oil company, said that my father's fee of five dollars was too little and gave him fifty dollars per visit—a large amount of money then—equivalent to a secretary's pay for a week's work. Others, too, overpaid, and were generous with their time and advice in helping him to improve his operation and to make useful contacts.

I still run into patients or children of patients who tell me of my father's kindness. One of his first patients was a Jewish woman from St. Louis who had severe crippling rheumatoid arthritis. Dad's treatments made her feel better. Her son became like an older brother to me over several years, and his son—her grandson—is a good friend of my son Josh. This gives me a little feeling of rootedness. Although my parents gradually became increasingly comfortable in St. Louis, they never felt at home anywhere again.

My father's staff was also very loyal. He had the same office assistants for nearly thirty years, Wanda Fabian and Mrs. Berry. My mother says that they liked my father because he was not a demanding boss. Whenever something came up that needed boss-like words to be spoken, my mother was called upon to do the dirty work.

My father maintained his office until his retirement in 1978. When he retired he was charging ten dollars per visit, and East St. Louis had become an impoverished, almost completely African-American city. The move of industries out of town and the Supreme Court's desegregation orders regarding schools, hotel accommodations, and restaurants resulted in "white flight" to surrounding cities.

At Home in East St. Louis

My mother was my father's strong support. He would come home after a long day at work, empty his pockets of the cash or checks that had come in that day, and never see the money again. My mother made the bank deposits, paid the bills, and made whatever purchases were necessary. The only time Dad became involved in shopping was during the purchasing of furniture either for the house or office, or of a dress for my mother for an important occasion. He had strong, definite tastes and wanted his tastes to be reflected in her choices. For the first ten years of our stay in the United States, my mother also did all housecleaning, laundry, and mending of clothes. Later, when they could afford it, she hired help. She cooked great-tasting meals daily, except for the infrequent occasions when they went out with friends or to some community event.

The house was strictly kosher, and neither of my parents ate nonkosher food outside the house. In restaurants they were limited to vegetarian food and fish.

Religious observance mattered much more to my mother than to my father. She was always meticulous and rigid in her observance of holidays, Shabbat, and Kashrut. It was she who insisted on a kosher house, not Dad. She steadfastly refused to ride in a car on Sabbath and the holidays. She felt *mitzvot* were obligations, and she always took her obligations very seriously. She also performed *mitzvot* out of gratitude, stating that our survival as a family was a miracle from God, that my survival was especially miraculous. This she felt placed special religious and ethical obligations on us to be generally charitable. My mother was convinced I had been saved for a special reason, but she was unable to tell me what that was, and no one else has enlightened me. For my part,

I was not convinced. Perhaps the writing of this memoir is a partial fulfillment of that obligation.

My father's religious philosophy was based on his generally pragmatic approach to life. His knowledge of science and medicine did not affect what he regarded as his sensible outlook. He believed in an afterlife, not because he was convinced that it actually existed (he professed agnosticism on this point) but because it was more comforting. He preferred seeing himself in heaven over merely rotting and disintegrating in the grave.

It was his emotional love for traditional Jewish religious music that drew him to be observant, not a reasoned acceptance of *mitzvot*. My father knew the liturgy very well and had a lovely high baritone voice. He frequently sang the liturgy at home a capella. He also sang along with the recordings of such favored *chazzonim* (cantors) as Rosenblat or Pinchik. He would at times be asked to lead services in the synagogue, which he enjoyed. In view of the strongly skeptical attitude that I developed following the camps toward God and His love of us, I find it surprising that neither of my parents ever spoke bitterly of God or religion. In fact, we did not speak of theodicy to each other.

We joined the synagogue in East St. Louis and my parents became its generous supporters. I taught Sunday school there for a few months while I was in high school. In subsequent years they also supported a couple of synagogues in St. Louis.

My parents worked as a team on their charities, becoming generous donors very soon after our arrival in the United States. They donated primarily but not exclusively to Jewish charities locally and nationally, as well as to Israeli educational and children's welfare institutions, and to hospitals. One of their longtime ongoing favorites was the Children's Town of Jerusalem where they established the Schonfeld Synagogue that serves both the institution and the neighborhood. They also supported Yad Vashem, the Shoah memorial in Jerusalem, the Hebrew University-Hadassah Medical School, several hospitals in Jerusalem, and both medical schools in St. Louis.

They also continued their European tradition of helping the family as our relatives gradually found their way to the United States or Israel. One memorable gift was that of a farm tractor that they sent from the United States to Esther and Rudy Tamir in Bitan Aharon, Israel, in the early 1950s. Despite the great deal of trouble that sending a tractor entailed, the Tamirs found that they could not use it because none of the farm implements available in Israel were compatible. They wound up selling it and used the money to set themselves up in the chicken egg producing business. Another gift was a large interest-free loan to the California branch to start a liquor business. I believe the loan was repaid after about thirty years, interest free. Packages of food and clothing were sent to relatives in Munkacs, Debrecen, and Budapest for the first few years until they were no longer needed. None of these gifts aroused much discussion. They were given as a matter of obligation to the family, and to Jews and Judaism.

School in East St. Louis

Within a few weeks of our move to East St. Louis in the fall of 1948, I enrolled into Rock Junior High School, housed in a large old building built of stone. Most people and teachers were cordial and I did pretty well scholastically. During my junior year of high school I was third in my class.

From the fall of 1949 through the spring of 1951 I attended the all-white East St. Louis Senior High School. The other high school in East St. Louis, Lincoln High School, was all black. Most of the public and private facilities in East St. Louis were segregated by color until the late 1950s. The area north of Bond Avenue was white and south of Bond Avenue, black.

There was much talk at my school about "dumb niggers," their criminal behavior and bad odor. The kids who made these comments had very little contact with or firsthand knowledge of blacks. I had to assume they learned their attitudes at home. I have often wondered how people professing Christ's teachings could so denigrate fellow human beings. Of course the similarity of anti-black sentiment to anti-Semitism was not lost on me. I am ashamed to admit, I kept quiet. I was not an activist by nature and my father warned me against speaking out and making waves. I kept my head below the radar to stay out of trouble, like many European bystanders when witnessing anti-Semitism in 1930s. I do not take pride in my quietism, but I understand it. Who knew what sort of reaction speaking out would have evoked? I had already been through the mill once. I was not eager to test the system. As I have become older and seen that the consequences of speaking out, at least in a small group setting, are not catastrophic, my hesitation has diminished. It simply feels too good to get some things off one's chest.

Two episodes from junior high school stand out. I was assigned to the choir led by Mrs. Kelsey, a fiftyish woman and a passionate musician. She loved my singing voice and strongly encouraged me to participate in the choir. She even kept me after school and gave me some coaching in the choir room.

After a while, during our private times together, she began to talk to me about her deep faith in Christ. She told me of the beauty and the comfort of faith, and of the wonderful feeling of knowing with certainty that if one accepted Christ, one would be saved.

I had absolutely no idea what she meant by being "saved." Gradually, I realized that she meant that I would be resurrected after death and reside in heaven with God, His angels, and deserving people. She felt I had a wonderful talent and was very much worth "saving."

I told her that I *could* wind up in heaven, even as a Jew, if I did what was right. She said no, that I could not be saved by "acts alone," that the "grace of God" (a phrase that I also did not understand) would be required, and the prerequisite for obtaining "grace" was my acceptance of Jesus Christ as my Lord and Savior. As a symbol of my conversion I would have to be baptized. Not to put too fine a point on it, I felt she was talking gibberish. I also felt she lacked any sense of propriety in asking a person who had so recently suffered on account of his Jewishness to throw his heritage away. She definitely needed to be sent to a school on tact and diplomacy.

The sacrifice of Jesus was also a strange concept. My God asked Abraham to sacrifice Isaac, his son, as a test of Abraham's faith, but in the end God did not demand a human sacrifice. He had a goat substituted for Isaac. By contrast, the God of the Christians demanded a *bona fide* human sacrifice. Perhaps because human sacrifice was not strange in Christian religion, the Europeans accepted the Nazi's plan for the Jews.

In my Bible we are warned against strange religions that sacrificed humans. I wondered, of what benefit to the world has Jesus' sacrifice been? Is the world not still full of strife, hatred, and murder? As a corollary, I could not understand why the death of Jesus has been held against the Jews. Had Jesus not died on the cross, would the Christian religion have come into existence? What would have been its symbol, a fish? Perhaps the Jews should be viewed as enablers of the new religion, rather than as Christ killers.

I kept saying to Mrs. Kelsey that I was not interested in converting, that I felt comfortable within my own religion. In fact, although I hesitated to tell her, her religion had been badly besmirched, in my mind, by my experiences in Europe. The last religious group in the world I wished to join in 1948 was the Christianity to which the murderers of Jews also belonged. I strongly suspected a heaven populated only by Christians would not be very comforting to people like me. Besides, if the Christians were correct, my relatives would all be in the other place, and I would have to face eternity in the presence of strangers.

But Mrs. Kelsey persisted. She even offered to take me to the preacher and to serve as witness to my baptism. Finally, after several weeks, I had had enough. I told Mom and Dad. I do not know what they did, but I was transferred out of the choir and Mrs. Kelsey's harassment stopped. In hindsight it is unfortunate that I was denied the opportunity of continuing in the choir because of her need to exercise her drive to convert a "pagan" Jew in a public school setting. It was she who should have been transferred or disciplined for harassing a student, and I should have been permitted to stay in the choir.

I am certain that many Christians genuinely believe as did Mrs. Kelsey, and that in her mind she was attempting to do me a favor. However, the superiority of her beliefs to mine was not obvious to me then and it is not obvious even now. Besides, I have suffered for being a member of my group, earned the right to belong, and would think it a betrayal if I left it. I am grateful that in the United States such convinced people do not possess the temporal power of the state. We have seen throughout history how "true believers" can torture and kill people "for their own good."

The second episode involved a classmate who was on the wrestling team and repeatedly said he wanted to wrestle me. I did not know whether to regard his insistence as an invitation to a sportsmanlike match or as a bullying threat. Chalk it up to my uninformed immigrant status. In any case, I was not interested and told him repeatedly to leave me alone.

One day in gym he approached me and began to grab at me. I grabbed his leg, sat on him, and began to twist it. He complained that I was hurting him and that what I was doing was illegal. I knew nothing of the rules of wrestling and did not care. I wanted him to stop badgering me. I told him I would continue to hurt him until he gave up and promised to get off my back—and so it was.

I made three good friends in high school: Sandor Korein, Jerry Arky, and Arden Sher. Each of their parents had businesses in the black areas. Sandy was two years older, and Jerry and Arden were each one year older than I. They were Jews in a sea of Gentiles. Sandy had been born in Hungary and emigrated at the age of three. His parents were both fluent in Hungarian. His cousin Jerry was born here but his father was born in Hungary. Thus, we had common backgrounds and our parents were also friendly.

I will always be grateful to them for taking me into the group. We did all sorts of things together, from hanging around the various houses and teasing Jerry's younger sister, to going on bicycle rides, the movies, ballgames, and ice-cream parlors. My friends introduced me to AZA, the high school branch of B'nai B'rith, where I met contemporaries from St. Louis. We went on a number of double and multiple dates.

I frequently slept at Sandy's house across the street from Grand Marais State Park, a large park with a lake in it. Mrs. Korein introduced me to the variant of chicken paprikas laced with sour cream. She was a fabulous cook and baker, and Mr. Korein liked to tell corny jokes. Sandy and I have remained close friends for almost sixty years. His friendship gave me a feeling of stability in the United States.

I made tentative attempts to fit into the various non-Jewish groups. I even took up smoking cigarettes at the age of sixteen, despite the fact that they made me vomit for the first few days. I suppose I wanted to look cool, to fit in. I went out for football much to my mother's horror (she nagged so forcibly that I quit after a few weeks), but I found becoming part of the general crowd difficult.

First, I was not certain about their feelings toward Jews. Second, I could not understand how they were able to confine their attentions to what I considered shallow matters, such as gossip about friends, girls, parents, sports, and teachers. The boys interacted by teasing each other or in friendly shoving matches. I was concerned about "more weighty" matters: questions of good and evil, and about the fact that in a short time we would all die in a nuclear war. I was convinced that political leaders in their arrogance and stupidity would incinerate us. I remained bitterly angry with the Hungarians and Germans, and thought it a cruel twist of history that the United States turned to Germany as an ally against the USSR. In sum, I was too busy with my post-traumatic neurosis for light conversation. I must have been a terrible bore.

I read, frequently staying up until three a.m. My cousin Alex fed me books by Carlo Levi and Ignazio Silone. He had read those authors in his high school years when he had socialist leanings, I suppose picked up from his uncles, and from the general feeling in Europe in the 1930s that the communists were the only ones with the guts to stand up to Hitler. (With the advent of the Molotov-Ribbentrop Pact in 1938, which divided Poland between Hitler and Stalin, communists were shown to have feet of clay, resulting in books such as *The God That Failed*.) I also read books by disillusioned communists, such as *Darkness at Noon* by Arthur Koestler, a Jewish-Hungarian refugee physicist who had been a staunch Communist in the 1920s and 1930s. He even risked his life in the Spanish civil war in 1936.

I also studied the Hebrew language, Talmud, Bible, and Jewish history, for two to three hours per day, four days per week at the St. Louis Yeshiva on Skinker Avenue, a trip of nearly one hour each way to and from East St. Louis by bus. The topics were of great interest—I wanted to know who I was, whence we came, and why the Jews had been chosen to suffer for so long.

Despite my activities, I was depressed. I felt that I was only going through the motions. I felt that my work would provide me no long-term benefits in face of the nuclear race. This underlying reality was enhanced by Senator Joseph McCarthy's scare tactics—he claimed there were communists under every bed, including in the U.S. Army. One of the highlights of those days was the bravery exhibited by Mr. Welch, the Army's gray-haired, soft-spoken lawyer, at the Army-McCarthy hearings televised by the networks. In addressing McCarthy's apparently baseless allegations, Welsh asked the senator, "Have you no shame, sir, no shame?" In the face of the near mass hysteria produced by the cold war and McCarthy's scare tactics, facing McCarthy down was a truly brave act, and encouraged those who were being unjustly hounded by the FBI and subjected to police encroachments on constitutional freedoms.

The crises in various part of the world, as the two "superpowers" faced off in a global pissing contest, culminated within five years of our arrival to the United States in a major killing-spree in the Korean War. These events, too, did not help my mood. I do not mean to imply a moral equivalency between the United States and the USSR. It is just that I found the chest-thumping manly joy some of our politicians exhibited to be repellant. Attitudes and behaviors that may be appropriate at a football game or a wrestling match are not appropriate during a discussion of bombing and killing, even of your enemies.

For several years I was confident that the hard-liners on both sides would eventually provoke a nuclear exchange that would destroy both us and the USSR. Fortunately, sometime during my junior year in high school I realized that I had absolutely no power to influence these events, and that if a war came, we would probably be dead before we realized what had happened. Even if we survived the initial attack, none of us would suffer for too long. Radiation sickness is a quick killer.

Employing the well-known technique of denial, I began to ignore news articles about the arms race and the daily fluctuations of the Cold War. "What if there is no nuclear war?" I asked myself. "For how long will you remain a prisoner of your fears?" I found denial to be quite effective. I could operate under the optimistic operational assumption that such a war would *not* occur. That bit of "wisdom" was liberating and permitted me to regard the future with guarded optimism.

Another issue related to the nuclear arms race bothered me: I found it difficult to accept that Germany had suddenly become our friend and ally, and that we were protecting them against the Russians to the point where we were willing to risk a war over Berlin. My initial response was let the Russians have it and teach the Germans a lesson. This issue, too, became resolved in my mind over time, as I came to realize that I had no say in the matter; and much later when the monstrosity of the USSR, on the one hand, and the willingness of many Germans to accept responsibility for the Shoah, on the other, unfolded.

In addition to the above, I continued to be nagged by questions relating to anti-Semitism and the Shoah, and thought that it was perhaps within my power to obtain some answers if I went to the right place and learned from the appropriate persons. Who better than well-informed rabbis in a theological seminary?

Who Am I? Why are the Jews so Hated? The Yeshiva and Academy in Chicago

I repeatedly heard from fellow students at the St. Louis Yeshiva that there were Jewish day schools and yeshivas in other cities where the issues in which I was interested were approached as serious academic subjects by learned rabbis whose powers I generally held in high regard. The day schools also provided a rigorous general curriculum.

The Chicago Jewish Academy, a Jewish parochial high school, and the Hebrew Theological College (the yeshiva) located near each other worked cooperatively to provide the advanced courses I sought. I requested that my parents send me to Chicago. After discussions with the local teachers and the people in Chicago, they agreed.

With great anticipation I enrolled into both the yeshiva and the academy for my senior year of high school in the fall of 1951. I was looking forward to learning, and to being free of my parents' hovering, protective presence. I understood the significance to them of my being their only surviving child. Nevertheless, at times this was a heavy burden for all of us.

The yeshiva was located at 3448 Douglas Boulevard, a four-lane street divided by a broad strip of grass containing a few trees. For about ten blocks the street was lined with three- to four-story apartment houses, populated mostly by Jews. The blocks to the east of the yeshiva had become settled by Hispanics and blacks. Over the ensuing few years, as more and more Jews moved northward in Chicago, the neighborhood would gradually become a black ghetto.

Within a block of the yeshiva were two enormous Orthodox synagogues that dominated the streetscape, and many small synagogues called *shtiblach* (little rooms). Across the street to the west of the yeshiva was the Jewish Community Center containing a swimming pool and meeting rooms. The yeshiva was housed in a two-story colonnaded institutional-looking structure. Its student body consisted of over three hundred males, encompassing both general high school and college students and students studying for the rabbinate. A few were married. The ground floor housed administrative offices and classrooms. The second floor was almost entirely occupied by a very large study hall (*beit midrash*) that was also used as a synagogue and a lecture hall, and several small classrooms devoted to classes in Talmud. The dining hall was in the basement. A two-story house next door contained the dormitory.

Several blocks west of the yeshiva the boulevard turned north. The Chicago Jewish Academy was located one block to the west, about a ten minute walk from the yeshiva, It was housed in a conventional school building and had a student body of both boys and girls totaling about 250 in four grades. The academy students were middle class, smart, highly moti-vated, and bound for college. The classes and labs were rea-sonably well equipped.

The vast majority of students were from Chicago, though a few were from other U.S. cities and Canada. The St. Louis contingent consisted of Joe Feder, Yitz Abramson, Marty Baron, Yale Miller, J. B., and Jerry Lefton. Joe Feder was older than the rest of us. He was married and attended both the yeshiva and the graduate school in biochemistry at the Illinois Institute of Technology.

We shopped on Roosevelt Road, a major east-west street two blocks north of the yeshiva, and also along the north-south streets between Roosevelt Road and Douglas Boule-vard. There were several kosher delicatessen, bakeries, and butchers, and Jewish gift shops and bookstores. The streets were full of people and cars. The area resembled the Lower East Side of New York, and Borough Park in Brooklyn. Chicagoans told me that the neighborhood was not what it had been before and during the war, when it had been almost exclusively Jewish. By 1951, many of the Jews had moved to the North Side of Chicago and beyond.

❦

During my first year in Chicago I slept in the dorm and ate breakfast and dinner at the yeshiva and lunch at the academy. That year was my only real taste of dormitory life and I do not regret it.

Boys of that age are sloppy about their persons, clothes, and personal effects. The rooms were always a mess. Many of us smoked, and we did not hesitate to scatter cigarette butts around the floor. The messiness was a shock because Mom was an immaculate housekeeper. In my room at home, everything had a place and was in its place. However, it did not hurt me to discover that sloppiness of one's room was still compatible with study and accomplishment.

The dormitory also had the advantage of built-in companionship. At almost any time someone was available for a conversation, taking a walk, picking up cleaning and laundry, or going out for ice cream. Many of the philosophical conversations I forced onto my fellow students took place in the dorm.

I came to know a few boys pretty well. One was a mathematical genius who studied trigonometry and calculus on his own and passed the appropriate placement tests in college allowing him to claim credits. There was a nice quiet dull boy from Winnipeg and a wise-ass guy from Chicago. I never understood how the latter was admitted to the yeshiva. He loved to mess with girls, to eat nonkosher food, and to flaunt the Sabbath laws. His rabbi would say to him with a heavy Yiddish accent, "Tatele, Tatele, ven I tawk to you, it's like tawking to a vall."

J.B., from St. Louis, was tall, strong, and very hirsute everywhere but on his scalp, which, at the age of sixteen, was already balding. He usually had a serious, look of concentration on his face and walked with a loping, bent-over gait, always in a hurry as if he had important matters to attend to. JB was earnest and above average in intelligence, with an unquenchable desire to help others to improve. His technique was to lecture others on ethical and religious behavior. For all of this he was not loved, and the younger boys took every occasion to irritate him.

He spent inordinate amounts of time in the bathroom, leaving an odor behind when he left. One day while he was in the bathroom a couple of the younger boys came by with some firecrackers debating the desirability of slipping some lighted ones under the door to hasten JB's exit. They said they wanted to do this but were afraid he'd kill them. I offered to be of help and threw two lighted firecrackers under the door, with predictable results. He came storming out of the bathroom, and found several boys standing there asking each other, "What happened?" No one admitted any knowledge of the prank so he took his anger out at the furniture, kicking and slamming some chairs around—so much for loving-kindness in the face of irritating behavior.

The summer after I graduated from high school in Chicago, I returned to St. Louis and took college classes at St. Louis University in developmental psychology and public speaking. I spent much time with Barry Eichenstein, the son of the chief rabbi of the Orthodox community in St. Louis, whom I came to know and like. His parents were very hospitable and expressed hopes for Barry's success in the rabbinate. Barry was bright, sympathetic, studious, and for someone of his background, quite broadminded. He eventually married the daughter of a rabbi, and founded a yeshiva in Jerusalem. In short, he followed the family tradition. My latest news of him is that he is a rabbi in Johannesburg, South Africa.

In the fall I returned to Chicago, to a rented a room in an apartment across the boulevard from the yeshiva. Jerry Lefton took the room next to mine. The landlord and his wife were both Polish-Jewish survivors of camps, in their forties with a couple of children. They lived in the other two bedrooms. The apartment was disheveled, badly in need of wall paint, furnished with decrepit furniture, and maintained just this side of dirty. We spoke to them in Yiddish. From time to time they offered us a glass of tea with sponge cake.

The husband had a large, soft belly that hung over his belt. The living room couch was so situated, that when he was lying on it, the first thing we would see upon entering the apartment would be his belly hanging over its side. If he was on the couch overnight, we knew his wife was menstruating.

We enjoyed being out from under the yeshiva's supervision, and could skip the occasional class or meal. I particularly disliked Friday night meals. The roast beef had a greenish sheen and a slight odor—not bad to most, but I found it offensive. I was used to much better at home. The dinner was preceded by singing, prayers, and ritual washing of hands. There was also singing during the meal and another prayer at the end of the meal. I needed an occasional night off, away from all the piety. Sometimes, I preferred just buying a half dozen Kaiser rolls and a jar of Hellman's sandwich spread, which I would eat either in my room or out on the green while reading a book.

Classes at the academy began at eight thirty a.m. We studied English, math, etc., in the mornings and Hebrew subjects in the afternoon. Upon enrollment, one was tested on one's knowledge of Talmud. Based on the test results I was placed into a class *(shiur)* held at the academy. More advanced Talmud students did their *shiurim* at the yeshiva. After school at about five p.m., I returned to the yeshiva for dinner and further study at the *beit midrash*. There was heavy emphasis on the need to study and the performance of commandments *(mitzvot)*.

The formal classes in Talmud were held daily except on Saturdays, in either academy or yeshiva classrooms. In each class the rabbi held forth to ten to fifteen students, frequently pausing to ask probing questions or requesting that a student read and explain a portion of the text under discussion. Each class learned a different tractate (volume) of the Talmud.

After *shiur*, we adjourned to the *beit midrash* for further rehearsing the text and its meaning until they became imbedded in one's mind. It was not easy. In addition to the complex legal concepts, the text is terse sometimes to the point of unintelligibility except to the cognoscenti, and written in Aramaic using Hebrew letters. Most of the commentaries surrounding the text are in Hebrew. Thus, it was essential to have some working knowledge of two ancient languages and a second alphabet. If one were to study a large folio page daily, which a *good* student can do, it would take seven years to complete all the tractates of the Talmud. Very observant men set themselves a lifetime goal of covering the whole Talmud at least once. Men who devote themselves full-time to study over many years with the support of their families or other benefactors, in institutions known as *kolelim*, proceed at a faster pace. They may cover the Talmud two or three times in a lifetime of study.

The *beit midrash* was a lively and loud place. It contained large wooden tables, armchairs, and unique wooden podiums (*shtenders*) upon which the large heavy folio volumes of the Talmud were placed. Bookcases lined the walls. They held prayer books, Bibles, biblical commentaries, sets of the Talmud, the writings of Maimonides, Nachmnides, later rabbinic responsa, and compendia of laws (Shulchan Aruch and Yora Dea), all in Hebrew or Aramaic. The hall was full of students loudly disputing in groups of two or three the fine points of Talmud with fervor at all hours of the day and late into the night. It reminded me of my grandfather's *beit midrash* in Munkacs.

The *mashgiach* (rabbi study supervisor), a mild-mannered European immigrant and concentration camp survivor in his fifties, always dressed in a brown suit that needed pressing. He wore his glasses low on his nose and his face frequently registered pain, the source of which I never ascertained. He was in attendance twelve to sixteen hours per day. The teachers of the various Talmud classes would also be present from time to time.

The rabbis would walk around the room joining one group or another to see how the "boys" were doing and to be of help. Frequently the rabbi would be requested to come to a group to help straighten out a difficulty. I was amazed at the facility with which the rabbis were able to enter into discussions on the great variety of topics dealt with in the different tractates: the laws of marriage and divorce, torts, pledges and vows, the holidays, the treatment of slaves and animals. (Incidentally, according to our law, slaves were freed after six years of service, and children of slaves were not slaves.) However, I slowly came to realize that anti-Semitism and the Shoah were not included among the many topics we were learning.

We prayed at the *beit midrash* three times daily. The "boys" prayed with fervor and *shukled* with great emphasis, just like in Munkacs. The weekday morning services lasted thirty to forty-five minutes, the afternoon and evening prayers ten to fifteen minutes each. Morning services on Saturdays and holidays lasted three hours. Students led the prayers. On Saturdays and holidays after the reading of the Torah, the rabbis would take turns giving sermons about the Torah portion of the week. Members of the faculty and occasionally outside visitors gave special intricate closely reasoned lectures (*pilpul*) on various topics covered in the Talmud.

The *pilpul* began with the posing of a paradox or contradiction between various texts on a point of law. The rabbis quoted verbatim extensively from the Bible, Talmud, and a wide variety of more recent commentaries. They mined the texts for their meanings and after many twists and turns reached a conclusion that brought new nuggets of insight and resolution of the topic. These lectures obviously required many hours of careful preparation and were quite impressive. Most lecturers used books and notes for their quotations, not trusting their memories to maintain their complex arguments in a logically flowing stream. A few lecturers amazed the audience. They wove their complex legal arguments and cited their texts from memory without hesitation, pause, or a single note.

Rabbi Kreiswirth of Antwerp, a tall, athletic-looking man with a few gray strands in his beard, attacked his topic aggressively in Yiddish. He was consistently amazing, and was said to have a photographic memory. Rabbi Regensberg, a small saintly man in his seventies, and a camp survivor from Europe, spoke very softly in Yiddish in the voice of an innocent little boy. The audience strained to hear him while their faces radiated bliss. These exceptional teacher/scholars had wide-ranging local and international reputations and drew big crowds to their lectures both from within and outside of the yeshiva.

All of the rabbis were treated with great respect. Students stood when a rabbi entered a room, and stayed upright until the rabbi sat. When rabbis walked by, people would stand and bow. I thought, *Surely these men will have the answers I sought.*

The schism between the "modern Orthodox" and the fundamentalist Haredim apparent in Munkacs in the 1930s also existed in the yeshiva and the academy in the early 1950s, and probably still exists. The academy was a relatively modern Orthodox institution. Its students were not segregated by gender, the principal and its Jewish teachers wore contemporary clothes, general subjects were valued, and it was assumed most pupils would go on to college and pursue careers.

The yeshiva was split in philosophy. The administration and some of the teachers were modern, but many of the teachers, particularly those who taught Talmud, were Haredim. They pushed the boys to study Talmud to the exclusion of much else, meticulously to observe the laws, and discouraged college attendance, where time would be wasted away from the Talmud and minds could be contaminated with strange ideas. This schizophrenia eventually resulted in the Haredi element splitting off and forming another yeshiva in Chicago.

Unanswered Questions

Although the sincerity of the religious fervor and the studious atmosphere impressed me, and although both my secular and Jewish studies progressed satisfactorily, the yeshiva disappointed me in some significant ways. The dean of the yeshiva, Dr. Rabbi Z. Fasman, was a sour man in his late fifties, mid-sized, kyphotic, meticulously and formally dressed. During the week he wore a black suit and black tie; on Shabbes he wore a morning coat and cravat. He wore his glasses low on his nose, peering over them with a dyspeptic expression on his face. He made smiling appear to be a chore. We said hello while passing each other in the hall, but I never had a conversation with him. I am probably being unfair, but I record only my limited knowledge of him.

The assistant dean for students, Rabbi Frimer, was in contrast to the dean hyperkinetic and friendly. Unfortunately, I had only one meeting with him. Shortly after I arrived, he invited me into his office for a get-acquainted visit. After I told him about my family and background he posed a question, which I suppose was meant to separate the earnest from the irreverent: "What would you do if I told you the

Russians will drop an atomic bomb and you had only a couple of hours to live? Would you pray, study Torah, or get yourself a woman?" I hesitated a minute and told him I would probably get a woman. He paused for a while and told me he was not certain my attitude was proper for the yeshiva. I never had a private conversation with him again—disappointing because it told me I was either beyond salvaging or not worthy of salvaging.

The bigger disappointment was that no one at the yeshiva helped me to understand the collective experience of the Jews during the war. Having been raised to respect religion and rabbis, I expected that these smart people would be able to provide some sort of explanation for anti-Semitism and the Shoah.

Why had the Shoah occurred? How could God have permitted it to happen? Did we deserve it? Were the Jews as nasty as anti-Semites claimed? Were we worse than everyone else? Did we deserve to be humiliated, to suffer, and to die violent deaths generation after generation? What criteria are used for judging? Who had the right to judge us?

What does it mean to be God's "Chosen People"? Did He choose us for good or ill? Where was He during the Shoah? Is the Shoah to be construed as some convoluted act of love? When we prayed was anyone listening? When we performed the commandments was anyone appreciating our efforts? Was He there at all?

How much of our putatively historic interactions with God and His alleged historic promises were factual rather than mythic? How much had been hallucinated by some feverish minds in the parching heat of the Middle East? How much of the putatively divine origin of the oral Torah did the old-time rabbis really believe? How much had they invented, imposed on credible folk, and perpetuated as a way of maintaining their influential positions?

These questions went to the core of my belief in God, religion, and the religious establishment. But, in my opinion, after the Shoah we needed to adopt a questioning, skeptical attitude about God and His proponents here on earth, toward those who felt duty-bound to persuade others to learn and to obey.

Although I very much wanted to honor my ancestors by believing as they did and performing the rituals they had done, Hitler's success in virtually eradicating the Jews of Western and Central Europe had made a questioning attitude mandatory. The fact that Jews may have recovered to some extent from the trauma in the ensuing sixty years does not invalidate the questions even today.

While the Shoah is a frequent topic of discussion today, in the early 1950s the yeshiva had no one on the faculty willing to address my questions. The yeshiva's aims were to turn out emotionally committed, educated laypeople and rabbis, not to address the questions of a rare injured Shoah survivor with a skeptical turn of mind. Questioning of basic tenets was a distraction from the major goals of the yeshiva and may have been regarded as subversive to its aims. Thus, when I raised my questions with rabbi/teachers, they were manifestly uncomfortable, their discomfort similar to that some people experience in the presence of the terminally ill. To be fair, I did not approach all of those who had the potential to answer my questions. I permitted myself to be discouraged by a couple of people who did not respond as I had hoped.

With hindsight it is perhaps easy to understand their discomfort. In the early 1950s the Shoah was an acutely painful topic for everyone. Only those who actually experienced it firsthand could discuss it freely among themselves. It took fifty years for the Shoah to become an acceptable topic in polite company.

When I raised questions about the Shoah and God, the rabbis encouraged me to immerse myself in Talmud, assuring me that with more knowledge, faith would come and my questions would be ultimately answered. They told me, "With faith there are no questions, with doubt there are no answers." To my query as to how long this might take, they answered "several years." I thought this was a dodge, since the topics being addressed related to observance of Halacha and *not* to anti-Semitism and the Shoah. Had I remained in the yeshiva another ten years, I would have learned about the laws governing prayer, interpersonal relations, the holidays, and kosher food in great detail, and my bothersome questions would still have remained unaddressed.

Good and Evil

The issues surrounding anti-Semitism and particularly the Shoah can be framed as questions of good and evil, which in a theistic setting become the province of theodicy and theology. These questions relating to why good people suffer continue to haunt me, albeit with lesser intensity and frequency as the years have passed, because I have found the framing of those problems in terms of cosmic good and evil less and less useful.

Several explanations evoking the supernatural are on offer. Perhaps the oldest, yet still invoked with some frequency, is that evil happens as God's punishment for evil. Several biblical and post-biblical stories illustrate the point. For example, Job's "friends" told him that he had fallen on hard times because he had sinned and God was punishing him. They did not find credible Job's protestations to the contrary. We the readers are told that Job, in fact, did not sin. He was made to suffer so that God could win a bet against the devil (not a high recommendation in favor of God's seriousness of purpose).

The Orthodox Jews accept the traditional explanation for the destruction of both the first and second temples in Jerusalem, namely that God punished the Jews for internecine hatred of Jew against fellow Jew. The Babylonians and Romans are not credited with having stronger armies against whom the Jews might have perhaps foolishly rebelled.

A few years ago, a train hit a school bus in Israel on a Saturday. About twenty children died. One of the leading Haredi rabbis said God had punished the children and their parents for breaking the law of Sabbath (not because the bus driver made an error).

In a similar vein, some rabbis say the Shoah was God's punishment for our sins, i.e., Hitler was a tool of God! When he reached the pearly gates, Hitler could have claimed, "God made me do it," and he thus should have been immediately admitted to heaven.

ঔ৵৹

The second approach follows from the axiom that God's intellect is infinite while ours is finite. He has complete information, while we have only a limited perspective. His judgment is superior to ours. This is the rabbis saying, "Trust in God." He knows what He is doing. Crudely translated, the rabbi is saying, "Damned if I know why He did it," which I find acceptable. But then they add, "But He must have had a good reason," which I find harder to accept. There does not exist any conceivable justification I could accept as valid for the murder of my brother and grandmother, and millions of others. I do not care how powerful or all-knowing God is.

The third "explanation" comes from the Kabala. Apparently, there are times when God chooses to turn away from us for reasons that are not clear, at least not to us. At those times evil may creep into our lives. This explanation provoked me to ask, "Why, when God decides to go off duty, does He not get someone to cover for Him?" Conscientious doctors must obtain coverage. Those who do not are subject to malpractice suits! Indeed, God has been sued in Jewish religious courts of law in Europe during the Middle Ages for permitting innocent people to suffer. As far as I know, God chose not to appear in any of the courts to defend His actions.

Finally, the Kabala also states that before God created the earth, His Being filled all of space, everything. Therefore, in order to provide some room for His creation, He had to vacate some of the space. This is called *tzimtzum*. The concept of *tzimtzum* could lead to the notion that after He created the world, God left it to us to run it on our own, leaving room for human free will. The part about leaving us alone seems to me the most believable and desirable. Accordingly, people are held responsible for their own actions. Where is our free will if God keeps on interfering with our daily activities?

In fact, I find none of the explanations invoking the supernatural to be credible. Certainly, none are verifiable by any method of proof I have come to accept as a scientist.

Thus, I have learned to accept that the cosmic meaning of the Shoah is unknowable, or that most likely there is none.

Pre-Med at Roosevelt College

Despite their support for my attending the yeshiva, my parents never wavered in their determination that I would attend college and pursue a career, unlike the Haredim, preferably in medicine. During the spring of 1952 I took a mechanically graded, standardized comprehensive exam meant to evaluate the college potential of Illinois high school seniors. About ten subjects were included. My grades ranged from the low ninetieth to the high ninetieth percentiles. Without pursuing it, I was offered a full-tuition scholarship at Roosevelt College (now University), which most of the yeshiva boys attended.

There were no college counselors at the yeshiva or the academy, and none of my American relatives was sufficiently conversant with the various universities to advise me on which to select. Dad thought Roosevelt satisfactory, saying, "I don't know any good schools, I know only good students." He also felt that college was a waste of time, to be gotten through as rapidly as possible before one entered medical school. Thus, I chose the readily available and comfortable alternative.

Roosevelt College at that time was the "streetcar college" for locals pursuing college degrees, many of them part-time. The college was in an old high-rise hotel, on beautiful Michigan Avenue across from the Chicago Art Institute. The classes were held in renovated old rooms, and the labs were pretty primitive. However, teachers and students were serious about the tasks at hand.

Love in the Yeshiva

Side by side with my philosophical meanderings were my biological and sexual urges, which were not to be denied their rightful places. PM was a bright, tall, slender, attractive, and assertive young woman. She had a commanding air about her that attracted attention. She was from a well-to-do, traditional family and apparently had set her eyes on me soon after my arrival at the academy. By the time I entered Roosevelt College we had been dating for several months.

In yeshiva circles early marriages were common, preventing premarital sexual experimentation, venereal disease, and unwanted children born to single parents. Parents who could afford it helped their children with the costs of college and/or postgraduate education, and rentals or purchases of apartments. Parents also helped to find jobs by making strategic phone calls, took the kids into the family business, or helped with business startup costs.

Alex Sonnenwirth told me that my parents panicked when they heard I was dating someone steadily. They had no business into which they could place me. Thus, I needed a profession. They were convinced that young people should not marry before they had their careers in hand, because the responsibilities of married life and the inevitable children to follow distracted one from demanding studies, resulting in aborted careers. I had heard this litany many times. Despite my protestations to the contrary, my parents were convinced that my "raging hormones" were in control, to the detriment of my future welfare. By "going steady" I had foreclosed my options too early and would be married before the appropriate time.

Mom illustrated this with the following story. A tomcat was crossing the street just as a tram was approaching. He ran to get across, but the front wheels of the tram cut off his tail. He quickly turned to see what had happened, and the rear wheels cut off his head. The moral of the story is, "He who follows his tail, loses his head." Then my mother said, "Gus, don't lose your head."

My parents then asked me how I intended to make a living. I told them I did not know, and added offhandedly that I might become a teacher in a yeshiva or a rabbi—not weird notions to be mulling over in a rabbinical college. (Also, those careers would have provided me with the time to seek answers to my existential questions.) My answer added the possibility of an unsatisfactory career goal to a frightening romance, and the panic level rose.

My parents began talking about moving me back to St. Louis to "finish premedical studies." This episode was the first of several episodes of panic over my dating, until I was married. My parents did not discourage my dating, provided I dated any one girl no more than once or twice.

By the end of the 1953 spring semester with panic in full bloom, my parents insisted that I return to St. Louis to attend Washington University in the fall. I have never been good at "winning" an argument against them, and I returned, with a great deal of anger and hostility. I did not want my pleasant life, free from their daily interference, to be interrupted; and I dreaded the idea of losing my autonomy, of living again under their daily gaze.

So, during that summer I lived with the Gottesmanns who, knowing the situation, were kind enough to house me. I went to East St. Louis only to pick up clothes and for an occasional meal. A few weeks into the summer, my parents tried to pacify me by buying me a used 1949 fire-engine-red DeSoto convertible. A few days later, I drove to Chicago. PM and I spent the day together. It was not a good day. By the end of the summer the romance was over and I was left with a feeling of stunning loss of love and autonomy.

Years later, when I was beginning my internal medicine internship at the NYU-Bellevue Medical Center in New York, PM called and said she was engaged to be married, but she was coming to New York and would like to have lunch. I said fine. Two days later she called to say she had changed her mind because she did not want to risk a negative reaction from her fiancé. That was my last direct contact with her.

However, about ten years later when Miriam and I and our two oldest children were in Boston (I was working at MIT), we met a couple several years junior to us. They invited us for dinner. During after-dinner conversation the wife asked me whether I had spent any time in Chicago. I said, "Yes, at the yeshiva and the academy."

She then reminded me that she was PM's younger sister. I, of course, had not recognized her. She also reminded me that I used to give her a quarter to disappear so I could be alone with her older sister. I was caught completely by surprise, blushed, and stammered like a boy. The sister then brought me up to date on PM. I was relieved to hear she was happily married and had children.

Washington University, School of Arts and Sciences

When I left the yeshiva, I also left behind almost all of the religious observance that was such an important daily part of it. Many of the intense questions about what was important to observe and what was not fell by the wayside. In essence,

I have remained a secular Jew, strongly identified with our history and traditions.

The reality of anti-Semitism and the occurrence of the Shoah continued to exercise me to a greater or lesser intensity, but the nature of the questions changed. I no longer sought answers in the realms of religion or the supernatural. I began to look to comparative history, sociology, and political science. Although these disciplines describe with more or less accuracy what has happened in various societies, at various times, and propose "theories" of human behavior, in general they have no answers I find satisfying either. I am hopeful a combination of neuroscience and genetics will provide some answers to human behavior, but this may not happen in my lifetime.

∞

I enrolled as a sophomore in the fall of 1953, the one hundredth year of the university. It began as Eliot's Academy near downtown St. Louis, and moved to its present site at the western edge of Forest Park at the beginning of the twentieth century. The athletic field (Francis Field) served as the site of the 1904 Olympics. Brookings Hall, named after a wealthy, farsighted St. Louis businessman, is the majestic fort-like administrative building on the hill, completed in 1904 at the time of the St. Louis World Exposition. Brookings also founded The Brookings Institution in Washington, D.C.

Until about 1950 the university was regarded as a fine local/regional school with an appetite for increasing its national reputation. Indeed, over the last fifty years the school has seen a steady enhancement of its reputation for the quality of faculty, its teaching, and research. In recent years, the university has been consistently ranked among the top ten among major research universities in the United States, and its medical school has been ranked among the top five.

I entered the university with the idea that I would pursue a premedical course, but without a great deal of enthusiasm—partly because I was not convinced I really wanted to follow a career in medicine, and partly because my father repeatedly reminded me that college was an unnecessary evil to be gotten through as rapidly as possible, so that one could enter the "real" school (that of medicine).

He had entered the medical faculty in the German section of the Charles University in Prague right after gymnasium at age eighteen. The course in medicine lasted for six years. In contrast, American students attend college for four years followed by four years of medical school, graduating with the MD degree two years later than Europeans. Dad felt the earlier completion of the MD degree could be accomplished without loss of information, because many of the liberal arts courses taught in American colleges are taken up in European gymnasia. Conversely, many of the premed science subjects taught in American colleges are taught during the initial "pre-clinical" years in Europe.

While my father was generously paying my tuition and upkeep, he kept pushing me to try to get into medical school after three years of college. I spent as much time as possible in St. Louis away from East St. Louis to escape my father's carping and my mother's anxious oversight. I needed some breathing space.

Gradually, I had become aware of my father's technique of getting his way by throwing yelling and screaming tantrums. On one occasion while I was in medical school, he threw a tantrum (I do not remember about what). I felt I was old enough not be handled as a child, said so, and left the house threatening not to return. Cousin Alex stepped in and made peace, bless him.

⚜

After considerable thought and discussion, I became convinced of the desirability of joining a fraternity because it would provide a place to hang out away from East St. Louis, and a rapid way to acquire a coterie of acquaintances and hopefully some friends.

Kurt Metzl of Kansas City was born in Austria about a year after me. His family was in horse trading. At the time of the Anschluss, having seen the hand writing on the wall, they ran into Switzerland. The Swiss welcomed them by placing them into a Swiss internment camp, not a luxury resort, but better than being exposed to Nazi horrors. After a few months, they were set free within Switzerland. After the war, in 1948, they came to Kansas City with the help of the Jewish community. Kurt's father Freddie opened a kosher butcher shop, worked very hard, and did pretty well. The fraters used to kid Kurt by saying, "Nobody beats Freddie's meat." We were at each other's houses often. His mother would save us double yolk eggs that she made into delicious omelets, and huge steaks. Kurt went to the University of Kansas Medical School, and then we both went off to New York for our residencies. In New York, he and his wife-to-be introduced me to Miriam, my wife-to-be.

Sanford Neuman was from Granite City. His parents were from Mezolaborc, the birthplace of my great-grandfather. They immigrated to the United States in the 1920s. His aunt and uncle, more recent arrivals to America, became good friends of my parents. Sanford became a successful corporate and tax lawyer in St. Louis. He and his wife Roz, a gifted quantitative geneticist at Washington University School of Medicine and one of my longtime scientific collaborators, have been our good friends for many years.

As mentioned, just because the yeshiva provided no satisfactory answers on the Shoah does not mean I ceased asking the relevant questions. One of the reasons I became active in Hillel was in the hope that it would be helpful in my search for answers. In the Hillel House I sought an intellectual and social home away from home, a place to meet people, make friends, and discuss current Jewish issues, history, and religion. In addition, there was a tradition to follow. Rabbi Jacobs, its founding director, had been welcoming to Alex Sonnenwirth and Tuli Schonfeld, who had emigrated in 1948 from postwar Germany, and attended college on Hillel scholarships. I was anticipating he would be welcoming of me, and indeed he was.

The House had a library where I discovered volumes that started me reading about the Holocaust, Zionism, Israeli-Arab problems, and Herzl, Weizmann, and Ben Gurion, the founders of Israel. While this did not answer my questions about the Shoah, I learned that not all Jews were content to wait for the messiah to come, as the rabbis had instructed them to do. Some took matters into their own hands. I thought, *More power to them.* Before departments of Jewish studies were established at American universities, one had to learn about Jewish history on one's own, or not at all.

Rabbi Jacobs, who over the years became a prominent personage in the city, was respected for his openness to multiculturalism way before its time. I respected him, too, but found one trait a little irritating. He cultivated a mellifluous, sonorous voice and a stilted, semi-Oxonian pronunciation in which he preached and spoke in public, typical of reform rabbis of the day. Perhaps unfairly, I found this to be pretentious, an attempt to imitate the speech of East Coast high-class WASP American establishment, and not to sound "too Jewish." To be fair, my efforts to lose my European accent probably reflected my own desire not to sound too different from those around me. In those days having an accent was not considered chic, certainly not in the St. Louis crowd I knew. I chose to sound like a Midwesterner. Not having a conspicuous accent placed me in a position of equality with my peers and provided me with the option of telling people about my European origins, or not. More attempts to keep below the radar.

My favorite courses were masterpieces of literature, zoology, and organic chemistry. Professor Lisolette Dieckmannn was middle aged, lively and bright, with an unusually pleasant voice and soft German accent. (I found most German accents to be harsh and grating.) She was a German Jewish immigrant, born in Frankfurt and educated in Heidelberg. In 1933 she and her academician husband ran from Hitler to Turkey, where they taught until 1937. They arrived at Washington University in the 1940s.

We read selections from the writings of what today are pejoratively called "dead European males." It was my first exposure to the New Testament, the classical Greeks and Romans, as well as to the great European novelists. It was an eye-opener. I carried away some notions about various ideas of virtue and sin, hubris and tragedy, and a feel for classical Greece and Rome and their gods. I did not fall in love with the classical societies. In comparison to the rules Jews lived by, the Greeks and Romans were cruel, although they apparently built longer-lasting buildings and had stronger armies.

I found the New Testament mystifying. I could not understand the virgin birth. Was this an example of parthenogenesis, which is not supposed to happen in humans? How can a man be a man and a god at the same time? For me, this reeked of Greek paganism rather than monotheism. The institutionalized representatives of Jesus as embodied by the Church also did not help me to be sympathetic to the Christian belief system. The Church throughout its millennial history was sternly authoritarian as an institution. It regularly terrorized its adherents to maintain its authority when it had access to temporal power. The purges of "heresies" by the early church, and its constant patrolling for heresies even today, also put me off. Is that how a loving god is represented on this earth? The wars following Luther's proclamation of his *theses* consumed many lives and wrought much havoc, to what purpose?

Dr. Victor Hamburger, another German Jewish immigrant, tall and slender with a twinkle in his eyes, taught us about comparative anatomy and embryology. He was a giant in embryology, having studied with the great Germans. He lived to be one hundred and won almost every prize except the Nobel Prize, which some people say he deserved. Hamburger was in charge of the course in comparative anatomy, a wonderful course on the structures and physiologies (functions) of various organ systems in a wide variety of phyla of the animal kingdom. We did a lot of dissecting of animals and viewing of gross and microscopic anatomy.

The beautiful microscope slides led me to take a course in histology with Dr. Stalker, who taught us how to prepare and stain slides. We examined many more tissues from a variety of animals.

Hamburger also taught an advanced course in embryology, which I took, and became fascinated by the transformation of the zygote to the embryo and the embryo to the fetus. This embryology course was my first experience with the seminar format. The course included a library research project and the writing of a scientific report, a process that eventually became a critical part of my career. Before computers, we used card files and searched for articles in bound volumes of journals in library stacks. Hamburger gave me a disappointing B+ as the final grade. He offered an oral exam to those who wished a chance to alter their grades. I wanted an A, and studied hard, but at the end of the thirty- to forty-five-minute, one-on-one session, he told me. "Let's leave it at a B+." I was disappointed, but it could have been worse. He could have reduced my grade.

There were eye-opening courses in political science, economics, and history. Dr. Eliot was a wonderful teacher of political science. He was a Boston Brahmin, the descendant of a president of Harvard and of the founder of Washington University. He was a lawyer, who, as a young man, joined the Roosevelt administration and helped to write the Social Security law, and served in Congress for two terms. He came to Washington University as a forty-four-year-old full professor of political science and soon became chair of the department. Despite his eminence he insisted on teaching the freshman course. He was clear and enthusiastic in explaining the procedures of governance in the United States and in other countries. Eliot later became a chancellor of Washington University.

In the fall of 1954, the beginning of my third year in college, my father convinced me to apply for admission to medical school for the fall of 1955. I applied only to Washington University and waited to hear whether I would make the first cut, i.e., an invitation for an interview. In the spring of 1955, I was interviewed by the admissions committee, chaired by Dr. Robert Joy Glaser, an assistant or associate dean at that time. Mr. William Parker was the registrar.

The committee asked me several questions, which I cannot remember, and then I left the room. In a few minutes Glaser came out and told me, "Gus, you're a smart boy and we will take you into the medical school if you get an A in organic chemistry." That meant that I had to stay in college for a fourth year. I was not surprised, knowing the importance of organic chemistry for medical education. When I told my father, he was deeply disappointed. However, he had no choice but to accept their judgment.

In the fall of 1955 I took organic chemistry. Dr. Goldstein taught the one-semester course taken by most premeds. Those with an interest in chemistry *per se* (not I) took the two-semester course. Goldstein was an acerbic paraplegic, bound to his wheelchair. He had a thin mustache and a distant, unapproachable manner. He was not reluctant to embarrass a student in front of the class. Premeds feared him because his course determined their fates to a disproportionate degree. However, he was impressive, and his lectures were models of organization, crystal clear. I was determined to do well. To my surprise, I enjoyed organic chemistry, in contrast to inorganic and physical chemistry, which I had merely endured. I studied hard and received an A.

Glaser was good to his word. I was accepted by Washington University for the fall semester of 1956. I had applied to several medical schools, but upon hearing positively from Washington University, I cancelled my other applications before even knowing their outcome, because I knew my parents wanted me to stay in St. Louis and would threaten to stop supporting me if I refused the local school. However, I made a deal with them. I would stay at Washington University for medical school, and definitely leave town for my internship and residency.

Interlude at Anheuser-Busch

One hundred and twenty semester hours were required for graduation with a BA degree. I had taken enough extra courses during the school years and in summer school to accumulate 124 semester hours by January 1956. I had had enough of school by then, and decided to work for the eight months remaining before entering medical school. Alex Sonnenwirth helped to find me a job.

Alex at that time was assistant director of the diagnostic microbiology lab at the Jewish Hospital of St. Louis and on the faculty of the School of Medicine. He contacted his colleague Harry Hoffman, PhD, who supervised a microbiology lab at Anheuser-Busch on south Broadway in St. Louis, the original home plant. A-B was attempting to produce vitamin B_{12} as a potentially marketable product. The vitamin was a by-product of the brewing of beer. Hoffman was in charge of the lab that monitored the experimental production runs. They needed a third technician to run routine bioassays of vitamin B_{12} on various samples collected at various stages during the runs. Fortunately, I was hired.

The lab was in one of the older buildings off South Broadway in a room adjacent to one of the beer production lines. Employees were then permitted to drink as much beer as they wanted while on the job. (I understand that practice was stopped.) Our location was most convenient; we needed only to walk out the door and come back with an armful of cold bottles of Budweiser or Michelob for our refrigerator. Hoffman would show up in the morning to set our tasks, and again in the late afternoon to collect the day's results and discuss the work for the following day.

The bioassay employed a bacterial strain that needed exogenous vitamin B_{12} for survival. The more of the vitamin present in the sample to be analyzed, the more bacteria would grow. Surprisingly, I was able to do the assay quite well after just a few days, in a rote sort of way. I became adept at preparing the culture media using sterile technique, pipeting, and the routine use and care of equipment such as centrifuges, pH meters, spectrophotometers, incubators, and shakers. Soon the technical aspects of the job stopped being challenging, and after just a couple of weeks I was able to produce reliable, useful data.

Alex told me Hoffman was satisfied with my performance, which became routine but not boring for a couple of reasons. First, although the assay was invariant from day to day, it nevertheless required ongoing attention. Small errors in technique would throw off the findings, resulting in a grumpy Hoffman and requiring a hunt to find the problem. Second, the personal interactions in the lab were interesting. My two fellow technicians had been there for several years. The senior was a short, chubby man in his forties. He taught me to do the bioassay. The other tech was a good-looking, muscular man of medium build of about fifty. He was almost completely deaf from a childhood disease, and was neither a good lip-reader nor a good speaker. His voice was nasal and his pronunciation was badly distorted. But we had no difficulty in communicating. He had fine handwriting and we wrote notes. The senior man was a Baptist and the deaf man Catholic.

Our conversations would range all over the lot: women, marriage, children (both were married and had children), education (both had some college), sports, and work. In the ten years I had spent in America, these men represented my longest and closest exposure to non-Jewish middle-class Americans. I came to like and respect them. They were basically decent, honest men, who did their jobs responsibly and had a strong sense of fair play. They showed me some deference because they knew I was headed for medical school. They ruefully predicted that I would leave them far behind but at times, when I made a mistake or said something stupid, kidded me about my "brains."

Generally the two got on well. During the eight months I was with them, there were a few testy exchanges over trivia such as "Why didn't you clean up the mess?" or "It's your turn to make the culture reagents, why didn't you do it?" These exchanges tended to occur when one or the other had exceeded his usual quota of four to six bottles of beer per day.

One afternoon when I had been there for several months a fight broke out without warning. The two seemed to be having a quiet conversation, writing notes, speaking and signing to each other. Suddenly, the deaf one erupted, "Some nerve you have telling me I drink too much. You drink, too. What kind of a Baptist does that make you?" They started pushing, kicking, and hitting each other. I yelled at them to stop and stepped between them, and they rapidly cooled off. No one was hurt. Both thanked me and apologized for the flare-up. That was the end of it.

But this episode caught my attention because religion seemed to be involved. When we first arrived in the United States, I was surprised that in addition to Catholicism there were so many different Protestant sects. In Europe, I knew only that all Christians in my part of the world, without distinction were hostile to Jews. I had not yet learned that many of the different "brands" of Christianity were hostile towards each other. The fight demonstrated that residua of old hostilities still echoed, at least in the 1950s.

In May of 1956, I attended my college graduation exercises in the quadrangle at Washington University. My mother, Flora and Alex Gottesmann, and Alex Sonnenwirth were there. My father was not; he was "too busy" at the office. I was hurt. Nevertheless, I savored the day. In the ten years since arriving from Europe I had done well, and achieved direction for a reasonably secure future.

On Becoming a Doctor, Washington University School of Medicine

In the fall of 1956 I entered medical school somewhat apprehensively, having heard stories of how difficult it was. But soon I came to love it, so much so that I never really left it.

The biomedical enterprise in every even semi-developed country has experienced a huge growth since the Second World War, as governments and the public came to appreciate the contributions of science and medicine to the war effort and to public health. Fortunately for the public good, the benefits of medical research and education were recognized by those in positions to affect funding.

War is good, especially for the development of surgical specialties. There are plenty of injuries to treat, and more than usual amounts of money to improve the treatment of "our brave soldiers." Internal medicine also benefits because there are plenty of sometimes exotic infectious diseases. No government ever seems to begrudge the funds spent on war. It is in peacetime that spending in the public interest becomes contentious, especially on behalf of those not well connected to the centers of power.

Lister Hill and his colleagues in Congress, responding to the prompting of eminent figures in academic medicine, succeeded in garnering enhanced support for the National Institutes of Health (NIH). The campus in Bethesda, Maryland, was considerably enlarged to house the burgeoning "intramural" program. In addition, a competitive extramural program of peer-reviewed grants was initiated to support biomedical research at universities and medical schools throughout the United States and in several other countries, enabling the building of infrastructure and the acquisition of research equipment, supplies, and personnel. Native and imported talents and their scientific offspring (including more immigrants) are responsible for much of the progress of the last few decades.

Advances on a broad front followed in both basic and applied biomedical sciences, which gradually became translated into advances in diagnosis and therapeutics. The positive results have engendered continuing public support, especially during forward-looking national administrations. As a result the United States has become the overall world leader in biomedical research and development of diagnostics and therapeutics. This has spawned an enormous private industry in direct support of the research itself, and in the pharmaceuticals and diagnostic equipment that result from increased knowledge.

It is worth noting that it takes decades to develop a premier scientific establishment. Conversely, it may take some time for a decaying situation to become manifest. At an increasing pace since the war, European countries, Korea, and Japan have been catching up with the United States, as these countries have invested in the training of a scientific workforce and in biomedical research infrastructure. Thus, the United States is falling behind in relative terms.

The increasingly rancorous battles over reproductive issues, contraception, and stem cell research are not helping. Neither is the excessive tightening of our immigration laws that in attempting to exclude terrorists who wish to kill us also tend to exclude graduate students and postdoctoral fellows who wish to study here. Surely, the wise people who govern us and the many bright ambitious colleagues who surround them should be able to devise specific and efficient screening systems that achieve the security we need, without compromising the immigration of the scientific talent essential to our progress. The question is what is more important, the winning of debating points or getting the job done for the benefit of the public? If the desire is there to get it done, the political quibbling will cease. Of course there is a more important reason for the debates than pride of winning—money—the economic interests of those benefiting from the current non-system. It will be a long time before this issue is settled, and you may be sure that the rich will benefit by whatever changes of health policy result.

The School of Medicine at Washington University started with the merger of the two local medical colleges in the 1890s, initially becoming the Medical Department of the university and eventually its School of Medicine. The ambitions of the founders were high, and they recruited the best available faculty willing to leave the hallowed halls on the East Coast. The visit by Abraham Flexner in 1910 and his critique of the school gave the founders and their supporters an added incentive to place the School of Medicine on excellent footing. Since then the trajectory of the school has been consistently upward.

The dean welcomed the freshman class at the initial assembly. Most important for setting our minds at ease, he told us that the medical school did not subscribe to the philosophy of schools that trained marines and air force pilots. At those schools the welcoming statements include the advice,

"Look to your right and look to your left. By the end of the year one or both will not be here." Instead, the dean told us that the administration trusted its own selection process, and made every effort to help those it had accepted to complete the courses leading to the MD degree. His statement was followed by a perceptible relaxation of tight shoulders and necks in the audience. In fact, only two men in our class of eighty-two men and four women left the school, both voluntarily, within the first two weeks, after they had a look at the cadavers in the anatomy lab. The school was faithful to its word and has retained that philosophy to this day.

The major courses for the first year were gross and microscopic anatomy (including neuroanatomy), biochemistry, and physiology. There were small courses in biostatistics, medical psychology, and preventive medicine. We were in class and labs several hours per day followed by several hours of study every night. We attended the lectures and labs as a class. To obtain more individualized attention one had to chase the professor to his or her lair, usually the professor's lab. When we moved to the clinical areas in later years, small-group teaching became the rule. Now, small-group teaching sessions are very common even in the preclinical years. Still, a cartoon widely circulated among us remains relevant today. It shows a fellow seated on a chair with the top of his cranium open, like a box top on a hinge. Another person is standing above him holding a funnel and pouring "knowledge" into his head.

We spent several hours of each week of the first two trimesters dissecting cadavers in teams of three to four students. Several teachers of anatomy were present, helping us to expose and identify important structures such as specific muscles, nerves, arteries, and veins. The background I had acquired in the comparative anatomy course in college helped, but the human body was much more complicated and we were expected to know it in greater detail than in college. I found the body fascinating and derived a great deal of satisfaction from coming to understand its structure.

Dr. Mildred Trotter, a physical anthropologist, was chair of the department. She was a medium-sized gray-haired woman in her sixties at that time, and a formidable, world-famous figure who did not suffer fools or lazy people. Despite her eminence, she was usually present in the cadaver room, patiently helping us to dissect our cadavers and answering our questions. She never married and lived to be ninety-two.

Dr. Cecil Charles was a retired surgeon. Thin, taciturn, he had a hoarse voice from too many years of smoking. He constantly amazed us. When we struggled in vain to find a structure, a nerve, or a blood vessel, we yelled for his help. He came over, placed a probe into the area, and told us to dissect down to the point of the probe. There we would invariably find the structure in question. I received an A in anatomy, but I never knew anatomy as well as my father, who had studied it for two years. He and I would pick a part of the body and he would recite the muscles, arteries, veins, and nerves in the region, without error. He obviously also had a better retentive memory than I.

Physiology seeks answers to questions, such as what does the liver do? How does the kidney make urine? How does the intestine digest food? How do intestinal absorptive cells move digested food from the intestine into the body proper? How do nerves and muscles collaborate to move our limbs?

How do lungs move oxygen into and carbon dioxide out of the body?

The faculty of the physiology department contained two unusual individuals. Dr. Gordon Schoepfle was a fortyish very bright PhD from Alabama with a slight stutter. He taught us neurophysiology. He kept several snakes in his lab as pets and would invite us to watch as he fed them mice. Dr. Albert Roos, a refugee from Holland (MD, Groeningen, 1940), was a short slightly built man in his forties, who spoke in a softly accented English. He used a long fishing pole made of bamboo as a walking cane and pointer. As he paced in front of the class he would tap the floor or desk for emphasis, pointing to various items on the blackboard. One day, someone tied a fishing line, hook, and fish onto the pole, and hid the fish under a newspaper. When the professor picked up the pole, he found a smelly fish swinging from it. There was much laughter, which, to our relief, Dr. Roos joined in with the rest of us. The incident was blamed on Sam Farley, a fictional member of our class, who was blamed for all sorts of pranks. Joe Eads, the leading jokester and prankster in our class, invented Sam. Joe eventually became a fine plastic surgeon in St. Louis.

The chair of biochemistry was Dr. Carl Cori, who, with his wife and scientific partner, Gerti Cori, had won the Nobel Prize in 1947 for studies in the metabolism of glucose, in particular the synthesis of glycogen. They had both graduated from the German University in Prague, my father's alma mater, in 1920. They came to the United States in 1922 and spent several years at the precursor institution of the Roswell Park Memorial Research Institute in Buffalo, New York, and then came to Washington University. His lectures were beautifully organized, but he spoke with a heavily accented English, in a low volume. Students would mimic him by saying "glucose six phosphate mumble, mumble."

Nevertheless, he was an Olympian figure whom students were most reluctant to approach, although he did attract very fine people to his lab and to the department and trained many academic leaders, including my future mentor, David M. Kipnis. Obviously there was a side to him hidden from medical students.

With the long hindsight available to me now, I marvel at Cori's good "taste" in his choices of young faculty. Sidney Velick, Robert Crane, and David Brown were associate professors who did most of the lecturing. I remember Velick because he seemed to me to be the most sympathetic and approachable, but they each worked hard to make a difficult subject intelligible. Young men, who were available for help with concepts and techniques, directed the student labs. Luis Glazer was tall and pear-shaped; he wore eyeglasses with lenses so thick that they distorted his eyes. He spoke with a dual accent, reflecting both his German and South American backgrounds. He was very bright, knowledgeable, and happy to pass on what he knew; and he eventually became chair of the department. Carl Frieden, originally from New Rochelle, New York, was a fellow at the time. He became an eminent biochemist, concentrating on enzyme structure and function. Eventually, he became a member of the National Academy of Sciences and chair of the department.

Despite the hectic pace, we found ways to relax with bridge, sports, laughs, and the company of women. A few years before us, a group of male students had cut the penis off their cadaver and placed it into the vagina of a female cadaver that was being dissected by a female student. The next morning, the young woman asked her male classmates, "All right, which one of you guys left in a hurry last night?"

The student nurses, whom many medical students dated, circulated doggerel such as, "TB or not TB, that is congestion. Consumption be done about it? Of cough, of cough, but it'll take a lung, lung time." Also, "At ease, disease, get off my back, you'll give me bacteria."

❧

I had my own room, two blocks from school, in a big old three-story rooming house on Forest Park Boulevard, which then was a quiet street lined with trees. The house was filled with male medical and dental students. I occupied the large front bedroom on the second floor with three large windows facing the street. My room contained a double bed, an easy chair, a table and chairs, a closet, chest of drawers, a bookcase, and a sink. The bathroom was shared by several of us.

Many of the occupants were sober, serious, and dull, rightly preoccupied with their studies. Down the hall was a dental student, TL, who livened up the place. He loved to drink and carouse with a colleague, who lived in another house but visited him several times weekly. They would begin drinking in the midafternoon, and by early evening were singing, telling jokes, laughing uproariously, and tossing their glasses into the sink. The studious ones would come to TL's room and ask them to shut up. Most of the time, there would be quiet for a few minutes, but soon the laughter and singing would start again. A few times TL would drop his pants and "moon" the supplicants, laughing all the while. The studious ones would turn away in disgust.

For reasons still not clear to me, I was able to concentrate on my studies, undistracted by the noise. I would come out of my room whenever I needed a break, enjoy the entertainment for a few minutes, and then return to my books. Late in the academic year, in the face of oncoming exams, TL's antics became more pathetic than funny. While the rest of us were putting in maximum effort, it became increasingly clear that he was either unwilling or unable to stop drinking.

We later learned that he had flunked out of dental school. I am not sure that any of us could have saved him, even if we had known the severity of his alcoholism or how to help. None of us attempted to directly, and it would have been unthinkable to report him to the school's administration.

For the second year, I moved into an apartment that I shared with FB, a charming, very bright Viennese fellow whose family had escaped from the Nazis to Burlington, Vermont, in the late 1930s. We got along well and spent many spare hours together. We each had our own bedroom while sharing the living room, bathroom, and kitchen. Thus, we were able to have privacy when we needed it.

The second year subjects were microbiology, gross and microscopic pathology (morbid anatomy), pharmacology, and pathophysiology. We also began to study the taking of medical histories and the performance of physical examinations, initially using our fellow students as "patients." Late in the year we were taken to the medical wards where we practiced on actual patients, with their consent, of course.

We heard sad stories, patients' heart murmurs, and felt their enlarged livers and spleens.

We were taught that disease was the manifestation of disordered function of an organ, or multiple organs. This could be detected by blood tests that would detect altered function of such organs as the liver, kidney, or bone marrow. Other tests of organ function are the electrocardiogram and pulmonary spirometry. The disordered physiology would at times alter the size or structure of an organ. This could be detected by physical examination or by various imaging techniques, in my day mostly X-ray. In the nearly forty-five years since I graduated from medical school, the frame of reference has shifted from organ and cell physiology to molecular biology and genetics. With the increasing knowledge in these areas, diseases have come to be understood as disorders of molecular structures due to defects in gene structures or defects in the functions of molecular pathways induced by external agents such as bacteria or viruses, or dietary indiscretions/sedentary lifestyles.

The contrast in the way my father's generation and my generation practiced medicine is enormous, and the differences continue to widen. His generation understood disease at the anatomic and physiologic levels, i.e., as abnormalities in the structure and function of organs or organ systems. By contrast, we have come to understand disease as disordered structures or functions of molecules, either inherited, as in genetic diseases, or acquired from the environment, e.g., from voluntary or involuntary ingestion of toxic agents like strychnine, mercury, or carcinogens; or infections by bacteria, viruses, parasites, rickettsia, or fungi; or nutritional excesses or deficiencies; all of which directly affect single or multiple molecules and hence single or multiple organ systems.

Diagnostic tests, based on this understanding, and noninvasive imaging techniques, based on advances in physics and engineering technology, have made major improvements in diagnostic speed and accuracy. For example, molecular biology techniques reduced the time required for the diagnosis of bacterial and viral infection from days to hours. Imaging techniques have all but obviated the need for exploratory surgeries for the finding of intra-abdominal tumors or infections. Lesions in the brain can be found without the prior invasive carotid arterial punctures. The number of diagnostic tests has increased from dozens to hundreds, and the number keeps climbing.

Increasingly, therapies are based on an intimate knowledge of molecular mechanisms rather than empirical trial and error, although much of that still remains. The body of medical knowledge and procedural skills exceeds the capacity of single individuals to absorb and to update on an ongoing basis. That is why medical and surgical specialties have developed, along with a large cadre of "paramedical" specialties, such as lab technicians in chemistry, microbiology, and hematology; radiology technicians; operating room technicians; and therapists of various sorts. Nursing, a critical profession in the delivery of caring medicine, has come to mirror the medical specialties.

Of course the expansion of knowledge has of necessity entailed the development of teamwork in diagnosis and therapy, many of which did not exist at the time my father was practicing or when I first started to see patients. This ongoing expansion requires constant updating of knowledge on the part of practitioners. A whole industry has developed primarily to deliver postgraduate courses. Much of this is funded by pharmaceutical companies, giving them access to physicians, whom they use to sell their products.

All of the above is costly, and while the public likes and rightly demands the latest and best in medical care, it is not always ready to accept the costs. Most people have some form of health insurance, but a large segment of the population does not (forty-six million and counting). Economic interests, their accompanying political theorists and spinmeisters, and supportive politicians have polarized the political classes, resulting in decades-old battles as to who should pay and how much. These struggles continue to hinder the achievement of solutions beneficial to the wider public.

A simple problem, such as a sprain or a viral cold, can still be handled by a single doctor in his or her office. Most problems fall into that category. But complicated cases can require complex diagnostics and therapies that may require visits to several doctors and therapists, as anyone who has experienced a serious Illness can attest. This can, although it need not, lead to loss of personalized service, depending on the time pressures under which the various components may be operating. Since the United States has come to follow a business model in medicine, rather than considering health as a social good, the richest segments of society can afford the best of care, while the poor wait in lines and worry about how they will pay the expensive bills.

With the hindsight gained from a long career of teaching and practicing medicine, I realize that the profession rightly has placed enormous emphasis on technical knowledge of health and disease. This is critical for accurate diagnosis and therapy—in a word, producing a cure. Unfortunately, many of the humanistic aspects of the doctor-patient relationship are left to be learned by indirection, from master clinician humanists, where those rarities are available. In recent years, some awareness of the deficiency in personalized approaches to patients has seeped into the consciousness of the profession, and teachers have begun to speak of the difference between curing a patient's illness and healing the patient. The adding of explicit teaching sessions on healing is becoming more and more important as the tendency toward gadget-induced depersonalization keeps rising.

First Steps in the Lab

Toward the end of the first year I was introduced to Melvin Cohn, a professor of microbiology, by GM, who later became my roommate. I spent the summer of 1957 in Cohn's lab learning about research; but before I began, I paid a visit to my cousins Charlotte and Fred Farkas in Los Angeles for a couple of weeks.

I had seen them only a couple of times since Prague and Pleš, and it was a pleasure to be able to spend some time catching up. We drove to Las Vegas and stayed for two nights.

I was also introduced to HH, the daughter of very wealthy people from our part of the world, who had earned an MA in economics from Harvard. She was a very bright young woman and fun to be with. Both families were very much in favor of our marrying. After she and I had seen each other a few times, her father offered me the income from a property on Park Avenue in Manhattan to help us live in the proper style until I finished my training. My parents' eagerness that

I marry was ironic, because despite my parent's fears to the contrary, I simply was not prepared for any permanent exclusive relationship that marriage required.

Mel Cohn was born in 1922 and educated in New York (CCNY, Columbia, and NYU). He was a brilliant, charismatic man, who had spent several years at the Institut Pasteur in Paris with Jaques Monod working on the genetic regulation of beta-galactosidase, an enzyme in E. coli, for which Monod later won the Nobel Prize. He was among the first to decipher how a nutrient can regulate the actions of genes in bacteria. The work served as a model for later work on the regulation of genes in eukaryotic cells.

The head of the department was Arthur Kornberg, who later won a Nobel Prize for unraveling the biosynthesis of DNA. Other members of the microbiology faculty were Paul Berg, another Nobel Prize winner, and Drs. Kaiser and Hogness, all brilliant and dedicated to research. People were working on their projects day and night with intense concentration and devotion. In an odd way the place reminded me of the yeshiva, where people also studied day and night.

In Cohn's lab I learned how to grow bacteria in culture, to count them, to isolate enzymes, and to assay enzyme activity, lab skills that have been useful to this day. Mel spent much time thinking about the right experiment to do. He used the phrase "trivial experiment" as a strong pejorative. He hated to waste his time on "trivial discoveries." This taught me about reading the literature of science and about design of experiments, particularly about the importance of control groups.

Unknown to me, Mel spoke with my parents about my love and aptitude for research. He urged them to support my taking extra time to obtain a PhD, and then finish my medical studies. Dad feared that this diversion would stop me from obtaining an MD (this was before MD-PhD combined degrees became available), there was a blowup, and that was the end of that.

As a second option, Mel suggested in the spring of 1958 that I take a year off for research. The school had stipends available to support travel and expenses for the year on a competitive basis. He had arranged it with a friend at the MRC unit in Mill Hill outside of London. This, too, was strenuously opposed by Dad. Nevertheless, I applied for the stipend. Unfortunately, I did not receive it. (I suspect because I had not done well in pathology. I loathed the professor who was widely known as a "pompous ass," and turned out to be an alcoholic.) Without a stipend, and in the face of strenuous opposition from my parents, I continued in medical school.

On the day I heard the negative news about the stipend, I faced myself in the mirror and said, "Schonfeld, you're never going to be a researcher." It would be several years until I changed my course to include both clinic and research. In the meantime, I missed important opportunities for research training.

Years later I missed another opportunity for basic science training during my endocrine fellowship. This time it was the Vietnam War, not my parents. When people ask me, "Is there anything you regret?" my answer is, "I regret only not having had more training in basic research. I would keep almost everything else as it was."

As a third option, I spent the summer between my second and third years working in Ed Lennox's lab at Illinois

University in Champaign-Urbana. Ed was a friend of Mel Cohn's, and he and Mel thought that it would be good for me to learn about viruses that infect bacteria (bacteriophages). I learned about growing phages, the plaque assay, purification of viruses, and infecting cells—for me, a new world of knowledge. I lived in one of the dorms, and frequently returned to St. Louis for weekends to be with my girlfriend, JE.

Clinical Rotations

FB transferred to Harvard Medical School for his last two years because he wanted a Harvard MD degree, so I moved into another apartment with Gordon Miller from Miami. He was a year ahead of me in starting medical school but had taken a year in London for doing research. He was a cheerful, bright young man, and a fun apartment mate. He eventually wound up back in Florida in the private practice of ophthalmology.

During our third year we spent most of our time with patients. We rotated through the large specialties— general internal medicine, pediatrics, general surgery—and the smaller specialties of OB-GYN, eye, ENT (ear, nose, and throat), neurology, and psychiatry. During our fourth year we took electives through the various medical subspecialties, e.g., gastroenterology, cardiology, metabolism, and hematology.

The chair of internal medicine was Carl Moore, the Adolphus Busch Professor of Medicine. Who would have imagined in 1958-59 that in 1996 I would become an occupant of that same chair? Moore was near fifty and tall, with a shock of white hair and an air of commanding calm. He frequently had a pipe in his mouth, which he used to good effect for deliberating before delivering himself of an answer to any question. On rounds, wearing his long white coat with his stethoscope in its pocket and surrounded by his retinue of junior faculty, fellows, and residents, he very much looked and acted the part of the distinguished academic that he was. In addition to being chair, he later served as dean. He was a member of the National Academy of Sciences and served as national president of several prestigious professional societies.

Sometime in 1958, Dr. Moore was expatiating on a case at one of the professors' rounds on Ward 1418, the major internal medicine ward for male clinic patients at old Barnes Hospital. He was surrounded by his large retinue of residents and staff. Suddenly, one of the associate professors fell to the floor, had what appeared to be a grand mal seizure, and stopped breathing. It was assumed that he had suffered a myocardial infarction with an arrhythmia. He was quickly lifted onto a bed, the curtains were drawn, and Dr. Moore calmly conducted the attempts at resuscitation. CPR was given along with injections of various sorts, but the attempt was ultimately unsuccessful. (This occurred before the common use of cardiac defibrillators.) Nevertheless, I was impressed by Dr. Moore's calm and competent handling of the situation.

Moore's area of specialty was hematology and his particular area of research was the metabolism of iron, which he studied mostly in people. These studies are considered classics of their type and are still cited. He also studied other hematologic diseases such as thrombocytopenic purpura, a bleeding disorder due to very low levels of platelets in blood. To discover whether the low platelet counts were due to a factor circulating in plasma, the plasma from one of the patients was injected into Carl Moore's vein. Rapidly, his blood platelets dropped into a dangerous range, proving his point but at considerable risk of bleeding into his own brain, kidneys, or other organs. Moore was hospitalized for several days and spent the time in bed writing his papers. Eventually his platelet count normalized.

Moore was considered a fine teacher and clinician, and given his accomplishments and status, and the way he carried himself, many of us viewed him as a distant, unapproachable deity. I certainly felt he was a different order of being, living and functioning at a level to which I could not aspire. It is still not clear why, but perhaps having to do with my wartime experiences as a Jewish boy in Europe or with my upbringing, I was left with an underdeveloped self-esteem, always surprised when I did well. I certainly did not feel worthy of barging into the big man's time and "wasting" it with any questions or requests I may have had.

To this day I am most reluctant to call on people for my own needs, although I am not nearly as bashful in pursuing the needs of others for whom I am responsible. However, I remain surprised by people's chutzpah in asking for special consideration, despite my later experiences with many individuals who did so. These persons, of course, are convinced that their activities have unique value, and that their opinions are so important that no one should be denied the privilege of hearing them—and so they barge into ongoing conversations.

My only contacts with Moore during my years in medical school were during my turns to present cases to him at Professors Rounds. It was a tension-producing experience. In a roomful of medical students, house staff, and residents, the medical students would stand and recite the patient's medical history, the results of the physical examination, and the outcomes and interpretations of various tests. We then listed the possible diagnoses (differential diagnosis), and discussed how we had reached a particular diagnosis. We were expected to know about the specific disease under discussion and something about its treatment. All of this was done without notes, in full knowledge that any errors would be noted.

It was not until the end of my endocrinology-metabolism fellowship, and then my military service in 1968, when I was looking for a job in academic medicine that I actually had a conversation with Moore. By that time he had aged considerably and had suffered from a Bell's palsy that left his face somewhat distorted. He briefly asked what I had been doing and what I hoped to do, and then offered me a job at the Veterans Administration hospital.

Moore died a few years later of a myocardial infarction while he was on vacation. People who knew him said that he had diagnosed his own angina pectoris several years before his death, but did not seek medical help.

I regret I did not approach him as a medical student. The awe that kept me from him precluded my learning about academic medicine as seen by a master clinician/investigator, early in my medical career, while still in medical school. What today is called mentoring was nonexistent in my day. I am one of those who could have used it.

The head of surgery was Carl Moyer, another distant deity. One day at rounds, he was presented a fiftyish woman who had begun vomiting two to three days after her surgery. He spoke with her, examined her with great concentration using only his hands and stethoscope, and made a diagnosis, which he confirmed by passing a tube into her stomach. His acumen and skill awed the three medical students surrounding the bed. Once again it is too bad that students who may have benefited from a conversation or two with him about academic surgery did not have the opportunity to do so. Mentoring of medical students by seasoned academicians is still not at the top of the agenda. This is unfortunate.

I found emotional satisfaction in the interactions with patients. It was wonderful to see a patient's health improve as a result of the actions of the team of which I was part. Nothing is as affecting as a patient saying the magic phrase, "Thank you, Doctor." However, the intellectual satisfaction of understanding the processes underlying the disease was even greater, and had greater potential of affecting diagnosis and treatment of many patients. I could foresee that diagnosing and treating the tenth case of pneumonia (or of any other disease) would not be nearly as fascinating as the first two or three, although becoming acquainted with patients' lives and personalities would turn out to be endlessly fascinating.

On rare occasions members of the faculty became patients of our teams. Some refused to be seen by the medical students. Others told us their stories and took our hands to guide them to their abnormal organs, helping us to outline the pathology. The first big spleen I felt was that of one of our professors.

Dad followed my medical education with great interest. He was a lifelong student of medicine, setting himself challenges and deadlines for taking state board examinations, e.g., in Missouri and California, both of which he passed. I still see him underlining the text he was studying with a red ballpoint pen using a ruler, or reproducing certain illustrations with his fine hand.

Elective Time at the Peter Bent Brigham Hospital (now known as Brigham and Women's Hospital)

During their fourth year, all of the medical students were offered the opportunity to take several elective courses in six-week blocks at Washington University or in other approved institutions. I decided to spend six weeks on the medical service of the Peter Bent Brigham Hospital (PBBH), one of the teaching hospitals of Harvard Medical School in Boston, followed by six weeks in Europe, split between visiting Paris and Hungary. These absences from St. Louis were strongly supported by my parents, who at that time yet again felt that I was dating someone unsuitable, and hoped that a twelve-week absence would break up the relationship.

My friend and former roommate, FB, who had transferred to Harvard Medical School for his last two years, helped to arrange for an internal medicine rotation at the Peter Bent Brigham Hospital (we called it the Bent Peter for short) in the fall of 1959. It had a sterling reputation for the quality of its teaching and was most highly esteemed for residency training in internal medicine. I was put up in Vanderbilt Hall and assigned to a team headed by a resident named Pitt, who turned out to be a pleasant and very knowledgeable man. Of course, I also spent much time with FB and his fiancée, M, getting to know Boston and its environs, which is quaint and interesting in the way old persons and antiques fascinate, leading me some years later to accept a job at MIT.

We would travel to Marblehead and Gloucester north of Boston. The ride took us through beautiful old towns, some dating back to the seventeenth century. We would stroll on the beaches and enjoy the salty smell and the screeching of the seagulls. I was raised in beautiful mountainous country but had not previously experienced the ocean. I soon learned why some people become beach bums, although I did not succumb.

For FB and M's wedding, they put me up at a pretty inn in Marblehead near the beach. I was privileged for the first time in my life to hear the roar of the surf as I fell asleep and awakened. Since then I have had many occasions to enjoy the ocean shore in many parts of the world, but I have not acquired the easy relationship with the ocean that persons raised near the ocean seem to have.

The physician-in-chief of PBBH hospital was George W. Thorn, the Hersey Professor of the Theory and Practice of Physic at Harvard Medical School. The title bowled me over until I looked up "physic." One of its meanings is laxative or cathartic, as in "a dose of physic." Trust Harvard to turn a cathartic into a grandiose title. However, I was greatly impressed at the time.

Harvard is very good about placing portraits of its notable professors and benefactors in strategic locations. Since Harvard is an old institution, some of the portraits date back a hundred or more years. Needless to say, the long line of luminaries impresses the impressionable, which I suppose is why the displays are so carefully crafted. Still, it is impressive that Harvard has managed to stay on top for so long in a very competitive field.

Dr. Thorn, an endocrinologist, was a man of many accomplishments, including the early use of cortisone-like drugs in Addison's disease, a condition of lack of cortisol, analogous to type 1 diabetes in which there is a lack of insulin. Replacement of cortisol saves lives, as does the replacement of insulin. In addition, the first renal dialysis occurred at the PBBH on his watch. Understandably, he was held in great regard by the house staff and treated with the deference accorded an army general (not unlike the treatment accorded Carl Moore at Washington University). Thorn headed the department of medicine at the hospital for many years and was a national leader in academic medicine.

Thorn's medical service was geared to teaching and clinical research. It also prided itself on the quality of care given to patients. Any team took only a selected and limited number of "good teaching" patients, who were kept in the hospital for many more days than is the practice now; affording each member of the team, even the medical student, the opportunity to obtain a detailed medical history, perform a lengthy physical examination, and come to know the patient in great detail. All of the medical and surgical specialties were represented in depth within the hospital, and consultations were unhesitatingly used when necessary. Each patient was discussed, the medical literature relevant to his or her illness was consulted, and the resulting best collective judgment was brought to bear on diagnosis and therapy—the opposite of today's industrial model of "maximizing throughput." Today, the pace is more harried, and by design patients are in and out before all their problems can be addressed. Perforce, only the most urgent problems are considered, and much is left for diagnosing and treating on an outpatient basis. This, of course, detracts from the quality of teaching and the thoughtfulness of patient care.

In sum, the PBBH epitomized the organization and practices extant on the medical services of the better teaching hospitals affiliated with the better schools of medicine, including Barnes-Washington University. So, the routine was familiar.

War stories dealing with great feats of diagnosis and treatment were commonly told by the house staff about giants such as Soma Weiss, Bernard Lown, and Samuel Levine, all cardiologists who had furthered the field and were highly respected clinicians. Stories were also recited of the tough love practiced by luminaries. Samuel Levine in 1959 was already quite senior. He was a small, energetic man with a magnetic presence. When he entered the ward, the word quickly passed around and house staff and medical students hurried in so as not to miss a demonstration of his history taking and physical examination skills. When he confirmed the findings of the house staff they were pleased, and when not, they were down.

On one occasion one of Levine's patients died, and he came in to speak with the family. I happened to be in the room, reading as he began to speak with them, and hoped I would be permitted to stay. However, he requested some privacy. I blushed and left, regretting the missed opportunity to hear how one of those rare master clinicians handled that sort of humanitarian situation. My discomfort was eased by an old story. The Talmud tells of a rabbinic student who hid under his master's bed in order to learn the master's approach to lovemaking. The rabbi found him, and although sympathetic with his student's reasons for wishing to stay, asked him to leave.

When I finished at PBBH, I went back to St. Louis and in the late fall of 1959 took off for Europe.

A Break in Paris

I flew into Paris and stayed in a small inexpensive hotel on the left bank. I spent many weekdays at the Institut Pasteur visiting Nissman's lab, helping out with isolating ribosomes from E. coli bacterial cells by ultracentrifugation. The people in the lab were cordial and helpful. Most spoke some English. Unfortunately I had no French.

Expecting that all French persons were gourmets, I was surprised to discover that many of them ate chewy, broiled beefsteak and French fried potatoes for lunch—not a gravy or fancy dessert in sight. During evenings and weekends I spent much time walking the center of the city, which was beautiful, not having been damaged during the Second World War. However, most of the days were overcast and gray, adversely affecting my mood. Also I missed my girlfriend. It would have been so much more pleasant to have visited the restaurants and museums in the company of a lovely woman. Nevertheless, I came to appreciate the beauty of the city and returned several times with Miriam as an academic.

The situation improved when a young American scientist several years my senior, who was on a sabbatical at the Pasteur from Johns Hopkins, befriended me. He was fluent in French, permitting him to get around easily. I was pleased I had found someone intelligent and well acquainted with Paris to relieve my loneliness and to show me some sights. We had several companionable meals and walks together.

On one of our after-dinner walks, which would turn out to be the last, we passed near his apartment. He invited me up and suggested I spend the night on his sofa bed. As we were about a half hour walk from my room, and it was late, I gratefully accepted. As soon as we came into the room he proceeded to undress and, to my utter surprise, standing by his bed, completely nude, invited me to sleep in his bed with him. It took a few seconds for me to understand what he had in mind.

I said no thanks. "I better go back to my room."

He tried to persuade me to stay, but I was not ready for whatever he had in mind. It is not that I abhorred homosexual persons. I simply happened not to be one.

I walked back to my room, regretting the loss of what I had thought of as a developing friendship.

Hungary in 1959, Fresh Wounds of the Revolution of 1956

After that episode, I had had enough of Paris and decided it was time to visit my aunt and uncle in Debrecen, Hungary. In early 1959, I flew to Zurich on Swissair and to Budapest on Malev, the Hungarian national airline, which was flying Russian airplanes such as the Ilyushin and Tupolev. The contrast with West European and American airliners was stark. The bodies of the Russian planes were smaller in every direction so that the seats were narrower, the leg room smaller, and one walked through the plane bent over. Fortunately, the flight to Budapest was less than an hour in duration, so I was able to endure the cramped position without permanent damage.

After disembarkation and stringent luggage and passport control, I walked out into the welcoming arms of Aunt Erzsi and Uncle Tibor Meisner. I had not seen them in fourteen years. It was heartwarming to be with the family.

They took me to their cottage on Star Hill (Csillag Hegy). The hill, on the western side of the Danube in the Buda part of Budapest, was the site of many cottages, ranging from small and simple to quite elaborate with many rooms. It was a place for the better-off inhabitants of the city to get away from the crowding and noise. My aunt and uncle used their cottage as a second home for visiting Budapest several times per year, where they visited friends and the cultural sites and events. I found it interesting that there was a clearly privileged class of Hungarians in what the communists were fond of saying was a classless society.

Budapest in 1959 was a gray, defeated, poor city, with many of its buildings badly in need of repair and maintenance. The damage had been inflicted during the siege of Budapest in 1945 by the Russian Red Army fighting against the German and Hungarian armies. In 1956 the city was damaged again during the nationalist revolution against the communists. In both instances the city was the battleground and both the city and its inhabitants lost.

Still, if one looked past the grime and bullet holes, one could detect many good-looking buildings built before the First World War. The contrast between the elegant past that had been experienced under the Austro-Hungarian monarchy and the shabbiness of the 1959 Democratic Republic of Hungary would have evoked pity in me, had I not experienced the actions of Hungarians in the 1940s. Knowing what I knew about recent Hungarian history, I felt they had earned their suffering.

We drove to Debrecen in about two and one-half hours, in a southeasterly direction, through the Hortobágy plain of Hungary, the area of the Hungarian "cowboy" and farmer, passing many villages. Debrecen is one of Hungary's major cities, a university town that includes a medical faculty and boasts of tram lines, major churches, a museum housing the paintings of Munkacsi Mihaly—after whom my street in Munkacs was named—and a nice hotel, the Bika (Bull), in which my parents were married in 1931.

Erzsi and Tibor lived in a duplex on a wide street with a strip of green in the middle occupied by the tram tracks. The house contained a sizable bedroom, a large living room with a tiled oven in one corner extending from floor to ceiling, a bathroom, kitchen, and hallway. There was a fenced-in backyard. I slept on the couch in the living room that contained fine handmade furniture, paintings, sculptures, and Persian carpets. Erzsi explained that since no one trusted the currency, people tended to place their savings into tangibles, such as furnishings, artwork, gold, and diamond jewelry, rather than into cash or securities. These items could be sold when necessary in order to obtain the cash needed for survival.

Tibor had never joined any political party. Nevertheless, he thrived under all political regimes because of his interpersonal and lawyerly skills. He was then the lawyer for the large farmers' cooperative in the region, and was instrumental in fashioning some of the relevant laws that were passed by the government. He also took on private work for which he preferred to be paid in kind, because private practice was to be kept confidential. They had a maid and cook who came in daily, a Lada automobile, and a barber who came to the house every other day to shave Tibor. The maid and barber were there under private arrangements. Clearly, they had provided for their own comfort, even under communism.

Their circle of friends consisted of the upper crust of Debrecen. The first person I met was Dr. Mrs. Suranyi, an internist, who came to treat me for a sore throat that began within a few days of my arrival and quickly degenerated to high fever and a couple of days of delirium. She treated me with antibiotics and made house calls twice daily until I was out of danger. She was very charming and very kind.

Soon, I also met her husband, Dr. Professor Suranyi, an obstetrician-gynecologist at the Medical University of Debrecen. Erzsi told me they were Jews who had escaped the camps by staying in protected houses in Budapest. Both had studied and worked in Hungary, but the professor husband had spent a year in Britain doing a fellowship in gynecology. He told me he had greatly enjoyed the experience and learned much that was new and useful. When I asked him why he had returned, he told me that he wished "to participate in the building of socialism in Hungary." I was unable to ascertain whether he gave me the politically correct answer, not knowing whether he could trust me with the truth, or if in fact he was a sincere socialist. In hindsight, I suspect he returned to Hungary because his family was kept behind, in effect as hostages against his defection.

I was certain that by 1959 no one could believe in communism, not after the show trials in Russia in 1936 during which "the revolution ate its own children," not after the execution by Stalin of his army's best generals just before the Germans struck, not after the Molotov-Ribbentrop Pact and many other acts that had disillusioned many devoted communists. Furthermore, why would a Jew wish to help the Hungarians to build anything, when our wounds were still fresh so soon after their hand in killing us? Perhaps I did not sufficiently take into account the strictures under which he lived. Nevertheless, it is possible that he was a sincere believer in 1959. I did not meet him after that, and do not know how his beliefs were shaped by subsequent events.

I also met the editor of the biggest newspaper of Debrecen. He was a large, well-fed, elegantly attired person, and when he spoke, everyone turned toward him, listened, and agreed, in word or by nodding. He turned out to be a convinced Communist. I asked the editor to tell me his story, which surprisingly he did.

He was born in the 1920s to a pig herder, a member of the lowest rung of the then socially immobile Hungarian society. Under the old regime he was doomed to spend his life in poverty and subservience to his "betters," e.g., kissing their hands and always being careful to bow and address them as sir and ma'am. I believed him because I had witnessed this sort of exchange in Nagyleta. His children would have had no opportunity for educational, social, or economic advancement. He joined the Communist Party of Hungary at the first opportunity at the end of the war, and helped to assure that when the new regime came to power, the old Hungarian society would be turned on its head. I must say I was sympathetic, having experienced the arrogant greediness of the Hungarian upper classes.

Indeed, when the communists ascended, the previously lower classes were favored in education, jobs, and government posts. The children of previously rich or even middle class parents were denied entrance to university and the better paying jobs. The editor resented the capitalists and the nobility that had kept him down. To him, the communist arrangement was just fine.

The professor of history at the university had a similar story of privation, followed by success under the communists. He, too, was convinced that the then current arrangements were just fine.

I was not surprised by these human reactions. When rulers consistently over long periods of time abuse those under them and give them neither sustenance nor an outlet for voicing their complaints, citizens become resentful and at the first opportunity help to bring the abuse-filled system down. What gave the abuses of the old regime in Hungary such a long staying power was the support of religion, which lectured the lower classes about the inherent rights of their "betters," i.e., that the upper classes were there with the approval of God. Later, of course, the communists, too, came to mistreat the people, and when they too got their comeuppance, they did not have the clergy and the "will of God" to fall back on.

Tibor, Erzsi, and I discussed on several occasions the then recent Hungarian Revolution of 1956 that was still a raw wound. They spoke of it only in their backyard or while strolling on the street, never inside the house, for fear of being overheard.

Having followed the events of 1956 as the U.S. media related them and as the Eisenhower government responded to them, I was intensely interested in hearing the local version. In America we had heard about the political terror, the knocks on the door in the middle of the night, the drive to Russify the schools, the command economy that confiscated people's property but produced no wealth, and the antireligious laws and practices. The countries behind the Iron Curtain were portrayed as part of a large prison whose masters were out to destroy us. Novelists, such as John le Carré, and the spy movies made huge amounts of money terrifying us. There was much truth to these reports.

As the 1956 revolution began, we in America saw heroic Hungarian "freedom fighters" with only rifles in their hands facing down Russian tanks. Television, the newsreels, and *Time* and *Life* magazines provided full and fulsome coverage. Our government and media lent the revolutionaries staunch moral support, thundering at the cruelty of the "godless" USSR and its Warsaw Pact allies.

The Hungarian revolutionaries initially had limited aims. They did not wish to change the system of governance. They wanted out of the Warsaw Pact. They wished to disengage from the Cold War, to become neutral, but were without luck, just as Horthy had failed to disengage from the Nazis in 1944. In effect, they were saying, "Stop the world, I want to get off," but the world would not stop for them.

Imre Nagy, the "moderate" Communist premier, went along. The revolution struck the chord of nationalism and soon the revolutionary forces occupied large parts of the country. The appetite increased with success. Flush with initial success and with expectations of help from the West—apparently, many believed America would come to their aid, since Eisenhower had praised them as heroes—the revolutionaries expanded their aims, seeking to overthrow the Communist regime and join the West.

This was too much for Krushchev, the first secretary of the Communist Party of the USSR. He sent Polish and Russian troops in force, shot and hanged hundreds, and jailed thousands. Imre Nagy was executed. Cardinal Mindszenty, the Catholic prelate, was forced to seek asylum in the American Embassy, where he spent the rest of his life as a hero of democracy and national freedom. This ended the dream of Hungarian independence for another thirty years.

Tens of thousands, including many who did not take part in the rebellion but saw the chaos as an opportunity to escape to the West, ran to Austria as refugees. We continued to thunder against "godless Communism" but did not get involved. Instead, we sent aid and generously accepted thousands of brave "freedom fighters" as refugees.

Erszi told me something that was not reported in the Western press or by Western government, namely that "one of the first acts of the 'freedom fighters' in the towns and villages they had occupied was to roust the Jews out of their homes and beat them. They also put up signs saying, 'We will finish the job Hitler left unfinished.'" She also told me that the "heroic" Cardinal Mindszenty was one of the most virulent of anti-Semites, consonant with the thousand years' philosophy of the Hungarian Catholic Church, and had been one of the staunch supporters of the Nazis. I do not recall the American press reporting any of this. During the Cold War anyone and everyone who opposed the communists was a hero.

Toward the end of my stay, we went to Budapest for a few days. The Meisners pointed out the spots where the Russians had parked their tanks to shoot at the revolutionaries, and where the Hungarian Nazis had shot the Jews on the banks of the Danube and thrown their bodies into the river. How could I feel relaxed in a country where that had happened to people like me only fifteen years before?

I visited Mom's first cousin Rozsi Nagy. She and her two children had survived the war in Budapest, but she had lost her husband in 1944 in a forced labor battalion on the Russian front. Her daughter Andrea was a very pretty eighteen-year-old at the time. She and I went to the Budapest opera for a lush performance of *Turandot*. Somehow word had leaked that an American was attending, and two thousand eyes followed us as we proceeded from the back of the hall to our seats in the front row. I vacillated between pride and resentment, respectively at being an American and spending dollars with the Hungarian communists.

Rozsi introduced me to her boyfriend Erno, a lawyer, who was supporting himself as a professional piano player in a nightclub. Erno was a wrinkle-faced chain-smoker in his fifties, about five-nine, slightly stooped, and very thin. I asked him, "How did you become a piano player?"

He said, "I'll tell you while we're walking." Everyone was convinced his place was "bugged." In a hoarse smoker's voice he told me his story. He was born into a Calvinist family in Budapest and became a politically active lawyer opposed to Hitler, but not so active as to draw attention to himself. (Rozsi was the daughter of a rabbi. A relationship with a Christian would have been unthinkable before the war, but the war changed everything for her, as it did for millions of others.)

After the war, Erno was asked to join the government, which, between 1945 and 1947 during a short burst of democracy right after the war, had been a parliamentary multiparty coalition government that included some Communists. He had been the minister of justice. But things did not go well. The Communists, bent on taking over, began to dictate policy and those belonging to or supportive of other parties would gradually disappear.

"Day after day, I noticed that people at work would be missing and others would take their places. The Red Army was in the streets, and no one dared to ask any questions." His turn came in 1947. "I was in jail for two years. I still do not know who denounced me or why." Some of those who disappeared were seen again in few months, some years later, some never again (at least not as of 1959). "Those of us who did return were given no working permits or food-ration cards and lived in the economic gray zone eking out a living, relegated to pariah status."

I also took the opportunity to visit the U.S. Embassy in 1959 because I wished to report that, contrary to the impressions I had formed from reading the American press, not all Hungarians felt enslaved behind the Iron Curtain, and not all anti-communists were noble, broad-minded, humanist democrats—in other words, to provide some subtlety, today known as nuance.

I was shown into an office where an American official was speaking on the telephone in what he imagined to be Hungarian. Unfortunately, his pronunciation was awful, barely intelligible. I told myself, *If this is the level of Hungarian on which the United States is relying, they certainly need my information.* He listened politely to what I had to say, asked me a few questions about who I was and what I was doing, and thanked me for "dropping by."

A few days later I was sitting in the airplane flying back to Zurich and then home to St. Louis. I kept asking when we would be crossing into Austria. When the pilot announced the crossing of the border, I raised my arms and cheered. The people around me smiled shyly and clapped.

A few moths later, when I was an intern at Bellevue Hospital in New York, the FBI called for "Dr. Skonfeld" and asked to speak with me. I readily agreed, thinking they wanted to follow up on my conversation at the embassy in Budapest. They began by certifying my identity and confirming the dates of my trip. Then, in a very matter-of-fact way, they asked me some formulaic questions directed toward ascertaining whether I supported the U.S. government and the capitalist free-enterprise system. I said yes, signed some papers attesting to what I had just said, and never heard from them again.

The FBI's visit left me with a sour taste. I thought our government to be more serious than to bother checking on my loyalty. It had also missed the opportunity to learn from someone who was reasonably fluent in Hungarian and had just spent three weeks with Hungarians—some successful, some unsuccessful under Communist rule. Instead, they were more concerned about my loyalty to the United States and had to have me go on record, in case they needed to make a case against me for perjury. I suppose they were protecting the United States against the possible danger that I may have been a Hungarian spy, plotting an invasion of the United States by Hungary. They succeeded. The Hungarians never did invade.

On my subsequent trips to Hungary, I did not bother to visit the U.S. Embassy again.

I had other occasions to test my reactions to Hungary and Hungarians, and to see Communism in action. In 1979, Miriam and I traveled downriver on the Danube from Vienna to Budapest in a hydrofoil. We had spent a few days in Vienna at the meeting of the European Atherosclerosis Society where I had presented an invited scientific paper. We spent two days with family in Budapest and two days in Debrecen. We stayed at the Grand Hotel on Margaret Island. Despite its idyllic location and elegant construction, the Grand had gone shabby under Communism. Our phone did not function and they had no replacements. Messages were brought to the room at a time convenient to the bellman and slid under the door. He had to walk upstairs most of the time because the elevator functioned only periodically.

Service left something to be desired. In the hotel restaurant I ordered one of my favorite dishes, paprikas chicken. A waiter, about whose personal cleanliness I was not convinced, brought the food and set it down without comment. The chicken turned out to be stringy and stale tasting. I asked, "Is this chicken fresh?"

The waiter replied, "No, it was cooked yesterday and rewarmed just now."

"Why didn't you tell me?" I asked.

"You did not ask," he replied with a typical Hungarian macho smirk.

Down the street was the Thermal Hotel and Spa, a new, attractive place built with much rose-colored wood. We had lunch there. The restaurant was full of uniformed soldiers from Poland, USSR, North Korea, and East Germany, all our enemies during the Cold War. These soldiers reminded me, if I need the reminder, of where we were—not among well-wishers of the United States.

We visited my Grandfather Gottesmann's grave in Nagyleta. It was in a small cemetery next to a farmer's house. The farmer kept Grandfather's plot mowed and neat, because Erzsi regularly paid him. The rest of the stones were leaning or fallen over, and weed- and moss-covered, leading me to believe that the cemetery would be converted to other uses in the not-too-distant future. My grandparents' house in the village, where I had played as a child, was now the headquarters of a collective farm, and the Gottesmann lumberyard had been converted to a huge commercial bakery. Erzsi, who had driven us, refused our requests to step out of the car and visit the house and lumberyard, saying, "Don't make trouble."

Further evidence of Erzsi's not wishing to rock the boat, was that she had not placed any claims to have the properties returned to the surviving family. During our most recent trip in 2000, we did not even bother to inquire of her about the disposition of those properties.

In 1983 I was invited to present a paper at the International Congress of Physiology in Budapest, and visited Erzsi and Tibor in their summer cottage on the hills of Buda. Miriam did not come with me because just six weeks before she and I had been in Rome on a separate trip attending another meeting of the European Atherosclerosis Society.

In Rome, we ran into one Hungarian man and four women between the ages of fifty and sixty. All of us were seeking shelter from a sudden downpour under the portico of a church in the garish Victor Emanuel Square, and they were thrilled to meet a "Hungarian-American." Suspecting from his demeanor that he was eager to tell his story, I did not confide that I was a Jew. I wished to hear his unvarnished thoughts.

His family had been of the rural nobility and had been rich landowners. He had been an infantry colonel in the Hungarian army on the Russian front during World War II. He volunteered, "I have lived under both the Nazis and the Communists. I preferred the Nazis. The Communists nationalized our land and discriminated against us." He was angry, but said, "I know what is going on. The Communists in Hungary are all Jews. They are avenging themselves for what we did to them." (In fact, Matyas Rakosi, the First Secretary of the Hungarian Communist Party after the war, was a Jew who had spent the war in Moscow. He was installed by Stalin and remained under Russian control.) At the end of our conversation, the colonel ruefully expressed admiration for the recuperation of the Jews. "You have to give them a lot of credit for the way they are on top again and running Hungary now."

I said, "But is not Janos Kadar Prime Minister? He is not a Jew."

"That does not matter. The people behind him are actually running the show and they are all Jews. Tell me, don't the Jews also run America?"

"No," I said. "America is too diverse for one ethnic group to run it."

"I don't believe it," he replied. "I bet if you really looked into it, you'd find the Jews are running things there, too. As a matter of fact, they are running the whole world again."

Six weeks later, with the colonel fresh in mind, I was sitting in Buda in Erzsi and Tibor's summer cottage listening to a veterinary pharmacologist complaining about America letting down the revolutionaries of 1956. I was not disposed to being sympathetic, although I thought it irresponsible of Eisenhower to have encouraged the revolutionaries without extending any help (encouraging the weaker boy to fight the bully: "Let's you and him fight.").

❧

By our last trip in 2000, after the fall of Communism, notable changes had occurred. The entry at the airport had been simple, nonthreatening. At the hotel desk the staff welcomed us with smiles and asked to see our passports; but instead of keeping them overnight which had caused us considerable anxiety in the past, they promptly returned them. The rooms at the Intercontinental were adequately furnished and clean, but not luxurious, though at least the utilities all were in working order. Parenthetically, as expected in that part of Europe, the hotel deserved four stars but claimed five.

We had not seen Erzsi in over four years, since she was last in St. Louis. Her surrogate daughter, Nellie (mostly known as Mutzi), is the daughter of Madarka, Tibor's secretary of fifty years. Mutzi and her live-in boyfriend Laci drove down from Budapest to Debrecen to bring Erzsi back up to Budapest to see us (and they drove her back home at the end of our visit). Laci and Mutzi (reader, forgive me) were "family." Erzsi ordered them around, as would an old aunt who expected to be obeyed. They respectfully and affectionately obliged. After a few minutes with us they departed.

Erzsi looked great. She had had hip replacement surgery in 1998 and limped using a cane, but she was well groomed, alert, and happy to see us. We chatted about Mom and the rest of the family.

The dinner at the hotel was a lovely buffet, freshly prepared, colorful, and tasty. While we were eating Erzsi told us that the Hungarian government in 1999, for the first time, had publicly admitted some regret and historic culpability for the war crimes committed against the Jews. After a lengthy and complicated applications procedure, Erzsi had been receiving sixty dollars per month in reparations, some fifty-five years after the event.

The next morning after breakfast, Mutzi and Laci appeared with their small old Fiat, ready to show us around the city. Mutzi is a small, energetic, pleasant looking woman in her forties, a senior secretary at the Department of Interior. She has a couple of teenagers by a previous marriage. Laci is about fifty, about five-ten and of medium build. He, too, has two children in their twenties.

He had a university post teaching computer science, under the Communists. He now teaches computer science at a technical high school. They live in Budapest, on a combined salary of one hundred dollars per month, and obviously are not among the winners from the changeover.

I asked, "Are you happy to be out from under Communism?"

Mutzi said, "Yes, we like the freedom to speak and to come and go, but we cannot afford to go anywhere. We are poorer now than we were then. Our salaries were larger and medical care, food, rent, and clothes were all less expensive."

Erzsi told us a similar story about her own economic situation.

I asked Laci, "Who has benefited from the change to capitalism?"

He replied, "The old-time communists who rapidly converted to being religious capitalists and took the best of the nationalized factories, and valuable properties for themselves and their friends and families. Also, the ruthlessly ambitious young people who know about capitalism and computers. They are able to adapt to the new system and to deal with their American and European counterparts."

The government has openly stated that the old generation would suffer for the benefit of the young.

⟨❧⟩

But not all young people wished to stick around once the jail doors opened to find out whether and to what extent things would improve. In 1992 a Hungarian colleague who was visiting St. Louis asked me to take one of his protégées into my lab for "a year." He gave her a very high recommendation. It took me only a few minutes to agree. I felt the young should not be blamed for the sins of their elders. (I had previously accepted a young doctor from Munich for two years of research training in the mid 1980s.)

JP arrived from Balaton in 1993 where she had been working in a cardiac rehabilitation hospital. She was a willowy, lovely young woman. Even more important, she turned out to be smart, determined, ambitious, and an asset to the lab. Several fine papers resulted from her work. After a few months she arranged for her boyfriend, a former classmate in medical school, to come to St. Louis and found him a job in another lab. They eventually married. The one-year stay turned into four years. She then took residency training in internal medicine in Chicago, passed her specialty boards, and is now in a fellowship, where she has continued her successful research career. Her husband is in a pathology residency. They have two children and are seeking to stay in the United States permanently. She is my most pleasant recent experience of Hungary and apparently has decided to leave it.

Mutzi and Laci drove us to the beautifully restored Moorish-style 150-year-old Dohany utcai synagogue on the Pest side. Policemen guard the synagogue and one enters via security gates, leaving packages outside. The synagogue, purported to be the largest in Europe, is very intricately decorated with mosaics and is truly impressive. Its main sanctuary holds more than three thousand persons. In the Orthodox style the women's section is upstairs and the men's downstairs. The main sanctuary is used only on the High Holidays and for special events. A smaller room is used for routine Saturday services, which draw thirty to forty people. The restoration, according to Laci, was partially paid for by the Hungarian government and by Jewish donations, including a large one from Ronald Lauder, whose mother Estee was from Hungary.

According to Erzsi, the youngsters are leaving the community. Many are products of intermarriages with Christians, and the trend continues—this despite the presence in Budapest of most essential Jewish communal services, such as ritual slaughterers, kosher butcher, kosher restaurant, ritual bath, Hebrew school, and even a rabbinical school (the only one in Central Europe).

The synagogue building also houses a two-story museum displaying ceremonial objects used on Jewish holidays and life cycle events such as circumcisions, bar mitzvahs, and weddings. There is also a fine, and horrifying, display of the Hungarian Holocaust.

At the rear of the synagogue, surrounded by an eight-foot-tall steel picket fence, is the stone-paved Raoul Wallenberg Memorial Garden, named in honor of the Swedish diplomat who saved thousands of Jews in Budapest during 1944-1945. In it sits a very realistic metal sculpture of a fifteen- to twenty-foot-tall weeping willow tree commemorating the child victims of the Holocaust, donated by the actor Tony Curtis, a.k.a. Bernie Schwartz, the son of a Hungarian Jew. Unfortunately, the gate was locked for "security reasons." There was no reasoning with the functionaries. In typical bureaucratic fashion they refused to open it. We were annoyed, having traveled a long way. Were they trying to secure the place against people like us, or against indigenous or foreign terrorists? Clearly, we were not terrorists. Use a little sense! It occurred to me too late that a bribe might have helped.

We strolled around the neighborhood and came across two other large synagogues, both in bad physical shape with gaping holes in their walls and windows. Laci told us one of them was being reconstructed.

It is worth noting that the restorations of many of the Jewish memorials we visited were initially largely paid for and kept up by Jewish money, not by the Hungarian government. Hopefully, by now the government realizes what good tourist destinations their Judaica have become, as I have mentioned before, and it is investing some money.

Laci was full of praise for what the Jews had accomplished as individuals and contributed and still continue to contribute to Hungary. He named people like von Dohnanyi, Szilard, Hertzl, and others unknown to me. He seemed genuinely regretful about the Holocaust.

I asked him a "trick" question. "How many Jews are there in Hungary today?"

He said, "I believe it's about seven hundred thousand."

I said, "the Jewish population of Hungary in nineteen-forty was about eight hundred thousand, and half were killed in the Shoah. The present population is generally accepted as being about eighty thousand."

He was surprised, but overestimating the numbers of Jews seems to be common. I suppose we have a disproportionate impact, which is both good and bad for the Jews.

We walked through the kiosks selling knitted goods on Mihaly Vörösmarty Square near the Vaci Utca shopping mall, and had lunch in Gerbaud, a 140-year-old classical patisserie featuring fine sandwiches and pastry delicacies, from strudel to dobos torte, and fine coffees, similar to Café Sabarsky at the Neue Gallerie at 5th Avenue and 86th Street in Manhattan. Having been at patisseries in both Vienna and Budapest, I prefer Café Sabarsky, where I can have all the *gemütlichkeit* of Vienna and Budapest without the Viennese or Hungarians.

That evening we ate in a restaurant called Kacsa (duck) featuring good Hungarian cooking and gypsy-type schmaltzy music. Then we attended a music recital at the Vigado, a 150 year-old recital hall, featuring singers and dancers; and Hungarian and Viennese music, much of it by Lehar and Strauss. The hall was located on the top floor the building with an imposing foyer and staircase. The cast of singers, dancers, and musicians was enthusiastic and talented. Many of the songs were familiar from my childhood, when my mother and father sang them or I heard them on the radio.

The next day we visited old Buda (*Obuda*), on the hilly west bank of the Danube. As we were crossing the Danube on the Chain Bridge, the royal palace on Castle Hill was directly in front of us. To the left was Gellert Hill and the Gellert hotel and spa dating back a hundred years. We saw the old St. Matyas church and the adjacent Hilton Hotel built into a two-hundred-plus-year-old monastery. Restored houses, some built in the 1780s, are now the up-and-coming gentrified area. The view across the Danube into the city of Pest was spectacular: the river below, Margaret Island, the bridges, the parliament, several hotels including our own, and the main outdoor shopping mall on Vaci Utca.

We returned to the hotel for lunch and packed our bags. In the afternoon we said our good-byes. Erzsi got into the Fiat with Mutzi and Laci and we got into a cab. Unfortunately, that was the last time we saw Erzsi.

On our way out of the city, in my thoughts, I wished Erzsi well, and hoped the Hungarians would find peace and democracy. I also realized that with this trip I had come to the end of any remnant of special feeling of connection to Hungary or the Hungarians, and had no desire to return. I was eager to get home.

The airport checkout procedures were as easy as the procedures at entry. We flew Swissair to London. This time I was the only one who seemed to notice when we left Hungarian airspace.

Graduation, MD at Last

In June 1960, I graduated with an MD in the top third of my class. Mom, Dad, the Gottesmanns and my then girlfriend, JE, attended the graduation ceremonies. My parents' joy and relief at my having successfully achieved their cherished goal was obvious for all to see. I, too, was pleased and relieved to be done with school.

I applied to internship programs in New York, Boston, and Cleveland, but not in St. Louis, because I was attracted to the Northeast. It seemed to me then that it was culturally and intellectually the most interesting part of the country. In the intervening years nothing has happened that has forced me to alter that opinion, despite the fact that a long career in St. Louis had turned out very well for me and my family. I decided to apply in internal medicine, because I found it to be the most scientifically based specialty, with the broadest and deepest base in research. It also provided the largest choice of subspecialties from which to choose, should I wish to do so subsequently.

I was matched to the NYU service of Bellevue Hospital in New York. Kurt Metzl, my friend from Kansas City, wound up at Maimonides Hospital in Brooklyn, and subsequently at Cornell-New York Hospital in pediatrics. When I reached NYU-Bellevue, I found that FB, my former roommate, had also matched there.

The chief of medicine at NYU was Lewis Thomas, the medical Renaissance man, who subsequently became head of pediatrics, and then CEO of Memorial Sloan-Kettering Cancer Center and a fine medical writer. His *Lives of a Cell* is classic of biomedical humanism. My dealings with him were limited but cordial. He was succeeded by Saul Farber, the head of nephrology, who held the job for about forty years.

Bellevue Hospital in the early 1960s consisted of a series of four- to five-story brick buildings housing a large emergency room on the ground floor, general surgical and medical wards, labs, and offices. The hospital, one of several charity hospitals in the city of New York, was one of the oldest. It had a distinguished history for medical care and invention. The several internal medicine wards contained forty beds each, lined along both walls with the feet facing toward the center of the room. There was also a row of beds down the middle of the room. Privacy was nonexistent except when people were dying or undergoing medical procedures, at which time movable curtains were wheeled into place. The nurses' station and a small physicians' office were near the entrance door. When entering the ward one saw the nurses' station and office, and three rows of patient-filled beds stretching the length of the room.

Call the Doctor

The first patient you are called to see is a memorable experience. You are faced with someone who has a number of complaints. As a student you were expected to obtain a medical history, to do a physical exam, suggest what tests should be ordered and perhaps which treatments should be provided; but before you actually did anything the intern or resident would have to check you out and approve. So, in the face of a clinical problem we were used to "calling the doctor." The first time I saw a patient at Bellevue I was tempted to react as before and call someone above me. Within seconds I realized that the nurse who had called for a doctor meant me; when I turned around I was alone.

❦

The hours of work during the first year of post-MD graduate training (then called the internship) consisted of being on call for thirty-six hours and off for twelve hours, with thirty-six hours off every other weekend and two weeks of vacation for the year. We began between six thirty and seven a.m. six days per week, drawing blood from our patients. The tests to be requested had been decided on the previous day. The nonemergency blood samples were sent to the labs for chemical tests or bacterial cultures. We did our own blood counts and urinalyses, examining blood cells and any cells in urine under the microscope. More complicated tests were sent to the clinical labs. The more ambitious medical students would be there to help us.

Medicine has its share of sociopaths. One of the interns repeatedly asked his colleagues for help in blood drawing. We found out he slept in for several mornings per week while the rest of us were doing his work. The same man would also request that we cover him for two hours on a Saturday or Sunday, so he could run an important errand. No one demurred. However, during a discussion of cross-coverage we discovered that several of us had been asked to cover for consecutive two hours, netting our colleague a weekend day off. Needless to say, we felt used and made our feelings clear.

We also heard rumors about one of our colleagues taking advantage of the dependency of female psychiatric patients.

He was tolerated, i.e., no one reported him to our superiors for further investigation—not because we either admired him or were afraid of him. We were simply too busy with our own patients, trying to survive a very busy and stressful period. No one had the time, emotion, or energy to lavish on chasing down what we suspected to be the truth. This attitude is probably common in all occupations, which is why sociopaths get away with so much.

Our resident (a second- or third-year postgraduate MD in training) arrived between seven thirty and eight a.m. We would then make "work rounds" on each patient, wheeling our patient charts with us. Nursing orders would be written. The attending physician would arrive at about ten a.m. for "attending rounds." Any patients he or she had previously not seen, or any prior patients for whom we wished his or her help, would be presented and discussed. At times, nursing orders were amended as a result. After a hurried lunch we would return to perform any diagnostic or therapeutic procedures, such as spinal taps or withdrawing of fluid from the chest or abdominal cavities or joints.

Routine new admissions were received and worked up in the afternoons. Late in the afternoon we revisited our patients, and then, on the days we were off duty, we left the hospital between six and seven p.m.

On the days we were on duty we slept at the hospital. We were almost always called for problems with already hospitalized patients, or to work up new patients admitted between six p.m. and six a.m. the next morning. Many of the admissions entered via the emergency room and we went down there to begin the workup and transfer procedures. We rarely slept more than three or four hours because there were usually new admissions, as well as some very sick patients on our ward. There were no intensive care units. We cared for the very sick alongside the less acutely ill.

We all remember a few patients for one reason or another. For sheer horror I remember a young man admitted to the emergency ward with dozens of deep razor cuts leaving his face, neck, and upper chest almost completely denuded of skin and muscle. Despite the surgeons' best efforts he did not survive.

Bertha was a frail old Jewish woman from the Lower East Side. She lived alone in a third-floor walk-up near Houston Street and had been admitted repeatedly over a period of a couple of years for vague chest pains, malnutrition, and insect bite-induced skin lesions. Several teams of interns and residents came to know her as a "steady customer." Examinations and tests, performed at each admission, revealed no cause for the pain. When we suggested that she was ready to go home, she always found new symptoms to complain about, such as in my case, "Doctor, it boins (burns) me under the tongue." She refused to go to a nursing home, much preferring the relative cleanliness and attentive service in hospital. So she would be discharged to her home but despite home care would soon be back. The teams became frustrated by the situation because she occupied a bed that was needed for sicker people.

Hospital staffs are familiar with such patients, who really do not need the intensive and highly expensive care provided; yet hospitals, especially non-profit, public hospitals, are *compelled* to keep them until appropriate "placement" is found. But the rest of the system in which care would be less expensive is *not compelled* to take anyone. Thus, these patients wind up consuming the most expensive part of the heath care system for weeks to months, generating bills that may run in the hundreds of thousands of dollars that will never be paid, leaving it to hospitals to swallow the costs.

One of the patients was to have a prolonged effect on my life. Mr. G was a seventy-eight-year-old Hungarian immigrant painter/artist, in the hospital with widely metastasized cancer of the prostate. He was impoverished, and in the hospital to die. He and I both knew it. During the four weeks of his stay, he had only one visitor, an elderly woman who came twice a week. She brought him a little chicken soup, stayed for a few minutes, and then left. Often, when I had a moment, I would sit and talk with him. He had come to the United States before the war as a young man; he lived a bohemian life, had had many women and much wine and song, but never married. Nor had he succeeded in becoming well known or fiscally well-off.

One day he told me, "You know, I have lived like a king, but I am dying like a dog, all alone. Don't be like me, get married."

I took his words to heart.

My most catastrophic mistake was in trusting the judgment of another colleague who asked me to cover for him in the emergency room for a "couple of hours." As he rushed out, he casually remarked, "There is an old man in a wheelchair in the back with asthma. I've treated him. He's ready to go home. His relatives will pick him up in a few minutes." I permitted the relatives to take him without double-checking his condition. Six hours later the relatives came back, furious. The old man had died at home. In hindsight, the man was probably in acute heart failure, which my colleague had failed to recognize. I had forgotten to apply a cardinal principle: always evaluate a patient for yourself.

In recent years, systems analysts working in medicine have come to realize that the changeover of shifts among house staff, i.e., the hand over of responsibility from one team to the other, is a dangerous time for acutely ill patients. The new shift does not know the patient as well as the doctors who initially examined the person and cared for him or her. Nor do they regard the person as "their patient," because the next day the original doctor will probably resume care. This problem in the "passing of the baton" is exacerbated by the currently mandated short stays in hospital and the relatively short working hours of house staff.

Farber, who was by then the chief of medicine, called me in for a chat. He started off asking me what had happened. However, I was very upset and rather than telling my story, I burst out and said, "Whatever you say to me cannot be as bad as the things I'm saying to myself."

I had two homes in New York. One was the room provided by the hospital, which was in a nonpatient wing of the several interconnected old brick buildings built in the nineteenth century. Maid service was minimal to nonexistent, assuring that the room was dusty and disheveled most of the time. The air in New York in those days was much more polluted than it is now. For example, I would put on a clean white shirt in the morning; by evening the collar of the shirt would be black with soot. When one blew one's nose, the returns turned the handkerchief black. The pollution made it imperative to thoroughly clean rooms, but this was rarely done by hospital staff. What little was done was done by me.

My other home was a former maids' room on the top floor of a lovely apartment house on the corner of 74th Street and Lexington Ave. It was sparsely furnished, but it was sufficient to serve as an escape from the hospital. There was a walkway around the roof permitting me to lean on the parapet and enjoy the views of the city. Jack Shulman, a real estate syndicator and distant cousin of my Aunt Lottie Schoenfeld, found the room for me. Rita and Jack Shulman, who were approximately my parents' age, were my surrogate, supportive, noninterfering parents in New York.

Miriam, My Partner and the Love of My Life

As I look back, it is amazing that despite the work schedule, I managed to date a few women, and to enjoy it. On December 17, 1960, I met Miriam Steinberg through my friend Kurt Metzl. By December, Kurt had been dating Marilyn Newman, his future wife, for a few months. Miriam was Marilyn's friend and colleague at the speech and hearing clinic of Columbia-Presbyterian Hospital. Both Kurt and Marilyn thought Miriam and I would be a good match. They gave me her phone number.

Miriam likes to recite the story of our first telephone call. When she answered I identified myself as Kurt and Marilyn's friend, and said, "I don't have much time to talk. I am waiting for a patient to die. Can we go out next Saturday night?"

Very soon after I met Miriam she and I both stopped seeing anyone else. Miriam was pretty, lively, intelligent, and had a good sense of humor. I found her very comfortable to be with, and her mixture of New York bravado and vulnerability was very affecting. It was clear that she knew who she was, that she strongly identified as a Jew, and that without equivocation supported Israel. We agreed on how we would educate our children and that we would have a traditional home. She listened to tales of my experience with attention and sympathy, without urging me to forget and move on.

We would meet for dinner at 34th and Lexington, pick out a restaurant, and I would drive to it. I paid for our dinners until my money ran out, then she would pay. When neither of us had money we would eat at Bellevue Hospital cafeteria. The open-faced toasted cheese sandwiches, prepared in the morning, were quite rubbery by the time we ate them at dinner.

Miriam's parents were small-business people; her mother and father were from Lithuania and Poland, respectively. Both emigrated from Europe as teenagers. Abe Steinberg had fought with the American Expeditionary Forces in Europe during the First World War, was injured, and survived a gas attack. Abe and Sophie Kanter met and married after the war. Two sons were born in New York. Then, in the early 1930s Abe took his family to Israel, hoping to participate in the building of the Jewish homeland. Miriam was born in Ra'anana, near Tel-Aviv. At the time I met him, Abe was of medium height and build, in his sixties. He was spunky, with a large well of stories and jokes. Sophie was tiny, cute, and quiet, except when she felt something needed to be said. She was then able to make her meaning crystal clear in a soft voice. Their stories of Mandatory Palestine were fascinating, and I came to admire their bravery and idealism. Sophie and Abe kept a kosher home and had raised Miriam in a traditional way.

By February 1961 we were engaged. When we called her parents to announce our engagement, they appeared to be very pleased and wished us well. My parents were surprised and initially not too happy. They had not expected such fast decisive action on my part. They were still hoping that I would come around and marry the rich girl of Hungarian-Czech-Jewish roots from California. Instead, I faced them with someone they had never met. Nor had they had a chance to "check out" her or her family. However, I was determined to marry her. Again, as in other arguments with my parents that had threatened a rupture, Alex Sonnenwirth and Alex Gottesmann intervened; and eventually they came around. The wedding date was set for May 28, 1961.

In April of 1961, the Berlin crisis, one of many crises during the Cold War, loomed. The USSR was threatening to occupy Berlin, and the United States was determined to resist. I feared that I would be drafted in case of hostilities. I was not eager to risk life and limb to defend Berlin. I thought if I already had a job in the U.S. Army Medical Corps I would not be sent to the front. I went to Washington, D.C., to explore the possibilities of obtaining a research job at Walter Reed Army Institute of Research. I asked Miriam to take the trip with me. When we got to Washington, I suggested we get married and keep it our secret. We could then marry publicly in May. We were married by Judge Hugh McCaffrey in Alexandria, Virginia, on April 14, 1961, with Mrs. McCaffrey as witness. I did not like the job offer at WRAIR and chose to gamble on not being drafted, a gamble I lost in 1966.

We were publicly married on May 28, 1961, in Kehilat Jeshurun Synagogue on the Upper East Side of New York. Both sets of parents, the Shulmans, the Gottesmanns, the

Sonnenwirths, the Koreins, and about 150 other relatives and friends were in attendance. Alex Sonnenwirth, Kurt Metzl, Sandy Korein, and Miriam's brothers Sam and Stanley were ushers. We have never told our parents about our elopement. Much, much later, we shocked our kids when we told them. It is now forty-seven years later, and we are still happily together.

Our honeymoon consisted of ten days in Bermuda, initially in a British-style overly elegant hotel, where it was the practice to dress formally for dinner. This was not for me. I never believed that I should dress for dinner merely to impress the waiters. Miriam, of course, thought that dressing up was a pleasure for its own sake. However, we both agreed that it would be preferable to be away from the older crowd and the stuffiness of the hotel. So, after a couple of days we moved into a cottage colony into our own little cottage on a hill overlooking the sea, with a veranda surrounded by flowers, on which we were served breakfast in privacy. Whom we saw, or whether we saw anybody at all, and how we dressed for dinner depended on our pleasure.

We stayed in our cottage for several days while it rained. On sunny days, we got around the beautiful, flower-filled island on small motorized bicycles. Miriam had given me the impression that she knew how to ride, but in fact she was clearly uncomfortable on a bike. However, she learned very quickly, taking a couple of nasty falls along the way, which caused some major bruises but no fractured bones. Nevertheless, she continued to ride. When we returned to New York, I found out how foolish we had been. One of the attending physicians told me that his daughter, while on her honeymoon in Bermuda, had been thrown from her bike, and did not survive the experience. In those days no one wore safety helmets.

We spent the first six weeks of our married life in my room at 74th and Lexington, using the shared bathroom down the hall. Miriam cooked simple meals on an electric plate and washed dishes in our bathtub. Within a few weeks of our honeymoon, we discovered that she was pregnant. We had not planned for the pregnancy to come so quickly. But did I have the slightest doubt that this was a very good thing? I experienced no ruminations about whether it was fair to bring a child into this "troubled world." On the contrary, I felt strongly that I wanted to share in replenishing our decimated people. If the population of the world needed to be controlled, there were many other groups who could benefit the world more by practicing birth control.

I was a little concerned for Miriam's and the baby's health, until her obstetrician reassured me that all would be fine. We then relaxed. However, we needed to find larger, more suitable quarters. Fortunately, Jack Shulman notified us within a couple of weeks that a rent-controlled apartment at 425 E. 86th St. would soon become available.

The apartment, consisting of one bedroom, a living room, a kitchen, and one bathroom, had been under lease to an old woman for several decades. With Shulman's influence, we were able to take over the lease after her death, at the then ridiculously low rental of $125 per month. Our friends and colleagues living in comparable apartments were paying $350 or more. The Shulmans directed us to stores where we acquired furniture and appliances at bargain prices, using the cash we had received as wedding gifts.

Life settled into the routine of my going to Bellevue Hospital and Miriam going to Columbia-Presbyterian Hospital. It was wonderful to come home to her from seedy, sad Belleview. One Sunday per month I took house calls for the New York Health Insurance Plan (HIP). I was paid fifteen dollars per house call and usually cleared $150-$200 per Sunday. Frequently, Miriam would accompany me and wait in the car while I took care of the patients. When the call took me to seedy neighborhoods, she would lie flat in the car to avoid detection by any unsavory characters in the area.

Most calls were not genuine emergencies, but on one occasion I saved the life of an old man. He was emaciated and breathing heavily when I arrived. I heard "wetness" in his lungs, a rapid heart rate, and a cardiac "gallop," all denoting heart failure. I treated him and called for an ambulance. By the time the ambulance arrived fifteen minutes later, he was much more comfortable. I heard from HIP that he had done well and after a few days of inpatient treatment was discharged from the hospital.

The income we made between us was sufficient to maintain us independently. We ate out and occasionally went to the Metropolitan Opera (the old house), the theater, and the movies.

Miriam worked until two weeks before her due date, climbing up and down the subway steps with her growing belly. I thought she looked beautiful pregnant, and told her so. She could not understand it. She thought she looked like a cow. Miriam went into labor on the afternoon of February 20, 1962. We drove down to New York Hospital along York Avenue. At 84th Street, a woman carelessly opened her car door directly into the path of my car. Fortunately, no one was hurt except for the cars. We were able to continue and reached the hospital in plenty of time. While we were waiting for the baby to arrive, Miriam and I listened to the reporting of John Glenn's space flight around the earth. Our son Josh was born in the early hours of February 21st. When I saw Miriam after the delivery, I thought her more beautiful than ever. As for my son, knowing something of embryogenesis, I marveled at his perfection and was grateful for it. I hoped he was only the first of several more. The Steinbergs were there with us and for us and the baby. My mother flew in from St. Louis as soon as Miriam went into labor and arrived within a few hours of the birth.

I had to find a mohel (one who performs the ritual circumcision, *brith*) who would come to our apartment on the eighth day of our son's life, perform the circumcision, and chant the appropriate accompanying prayers. On the day of the brith our apartment was filled with relatives, friends, and the rabbi of Kehilat Jeshurun Synagogue. Miriam's uncle Joe Kanter held the baby (i.e., he was the *sandeg*) as the mohel performed the circumcision. After the ceremony, the women became teary-eyed, everyone said, "Mazal tov," and the men had shots of whiskey, followed by breakfast, which our mothers and friends helped set up. Sophie, Miriam's mom, made the gefilte fish. In sum, it was a traditional brith.

Then I thanked Miriam for giving us a wonderful son. "You have done so well, and we have to build up the family again, so let's have six children."

She replied, "Wait a few weeks before we discuss it" — a wise woman, my wife.

My father was still very busy in his practice at that time and wished to be absent from his office for the absolute minimum of time. Rather than arriving a day or two in advance of the brith, he planned his flight to arrive two hours before the scheduled time. Unfortunately, a snowstorm caused the cancellation of his flight, so he missed the whole show.

Miriam turned out to be a good breast-feeder and attentive mother, and Josh flourished. In the spring of 1962 Miriam's parents fulfilled a long-term dream and returned to their house in Ra'anana, Israel. It would be a few years before we saw them again.

Back to St. Louis

I wondered what I should do at the end my year of internship and two years of residency in New York. The options were a third year of residency as chief resident or as senior resident, a fellowship in a subspecialty, or entering practice. The advantage of a chief residency was that chief residents were routinely offered hospital privileges at NYU Hospital and had a better pick of the practicing opportunities in the premier small-group practices then in existence in conjunction with the NYU Medical School. Although I was not certain I wanted to remain in New York, or to practice private medicine, I was somewhat disappointed when offered only a senior residency. That, it seemed to me, would just be more of the same, more subspecialty rotations, some time on the wards—not very attractive—and not necessarily leading to anything special. Subspecialty fellowships were not as well developed at NYU then as they are now, and I was not attracted to any of the division heads; so it looked as if we were leaving New York. Miriam was quite content to do so.

I received an inquiry from the head of the Stanford University's medical service at the Palo Alto VA Hospital about becoming a senior resident there. Again, it seemed more of the same, with the added disadvantage of it being a place where we knew no one, and where it seemed to us in 1963 a lot of hedonistic crazies resided. Miriam and I were not interested in raising our children in California.

Fortunately, I received a phone call from Al Eisenstein who was then chief of medicine at the Jewish Hospital of St. Louis, a teaching affiliate of Washington University School of Medicine, asking me whether I would be interested in returning to St. Louis as chief resident on his medical service. The idea was tempting. My father had done his internship at the Jewish Hospital; and Alex Sonnenwirth, my cousin, who was like an older brother, was working in the diagnostic microbiology lab at the hospital. Also, I knew many physicians from my days in medical school. In sum, this seemed like a good opportunity, perhaps ultimately to settle into practice after a chief residency or to see what opportunities arose in academic medicine. My parents would be able to see Josh on a regular basis. They were thrilled.

So we returned. Miriam found a job at the Central Institute for the Deaf. Ironically, soon after I began the job in St. Louis, Eisenstein was relieved of his duties at the Jewish Hospital and moved to New York. As a result, I spent the year working for several interesting temporary bosses, some in private practice, most in academic medicine, some at the peak of their careers, others near to retirement. Among them were Michael Karl, the doctor's doctor; Burton Schatz, a premier private gastroenterologist; W. Dickinson Richards, the world-class pulmonologist from New York; William Dock, Jr., retired chief of medicine at the New York VA and son of one our early chiefs of medicine at Washington University; Eric Reiss, a professor of medicine and endocrinology at Washington University and fine classical pianist; and David M. Kipnis, cohead of endocrinology and metabolism, and a sparkling, energetic near genius in medical research and many other facets of life and business. He would become my longtime mentor and friend, who encouraged me to enter academic medicine, supported me at critical moments, and generally enhanced my career.

Children

Josh, our oldest son, was born on February 21, 1962 at the New York Hospital, while I was a resident at NYU-Bellevue Hospital. Our daughter Julia was born at the Jewish Hospital of St. Louis on January 23, 1964, and so was our youngest child, Jeremy, on January 30, 1970, a few months before we moved to Boston. All of our children were perfect, healthy babies. It appeared Miriam and I made a good combination. Josh has given us three good-looking grandsons; Julia, two beautiful granddaughters and a handsome grandson; and Jeremy, one tall, willowy granddaughter. We have been blessed, but raising children is not for sissies.

Miriam and I have fond memories of long years of watching the children grow in size, agility, ability to express both verbally and nonverbally, and in consideration for their siblings and others. We remember long days of play, song, conversation, and many hugs and kisses. These memories have a glow to them like a summer sunset.

Being a physician is helpful when the children become ill. We have some idea about what may be happening, and we usually are provided with prompt, caring, and careful service by our colleagues; but we also know enough to be frightened about possible serious diagnoses or complications.

When Josh was a baby, he developed a viral infection followed by a severe drop in his blood platelets. I was worried about leukemia, then a uniformly fatal diagnosis. But he recovered completely within a few days. When Jeremy had the croup, I repeatedly called our pediatrician who is a patient man, worried Jeremy would choke. He reminded me to behave more like an objective physician than a frightened, panicked, ignorant dad. Fortunately, Jeremy, too, survived without any serious sequelae. A more recent episode also gave us a fright. A few years ago, Julia developed obesity, which her primary internist and gynecologist failed to diagnose as Cushing's syndrome. It fell to me to make the diagnosis and shepherd her through a successful surgery.

The children were sufficiently good students to prevent us from worries on that score. We had decided while on a trip to Israel in 1968 that we would send them to Jewish day school. We wanted them to know about the history of their people, the Hebrew language, and the basic customs of Judaism. Josh and Julia seemed to enjoy the school, and did well scholastically and socially. Jeremy, someone who always went his own way, did much better when he attended Clayton High School, where he excelled in water polo, drama, and music. He wrote the senior musical and played a starring role in it. He has chosen to follow a career as a singer/ composer/ songwriter, and is married to Sarah Jane Casey. Julia became a geriatric social worker and housewife-mother. She is married to Michael Zeuner. Josh became a lawyer, doing great work at Freddie Mac, in housing. He is married to Suzanne Kay. Josh and Julia are sending their children to Jewish day schools. The marriages seem to be happy and stable. Thus we are content as parents and grandparents.

As to our contribution to the further survival of the Jewish people, we have contributed our share, not only by providing loyal progeny, but also good works and funds on behalf of Jewish and Israeli organizations.

Super-Specialization in Metabolic Diseases

At the end of my chief residency I decided that I would attempt to follow a career in academic medicine. Eric Reiss gave me friendly advice: "Apply to Kipnis' lab." On July 1, 1964, at the age of thirty, I began a fellowship program in metabolism and endocrinology at Washington University, headed by William. H. Daughaday, the discoverer of IGF (an insulin-like growth factor), a critical regulator of growth, and codirected by Kipnis. It was Reiss' advice and Kipnis' charisma that persuaded me to enter the two-year program of combined clinical and research training. The clinical part was carried out in the Barnes Hospital metabolism and endocrinology clinic, and the department of medicine's inpatient floors. We confined ourselves to seeing only those patients appropriate to our subspecialty. The clinical training also included didactic lectures and a weekly research/journal club to which we were expected to contribute.

My research training was in Kipnis' lab, where I was assigned to a research project dealing with the interaction of glucose and fat metabolism. I did not become a whiz in the lab, but my intellectual appetite for basic research, first peaked in Mel Cohn's lab in medical school, was renewed after several years of dormancy. It was great to have the leisure to study and think about normal and disturbed human biology, with some detachment from the pressure of caring for very sick patients. The atmosphere was filled with the fun and importance of research and learning (again reminiscent in its intensity of the yeshiva in Chicago). Since all the fellows were in the same boat, we developed a camaraderie fostered by the chiefs.

Kipnis was a very busy academic, even then sitting on a variety of committees entailing much traveling; but he was also very helpful when necessary. A short time with him was worth hours with others less astute than he. One difficult biochemical assay required that I isolate an enzyme from liver. Since I had no experience in doing that procedure, Kipnis spent parts of several days helping me in the cold room and the lab. The first two research papers, resulting from my stay in the Kipnis lab, dealt with the effects of fatty acids on insulin action in muscle.

During the course of my readings, I ran into a three-part series of review papers by Fredrickson, Levy, and Lees in the *New England Journal of Medicine* on disorders of lipoprotein metabolism. It struck me that this could become an interesting relatively new area to enter, but I was unable to pursue the idea until a couple of years later.

Since I was interested in further training in basic biochemistry, Kipnis arranged for me to spend a year in the lab of his friend Ernst Helmreich, a pleasant and gifted man in the department of Carl Cori. I was looking forward to the year, but the Vietnam War intervened.

My Vietnam War in Texas

Miriam and I followed the events of the Vietnam War with great interest, wondering how our lives would be affected. In addition to the all-pervasive media, I read books by Bernard Fall, Graham Greene, David Halberstam, and others.

We also began to learn of the experiences of some friends and medical school classmates who served. Some returned convinced of the rightness of the war; others became radicalized and came to resemble hippies in both philosophy and appearance. For example, one who had become a surgeon upon his return from duty made the rounds with a set of graphic slides showing the horrendous injuries sustained by Vietnamese children and our own troops, speaking wherever he could, hoping to convince his audience of the wrongness of the war. He divorced his wife of long standing, leaving several children behind, and married an artist with children of her own. This caused a stir in our socially conservative, sedate community of physicians.

I tell the story to illustrate that few remained unaffected by the war, because the Vietnam War was fought by draftees, placing every young man at risk, at least in theory. In fact, the poorer, disadvantaged fought in disproportionate numbers, as the better off and more savvy found ways of obtaining deferments or duty in units guaranteed not to go overseas. Mr. Cheney, our recent vice president, is reported to have obtained five deferments, and President Bush Forty-Three served in the Air National Guard, which kept him at home.

Miriam and I were against the war for obvious personal reasons, but we were also well aware of the other arguments against the war. In my opinion, we were continuing to fight an anti-imperialist war lost by France, followed by a civil war. France had attempted to regain her pre-World War II position in Vietnam but had been beaten by the mostly Communist

Vietminh. After the final battle at Dien Bien Phu she with-drew from Vietnam. The Communist and anticommunist Vietnamese then began a civil war. The United States—more accurately, the leadership of our government—became deter-mined to beat the Vietminh because they regarded them as proxies of the Soviets and feared that if they won, the neigh-boring countries would fall to Communism like dominoes.

The counterarguments were that we had no business get-ting into the middle of a civil war to return to power those Vietnamese who had favored the French. After all, we had proclaimed during the Second World War that in addition to beating the Nazis and the Japanese, we wanted to see the end of imperialism. Following that principle, we had forced the British and French to retreat from the Suez Canal in 1956, when they attempted to recapture the canal from Egypt's Nasser, who had seized it from the British-French company that had run it since its construction.

Further, even if the Vietminh won, the opponents of the war said, the neighboring "dominoes" need not fall if we strengthened them. To the supporters of the war this argu-ment seemed to represent a callous disregard of the cruel fates that would await the "gallant" South Vietnamese should the Communists win. This argument sounded very humanitar-ian, but it disregarded the dictatorial cast of our "gallant" allies—who, it turned out, were unable to garner sufficient support for their own cause to win the civil war, despite our extensive aid and sacrifices. Further, had these right wing dictatorial types won, they would have treated the Commu-nists with the same consideration we feared from the Com-munists. Leaving considerations of morality and politics aside, an economic argument was also made. Who would control the natural resources of Vietnam—our side, or the

Communists? The pro-war side magnified the resources; the antiwar people minimized them, saying there were insufficient resources to justify the sacrifices.

These arguments made for interesting public theater, but after fifty-eight thousand US deaths, and thousands of allied deaths, and hundreds of thousands of injured, Nixon and Kissinger decided it was up to the southerners to save themselves. So we "Vietnamized" the war, giving them equipment and logistical support but withdrawing our troops. Soon thereafter, the North defeated the South, and we were treated to the sight of Americans escaping from the roof of the U.S. Embassy in helicopters.

In the ensuing years information trickled out about the brutality of the communists. Yet despite the fears of the war party, the dominoes did not fall. Perhaps the final irony was that Robert McNamara, the secretary of defense under Presidents Kennedy and Johnson and one of the staunchest supporters of the war, much later came to see the war as a tragic mistake.

Many similar arguments are currently being used pro and con about our involvement in Iraq. It appears that after four-plus years of a failing U.S. policy we are in the process of "Iraqizing" that war. One wonders if any policymakers in our government had read the history of the Vietnam War before embarking on Iraq.

One can carry the argument further. Strong objections have been made against the wars in Korea, Vietnam, and Iraq. Some believe that all represented misjudgments on the part of our leadership, which raises the question about the capability of our political system to place the most gifted of our citizens into leadership positions.

Despite my feelings, there was never any doubt that if called up, I would serve. I was drafted in the spring of 1966 and given the choice of being drafted as a private or "volunteering" to serve a captain physician. Kipnis suggested that I volunteer for the air force. Then, he arranged for me to be assigned to the School of Aerospace Medicine at Brooks Air Force Base in San Antonio, Texas. They assigned me to a "research flight medical officer" slot.

The training leading up to my exalted status consisted of ten weeks of basic training at Brooks AFB. We were taught to march in formation using an old concrete airstrip not used since World War I. Our trainer, a captain of medical administration, told us not to work up a sweat. If we felt sweaty we were to report this to him immediately, and we would repair to the officers' club for a cooling beer. This was in contrast with some of my classmates who lived in tents for days to weeks at a time and had to crawl under barbed wire while live bullets were flying overhead.

We learned how to put on and take off a parachute harness, and to jump from a low tower. Those who wished could qualify with a revolver. I did. There were also interesting courses in aerospace medicine, about the various layers of the earth's atmosphere, the pathophysiolgy and treatment of the "bends," aero-sinusitis, and aero-otitis. In addition, the FMOs were required to fly in airplanes for a minimum of four hours per month in order to retain "flight status." During my work on the base and while I was flying, I met many pilots and some astronaut candidates. I came to respect the group as bright, competent, highly energetic, and motivated. As a result of my background in metabolism, and my Air Force training, I was able to be of some use in "space-feeding" studies in preparation of the crewed orbiting laboratory. I was also able to continue some of my research on lipid metabolism.

Our life in San Antonio was pleasant. We joined a synagogue and attended services occasionally. We were received with great friendship and became active in B'nai Brith. Through that connection, I was invited by one of the large Baptist churches to speak about how Jews observe the Sabbath. It was my first experience of that sort, and I was gratified by the interested and friendly reception I received. Miriam was able to pursue her interest in art at the local art museum.

In 1967, Miriam received a telegram from her father reporting that Sophie, her mother, had died suddenly of a hemorrhagic stroke two days before the posting of the telegram, and had been buried in Ra'anana. Clearly, it was too late for her to attend the funeral, and she was unable to get away for the initial mourning period of seven days (*shiva*) because no one else was available to take care of the kids. So, she sat *shiva* in San Antonio. The members of the congregation that housed the preschool program our children attended came to our house to offer condolences and for services so she and I could say the prayer for the dead with a quorum of ten men (*minyan*). To this day Miriam regrets not having been able to be at the funeral of her mother, or to sit *shiva* with her father.

At the end of my two years of service, in addition to having performed my duty for the air force, I had passed my specialty board examinations in internal medicine and had published two scientific papers reporting on work done in the service. Miriam and the children had enjoyed the experience. I had also made a good friend of David Kudzma, a career air force physician, with whom I had collaborated on one of the papers, and who had helped me make the connections I needed to study for my board exams. Unfortunately, I had missed the opportunity to spend the time with Ernst Helmreich in biochemistry, which Dave Kipnis had set up for me. But I did have my clinical investigator slot at the VA Hospital in St. Louis.

First Trip to Israel

I was discharged in early April 1968, but the job at Washington University did not begin until July 1. This gave us nearly three months to visit Miriam's father in Ra'anana, Israel, a small town near Tel Aviv that Miriam's parents had helped pioneer, now a burgeoning suburb of Tel Aviv heavily populated by immigrant Jews from South Africa and the United States. With our two older children we lived with Abe Steinberg in the house he had acquired in the early 1930s. It was a single-story house coated with stucco, with a large porch in front and a roof made of brick-red tile. The house was surrounded by two *dunam* of land (about half an acre, or 2000 square meters) filled with fruit-producing orange and lemon trees on Borochov Street, a side street half a block from Ahuza, the main thoroughfare. For breakfast, Abe Steinberg would walk out of the house, pick a few oranges, and prepare us fresh orange juice.

One of our first acts was to visit Sophie's grave a few blocks from Borochov Street. Miriam wept with sorrow and regret at not having been able to be at the funeral. I, too, wept, saying, "You are lucky, at least you have a place to visit.

I have no place to visit my brother, grandmother, and other relatives, who went up in smoke in Auschwitz."

Abe had many friends among the original settlers, who would come to visit. We heard many stories of the old pioneering days in the region, when relations with the neighboring Arabs could be friendly one day and deadly the next. I spent several morning hours with a neighbor, Mr. Greenstein, whose wife would serve us strong Turkish coffee, while he and I would sit in front of his house as he told me stories, in Yiddish, of his time as a telephone lineman who had traveled all over the country installing telephone lines in the 1920s and 1930s.

We spent a good part of the two months traveling about the country, visiting Jerusalem several times, and becoming acquainted with Galilee. Our children played with the neighborhood children and began to chatter in Hebrew. Over the years and many visits, spanning from Metullah in the north to Eilat in the south, we have, each of us, come to feel comfortable in Israel. It is wonderful to be able to associate physical places with the Biblical, postbiblical, and modern stories one has learned over the years.

The lightning victory over the combined Arab armies in the summer of 1967 was still very fresh in people's minds in the spring of 1968. Israel had captured all of the Sinai Peninsula and Gaza from Egypt, the Golan Heights from Syria, the West Bank, and, above all, East Jerusalem from Jordan. There was a feeling of great relief and exhilaration. The more religiously inclined thought the victory was a divine miracle.

We went to East Jerusalem for the Israel Independence Day Parade, accompanied by Menachem Porush, a good friend, seventh-generation Israeli, and member of the Knesset from the Haredi Agudat Israel party. Rabbi Porush gave us an account of the recent war as experienced by a well-placed Israeli. Included were stories of decisions taken by Moshe Dayan and members of the government, most of whom he knew on a first-name basis. At various times he introduced us to Menachem Begin, when he was prime minister. He greeted us most cordially and made a little ceremony of kissing Miriam's hand. We also met Ben Zvi, the president of Israel, in his official home for a chat. We came to know the Knesset building on repeated visits, and ate in the Knesset members' cafeteria more than once. We were impressed by the easy, informal camaraderie of the place.

At the 1968 parade we sat in VIP seats in the grandstand constructed especially for the occasion in East Jerusalem, which at that time was empty land. We saw the enthusiasm of the huge crowds, as the massed Israeli tank corps and infantry paraded in front of us, including the fabled Golani Brigade and the paratroopers. The air force's French Mystere fighters flew over, forming a thundering Star of David. Tears flooded our eyes, and we felt empowered, knowing that the days of kicking Jews around were not over, but the days of kicking with impunity were behind us.

We also felt profound regret that Israel had not existed as a country in the 1930s, when its presence could have saved many Jewish lives. We could not help remembering that in the 1930s it was within Britain's power to have opened the gates of Palestine to Jews wishing to run from Hitler. Instead they closed the gates. One of the less pleasurable aspects of being a Jewish survivor of the Shoah, in addition to having experienced the physical and psychological shocks imposed upon us by the European anti-Semites, are the memories of such acts that live on in our minds long after the acts themselves have been perpetrated, cluttering our memories with unpleasant images that tend to crowd out more pleasant ones that may have come our way. I am confident Jews are not unique in that respect. All who have suffered at the hands of others must have similar remembrances of suffering that occupy their minds, impelling them to pass the memories on to their children, thus keeping the misery and enmity going generation after generation.

Back in 1968, in the now naïve-appearing days, we dared hope that the Israeli victory would cause the Arabs to rethink their attitude toward the Shoah survivors who occupied less than one percent of the land mass in comparison with the Arabs, and owned none of the oil. Perhaps they would permit the Israelis to reside in the neighborhood in peace. Instead, they have chosen to deny the Holocaust, to deny Israel's historical connection to the land, and to consider Israel an extension of Western imperialism, a constant reminder of their historic defeats by the West and an intolerable affront to their pride as Muslims, the chosen of Allah.

In the intervening years instead of abating, the virulence of Israel's enemies has intensified. The Palestinian Muslim extremists appear to be in the ascendancy, while those who passed themselves off as moderates willing to negotiate peace with Israel continue the late Yasser Arafat's practice of alternating between an unwillingness ("we do not want to provoke a civil war") or an inability to suppress the extremists ("we are too weak to do it") in order to progress toward peace.

Despite the wide-ranging hostility, Israel has increased its Jewish population severalfold, developed a strong modern economy, and is defended by the strongest army in the region. These accomplishments are a source of pride to her supporters and serve as constant irritants to those who wish her ill. Since I am one of the supporters, I relish Israel's victories and continue to hope that at some point soon, the Arabs will value keeping their children alive and having their own country more than destroying Israel. But my level of hope is not high, given the religious nature of their feelings. We know how bitter religious wars can be when they are nurtured by additional rehearsed stories of injury and victimhood, and how long they can last.

Life in Academic Medicine

At the end of my military service, I (along with many colleagues) was asked to stay on with an elevated rank as major. There were many positives to the military medical life: a feeling of service to a beloved country, a fairly certain career path, elite status within the service, and the possibility of early retirement after twenty years followed perhaps by a second career.

But there was the near-certainty of frequent moves around the country or the world, without much control as to where the next tour of duty might be. This could have disrupted the schooling of the kids and our family life. However, in the final analysis, it was the attraction of a career in academic medicine that drove me to decline the offer and to return to Washington University.

When we returned from Israel, my first job was as a clinical investigator on the Washington University Medical Service at the St. Louis Veteran's Administration hospital. The position was achieved by a competition and provided my salary, the salary of a technician, and supplies to do research.

The space and equipment were provided by the hospital. My boss was H. Mitchell Perry, a well-known expert in hypertension, who graciously welcomed and supported me. The VA provided my first technician, who proved to be a benchwarmer. Characteristically for a government position it took several months to get rid of her. Then I was able to hire Barbara Pflager, a gem who worked with me for the next twenty-five years. Barbara had had polio as a senior in high school, which left her lower extremities weak, requiring that she wear leg braces and use a cane. But none of that interfered with her enthusiastic embrace of the work. She was an effective teacher of lab techniques to those who came to the lab and is remembered by them even now, decades later. She was an absolutely essential aid to me and to the proper functioning of our lab.

We decided to study the factors that affect lipoprotein production in liver, using the perfused rat liver system. This was a complex technique requiring intricate surgery and sterile technique. I spent a couple of days at Vanderbilt University in Nashville in Murray Heimberg's laboratory. He and his people graciously taught me the technique.

On January 30, 1970, our son Jeremy was born at the Jewish hospital, to the joy of his parents and grandparents and all who have come to know him.

Although Barbara and I published several decent scientific papers, it soon became clear that I needed to learn more about the techniques for isolating lipoproteins from plasma and characterizing them. Therefore, I arranged to spend six months at MIT in Cambridge, Massachusetts, in Robert Lees' group, with the permission of the VA and the medical school. Lees was well funded and headed the clinical research center that was administratively located in the department of nutrition and food science. Barbara agreed to hold down the fort in St. Louis.

So, in the late spring of 1970 Miriam, Josh, Julia, Jeremy the baby, and I drove to Boston and moved into an apartment in a very pretty area of Weston. I commuted by car. The time was well spent, and we enjoyed living in the Boston area.

After a couple of months Bob Lees and I decided that I would stay on as his assistant director of the clinical research center. It seemed like a good idea. I was engaged in a project of trying to develop immunoassays for the protein portions of lipoproteins, a project I thoroughly enjoyed, and I was learning a lot. Lees agreed to have Barbara join me, and became responsible for her salary.

Lees obtained a courtesy appointment for me at the Harvard Service of the Boston City Hospital so I could keep a hand in clinical skills. I also took on a job at the student health service to generate additional income.

It appears to be the practice in Boston's premier academic institutions to underpay the younger people. The underlying philosophy seems to be that the young faculty should feel so honored to be affiliated that they would take less pay, a syndrome called "Bostonitis." Nevertheless, we enjoyed living in Boston. We made some friends and so did the children, who attended the Maimonides Day School. During the summer of 1971, we spent a very pleasant ten-day vacation on Cuttyhunk Island outside of New Bedford, Massachusetts. Thus, I was content to be Lees' assistant, for a while. However, it was my goal to become an independent investigator and eventually to earn tenure at MIT. I assume my desire for independence was in part inbred, and in part a result of my experience as a Jew in Europe. I simply did not wish my daily existence dictated by someone else.

It was my hope and expectation that Lees would help me in my goal. I had given up my independence to move to Boston to learn some things, but I did want my independence back, eventually. When I raised the question, it became clear that this was not Lees' plan. His interest was to keep me as a permanent assistant.

He told me, "If you want to be independent, I don't need you."

His reply was a huge disappointment. Much later, I was told by one of his previous assistants that this was his pattern of behavior with others as well. I resented that he had not warned me, but I could do nothing except to find a job more compatible with my ambitions.

I started on a job search. Since I was determined to have my own program wherever I wound up, I wrote applications for two separate grants to the NIH. Job opportunities presented themselves at the SUNY Downstate Medical Center in Brooklyn, and at Einstein Medical School in the Bronx—both of which were all right but did not fill me with enthusiasm. After a conversation with Kipnis at a meeting in San Francisco in late 1971, he called me to tell me he had arranged for me to return to Washington University. I was happy to do so and we returned with Barbara and my family in late June of 1972. My primary appointment was in preventive medicine, with a cross appointment in internal medicine.

Both of the NIH grants for which I had applied were funded. In addition, within a few days of our return, Kipnis and I began writing an application to obtain one of the Lipid Research Clinics, a large NIH contract meant to test the hypothesis that lowering of plasma cholesterol would prevent heart attacks. We spent several weeks writing and were successful, largely due to Kipnis' reputation as a star researcher. A short while later, Kipnis generously turned the direction of the Lipid Research Clinic program over to me. Kipnis became Busch Professor and Chair of Internal Medicine in 1973 and served until 1992, when John Atkinson took over.

The funding of the contract and the two grants gave me the opportunity to form and lead a sizable program. This start and the uninterrupted funding of my grant requests by the NIH for the next thirty-five years (as of 2007) permitted me to publish 211 original scientific papers and eighty reviews and chapters. In addition, I presented my findings at national and international meetings and was elected to various honorific academic societies. I sat on scientific advisory boards for the NIH, FDA, and AHA and on various expert committees. The local chapter and national organization of the American Heart Association and my medical school honored me. I also became a consultant to several pharmaceutical firms, and members of my group performed drug testing of the original statin (Mevacor) and other drugs for lowering cholesterol. Some individual private gifts were also given to the program. The pharmaceutical and private funds permitted me to pay for equipment and salaries not funded by the government, and extended our capabilities in research. The university obtained overhead to cover its costs on all of the research dollars my group was able to garner. I was proud to be self-supporting, i.e., being a plus on the books of the university.

I have attended many scientific meetings, but one stands out. In 1971 I attended a meeting of the American Heart

Association. At one of the scientific sessions, Paul Roheim from Albert Einstein College of Medicine in Bronx, New York, gave a presentation of his work on apolipoproteins. I had, of course, heard of his excellent work but had never met him. As soon as he opened his mouth I knew he was from Hungary. At the end of his presentation I approached him, complimented him on his science, and told him I recognized his accent. Soon we were telling each other our life stories. He was from Budapest, and migrated to the United States during the revolution of 1956. He had spent a year in various German concentration camps. It turned out he and I were both alumni of Muhldorf Waldlager, at the same time. I was very pleased to see another survivor who had picked himself up, and done so well.

Through the Lipid Research Clinics contract I also met George Steiner of Toronto, who was director of Toronto's LRC. George was born in Munkacs and came to Canada in the late 1930s with his parents, managing to escape the worst of it. We have been good friends for over thirty years. It is certainly true for me, as it seems to be for other survivors, that we feel most comfortable with persons of similar background who have some understanding for what we have experienced.

Dozens of postdoctoral fellows and visiting scientists came to the lab for two to three years at a time from the United States, Japan, China, and various parts of Europe. Some stand out: Joseph Witztum, my first fellow who carved out a distinguished academic career in atherosclerosis research at the University of California at San Diego; and Maurizio Averna, who in 1990 came as a visiting scientist from the University of Palermo for two years and subsequently every other summer for two months. We became warm friends with him and his family, visiting back and forth on several occasions. Maurizio recently became a full professor, a big deal in Italy. Wolfgang Patsch from Austria, Klaus Parhofer from Munich, and Carlos Aguilar-Salina from Mexico City have also done very well. It has been heartwarming to see the progress of the visitors to the lab.

I have also been fortunate to have had several people who have proven to be essential for the productive functioning or the lab over twelve to twenty-five years: Barbara Pfleger and Tom Kitchens as technicians, and Drs. Elaine Krul, Thom Cole, Rai Ajit Srivastava, and Zhouji Chen, creative PhDs to whom much of the credit for the productivity of the lab belongs. They have all gone on to productive careers in St. Louis and elsewhere. The excitement of the chase and the meeting of colleagues from all corners of the globe were very interesting and nourishing.

Another memorable fellow was Aviv Shaish who came from the Weitzman Institute in Israel. He was about five-seven, good looking, and of dark complexion. I assumed his ancestry was from Yemen or North Africa. Two days after his arrival, I called him into my office and asked him to tell me about himself, as was my custom. I was particularly interested in his last name, and asked him its source. He told me that *Shaish* means "marble" in Hebrew.

"What is the significance of marble to your family? Is it a common name in Yemen?" I asked.

He said, "No. My mother is from Yemen. But my father was from Europe and his name was Mermelstein, 'marble' in German."

"From where is your father?" I asked.

He said, "Hungary."

"Where in Hungary?"

"Munkacs."

We were speechless for the next few minutes. Aviv did very well in my lab, and has done well back in Israel. He has a wife and family and continues to be successful. I am always pleased to hear good news about Munkacsers and their descendants. It demonstrates that Hitler's victory was incomplete, that we were able to outlive him.

My Father's Later Years

While I was busy with my own life and career, my father continued his practice in East St. Louis. He saw about eighty people per day, with all sorts of health problems. I came to know what he experienced because I covered his practice several times while he took some time off. He worked very hard and very long hours. During the times I covered his practice it was customary for me to lose about ten pounds.

Following the Supreme Court's ruling on the desegregation of schools in 1954, the emigration of whites from East St. Louis continued. By the mid-1960s the city was over ninety percent black. Many houses became empty and were vandalized. Whole neighborhoods turned shabby and ugly; lawns were neglected, showing many areas bare of grass. Streets acquired potholes that were not fixed. Papers and garbage were left where they were thrown by uncaring inhabitants.

Previously prosperous businesses, whose Christmas windows had attracted crowds, shut down and moved out; banks shut their doors. The major movie theater on Main Street became garbage strewn, a hulk, with its windows broken. Those businesses that stayed placed metal bars in front of their doors and windows to protect themselves against the increasing crime rate. The school system went into a long decline. At some point the state had to take over its governance for a time. The police department repeatedly came under supervision by the state police. In sum, East St. Louis declined from a blue-collar city to a third-world city complete with failed government services. Whites abandoned the city so completely that they did not even drive through it, bypassing it whenever possible. I have not been able to discern any improvement for the past forty years.

This situation, perhaps more than any other failing, demonstrated for me the basic irresponsibility of politicians, despite the many noises they make to the contrary. That this sort of decline should have been tolerated by the political classes in America—the rich, beautiful, and bountiful—is unconscionable.

Of course my father's practice reflected the population. Payments went from cash and checks to "green cards" identifying those on Illinois state aid. He was not particularly bothered by the change in his patient base and continued to treat his patients as always, but life became more dangerous concomitantly with the rising crime rate, which he experienced firsthand. His office was burglarized on several occasions. The thieves took typewriters, instruments, and whatever drugs they could find. In mid-1970s someone came in with a gun and asked for his money. Thereafter, he had an armed guard sitting in his waiting room.

He had a mild heart attack in 1970, which depressed him but did not impair him physically. However, he lost much of his drive and gradually slowed down. First he gave up delivering babies and assisting at surgeries, then he stopped going on house calls. Finally, he stopped seeing hospitalized patients. Whenever someone needed hospitalization, Dad turned him or her over to another doctor, somewhat reminiscent of what he used to do in Europe. He closed his office during weekends and referred emergencies to the emergency rooms of the local hospitals.

Around that time, my parents rented an apartment near us in St. Louis and spent the weekends visiting us, the rest of the family, and their friends. Eventually, they sold their house in East St. Louis and lived at their apartment full time. One of Dad's employees would drive him back and forth to the office.

My mother became increasingly worried about my father's safety in East St. Louis, and began to push him to retire. After thirty years of practice, in 1978, at the age of seventy-six, he closed his office. Thereafter, he would spend several days a week at the doctor's lounge of the Jewish Hospital in St. Louis, talking to colleagues. Dr. Hyman Senturia, the head of radiology, invited him to sit in the radiology reading room, where he enjoyed reading X-rays. For several winters he and my mother would lease an apartment at the Roney Plaza on Miami Beach. We would drive down during winter break to visit. The kids loved the pool—and Grandma's spoiling them with her cooking. Miriam and I had a chance to spend some time alone.

During the last three to four years of his life my father became increasingly depressed. To his coronary heart disease was added the family curse of diabetes. They began spending winters in Jerusalem, where my father returned to the practices of his youth, studying the Talmud and praying three times every day.

My mother was constantly with him. The people they had met through their long-standing benefactions, cousins who had survived the camps and migrated from Europe, and some old-time St. Louisians, along with the Porushes and Heftlers, kept them company. Our good friend Mel Heftler kept us apprised of their doings. My parents decided that when the time came, they would be buried in Jerusalem, and bought grave sites in the Har Nof cemetery. The sites are located on a hill at the western edge of Jerusalem, overlooking the plain westward toward Tel Aviv and the Mediterranean Sea.

The change in the leadership of the Seders during Passover confirmed my father's declining strength. For many years my father led the two Seder meals during Passover at their house and later the apartment. Starting in the late 1970s the Seders would be held at our more spacious house with my father presiding. In later years, when he became too weak, my father asked me to take over leading the Seder. This was an act fraught with symbolism. I felt that he had placed his mantle on my shoulders. Was I ready?

During the last two years of his life my father hardly ever left the apartment, except to visit doctors or to visit Israel in winter. In late March 1987 shortly before Passover, he asked me to accompany him and Mom to Jerusalem. He apologized for having to miss the Seders at our house, but he told me felt he was close to dying and wanted to die in Israel, thinking it would be easier to bury him if he died there rather than having to transport his body. I accompanied them. He thanked me, saying I had done him a great kindness. We parted with hugs and kisses. I wondered whether this was the last time I was to see him alive.

Indeed, the celebration of Passover was truncated that year. I received a call from Heftler that Dad had been hospitalized with a stroke, but was expected to do well so I need not come. A few days later he called and said I had better hurry. Fortunately, our good and considerate friends Ron and Sharon Burde were visiting us when the call came. Ron arranged for my flight, furnished me with some cash and books to read on the airplane, and accompanied me to the airport. He and Sharon have the rare gift of natural goodness and generosity.

When I arrived, Father was in coma at Bikur Cholim Hospital. My mother was sitting with him, mute. My father's coma deepened as we sat with him all day and into the night. On April 24, after five days of a deathwatch, my mother and I were called at six a.m. and told that he had died peacefully at the hospital. With tears running down my cheeks onto his face, I kissed Dad's forehead, thanked him for all he had done for our children and us, and wished him a peaceful rest.

His funeral was that of a VIP. He was transported from the hospital in an ambulance-like hearse, to the Sanhedria funeral facility where his body was washed, dressed in a white robe and prayer shawl *(tallith)*, and placed into a simple wooden casket. The collars on my suit jacket and my mother's dress were torn, as a sign of mourning. The chief rabbi of Jerusalem, Rabbi Kulitz, delivered a moving eulogy about my father's love of Judaism and of Jewish scholarship.

Followed by busloads of scholars and students, the casket was taken to Children's Town, his favorite charity, where the great synagogue had been named the Schonfeld Synagogue. The casket was placed on a bier in the front courtyard where hundreds of scholars, students, and people of the neighborhood had gathered. My parents' great friend Rabbi Menachem Porush, a member of the Israeli Knesset, delivered an emotional eulogy in Hebrew and Yiddish, reciting my father's various fine qualities as a doctor and kindly man, and his charitable gifts that qualified him as a "builder of Jerusalem"—among the highest honors an observant Jew can

Fig 8. Captain Gustav Schonfeld, flight medical officer US Air Force, San Antonio, 1967.

Fig 9. Miriam, Josh and Julia at Grand Canyon 1967.

Fig 10. Family vacation on Sanibel Island, FL. The kids decided to call us "Camp Gus" and gave me a whistle and clip board. 1986.

Fig 11. With my son Josh, and David, my first grandson in the Chairman's office, 1997.

Fig 12. At my appreciation dinner with Julia, Josh, and Jeremy, Ritz-Carlton Hotel, St. Louis, MO. March, 2000.

Fig 13. The Schonfeld family at my grand-daughter Rebecca's bat mitz-vah, New York, 2008.

acquire. Then, his body was transported to the cemetery on Har Nof. More speeches and special prayers were said on his behalf. The casket was lowered into the ground, and various people threw earth into the grave. With a broken voice, on the verge of tears, I said the Kaddish prayer. I had lost a precious man, who, although hard at times in pushing me toward what he saw as a proper goal, did so out of love. In the final analysis, he accepted my career goals in academic medicine, and came to bless Miriam and to love and enjoy his grandchildren.

I sat *shiva* with Mom for seven days in Jerusalem, receiving hundreds of visitors whose lives he had affected, hearing many stories of his strength and kindness from the hundreds of visitors who came by to pay their respects.

I then returned to St. Louis. I kept my beard for the first thirty days of mourning, and attended services every day for the eleven months following Dad's death. I lead the services during the weekdays. These are the practices of mourning among traditional Jews.

Not a day has passed since my father's death that I have not thought about him. He kept me on a tight leash, but having raised my own children I now know how difficult it is to gauge how tight the leash should be. My father was an exemplar of an energetic, ambitious man, who was determined to build a secure life for himself and his progeny after the destruction of the Shoah. At the same time he worked not only for himself and his family; he shared his wealth with many others here in the United States and in Israel. He loved his profession, a passion his patients sensed and appreciated. For me, he represented a source of moral instruction, support, and in his later years when he permitted himself to express it, of loving kindness. He continues as an advisor even now. When I am at a loss, I wonder what he would do.

After his death, my mother chose to stay in Israel, but over a period of a few months became increasingly anxious and depressed to the point where she was hospitalized. I went to Israel and brought her back to St. Louis. For the first years back in St. Louis she lived independently, taking care of her apartment and finances, visiting with friends. Subsequently her care would rest with me and Miriam, increasingly as she became older.

Dipping My Toes in Academic Administration

My working life consisted of overseeing my own operation, which consisted of forty to fifty professional and support people. My research interests consisted of clinical and basic research in lipoprotein physiology, immunology, biochemistry, and of late, the genetics of disorders of lipoprotein transport. I taught the postdoctoral fellows in my lab, residents in medicine, and medical students, and cared for patients with lipid disorders and diabetes in my weekly clinic.

In academic life, the adage of publish or perish is very true. Medical academics really work primarily for two groups, neither residing at their home institutions. The first is the members of the NIH study sections (peer review committees), who grade one's applications. The grade largely determines whether or not one is funded, and in what dollar amounts. The second consists of the editors of biomedical journals, who publish one's work. One must have good (fundable) ideas for research and one must publish. While the local administration provides the laboratory space necessary to get the work done, and one's academic titles, it rarely interferes with productive, well-funded researchers who in effect pay their own way. It is only when either publications or funding or both are lacking that visits to the administration become necessary. Persistent lack of funding is hazardous to an academic career.

oⅧo

Throughout my time at Washington University I have been happy to be of service to the school when asked, but I have never considered myself to be a political person. Nor have I volunteered for or pushed myself into positions of leadership or greater administrative authority. I must have learned in Europe that being conspicuous is hazardous. Therefore, I was content to lead the relatively unobtrusive life of a professor with a primary appointment in preventive medicine and a cross appointment in internal medicine, a closely allied department.

The department had been established in 1947 with Robert Shank, MD, an eminent nutritionist, as its chairman. His department was always small, consisting of less than a half-dozen MD faculty as the core of the department, plus the programs in physical therapy, occupational therapy, and biostatistics, which he oversaw.

Upon Shank's retirement in 1982, questions arose about the need for continuing the department as an independent entity. In 1983 I was asked to become acting chair of preventive medicine, while its fate, a contentious issue, was being decided upon. Some school leaders wished the department to continue, hoping to attract a dynamic individual to enlarge it and provide the school with research and service programs in epidemiology, public health, population genetics, and clinical trials, all necessary components of what today is modish under the title of "translational research." Others saw no need for it, saying that internal medicine already contained most of the necessary components, and wished it abolished.

The school is largely governed by its executive faculty, consisting of the chairs of all component departments and chaired by the dean. Most decisions are reached by consensus. Contentious issues take a long time to settle. Finally, in 1986, the department was abolished. Its core faculty and their programs and activities were folded into internal medicine. The programs in physical and occupational therapy and biostatics became answerable directly to the dean. As a reward for my service during a tense time, I was honored with my first of what were eventually to become three endowed professorial chairs. I became the William B. Kountz Professor in Internal Medicine, named after a successful and obviously generous clinician with an interest in nutrition.

I was relieved to be rid of the administrative burden and pleased to return to my patients, lab, and fellows, content that I had served the school that had supported my career and expecting a relatively quiet time during the far side of my career. But a speedup was in the offing.

The change came gradually. In 1993 I was asked to stand for faculty representative on the Executive Committee of the Faculty Council of the medical school, which represents the faculty to the dean. The job required a small commitment of time and had the potential of being interesting. I was elected in a medical schoolwide vote. Within a few weeks, I was appointed to represent the medical school faculty to the university's Faculty Senate Council that represents the entire faculty to the university's administration and considers issues important to the university faculty as a whole. The chancellor (president of the university) regularly attends its meetings. I was elected chair of the council for two one-year terms, and by virtue of that position became the representative of the university's faculty to the Board of Trustees of the university, and to the committee of deans and senior administrators known as the University Council. It is chaired by the chancellor. Issues of importance to the individual schools and to the university as a whole are aired at its meetings, such as building projects and personnel policies (e.g., on sexual harassment). Suddenly, I began to see a bigger vision of the university and how it plays its pivotal role for individuals and in society. Exciting!

My first year as chair coincided with the last year of William Danforth's twenty-five-year term as chancellor, and my second year with Mark Wrighton's first year. When Dr. Danforth left, he told me to do "a good job of breaking in Wrighton."

I had the honor to represent the faculty at Wrighton's public investiture and welcomed him on behalf of the faculty in front of three thousand people gathered in the quadrangle of the university. My service ended in the summer of 1996.

Coming to know more about the substance and governance of the university and the issues of importance to it was a wonderful and interesting privilege. I also came to know deans, faculty members, and board members I would otherwise not have come to know. My affection and respect for the university rose to new levels as a result.

The Busch Professorship and Chair of Medicine

In 1995 and 1996 I was hearing increasingly insistent rumors at the Barnes-Jewish Hospital's doctor's lounge, where I frequently ate lunch—the camaraderie is great—that the department of internal medicine was having problems in its administration. I listened but did not seek any details. Frankly, I felt this was not my problem and left it for the "big shots" of the school to sort out. I fully expected that things would improve since the then sitting chair of medicine, John Atkinson, is a very bright man, with a substantial internationally respected research program, great clinical acumen, especially in rheumatology (I had sent my mother to him for a consultation), and gifted as a teacher. He was appreciated and esteemed by many inside and outside the department.

Given, my largely apolitical history, I was somewhat surprised when in early 1996 the dean asked to meet with me. Bill Peck, who has since retired as dean, had been cochair of the Department of Medicine of the School of Medicine, which Dave Kipnis headed, and head of the Department of Medicine at the Jewish Hospital of St. Louis, which was then an independent community hospital closely affiliated with the School of Medicine. (In 1995 it was merged into Barnes Hospital, to become the Barnes-Jewish Hospital of St. Louis.) Peck is also a great raconteur and jazz pianist. Under his fourteen years as dean, the school experienced a great spurt in the construction of new buildings and improvement to the existing facilities. He made some very good choices for chairs of several departments, followed by improved quality in clinical and research programs.

The many various clinical practices of the faculty were scattered helter-skelter throughout the medical campus, confusing the patients. Under Peck, the practices were rationalized under a faculty practice plan (Washington University Physicians) and moved into a new fourteen-story building, the Center for Advanced Medicine (the CAM). In addition to the practices, it also housed all of the necessary diagnostic, therapeutic, and administrative facilities in one place, converting the hitherto confusing welter of places patients visited for diagnostic and consultative services into a single "patient-friendly," one-stop facility. The school also organized the Siteman Cancer Center that rapidly gained national recognition and status as a premier clinical and research enterprise. On the research side, the school achieved very high rankings in NIH dollars received, in the contributions of its faculty to medical knowledge, and in national ranking for medical education.

Under Peck the difficult step of merging Barnes and Jewish Hospitals—which were just two blocks away from each other in the central west end of the city of St. Louis—was achieved. Although the merger was deemed necessary by members of the boards of the two hospitals for financial reasons, it was a highly contentious decision, strongly opposed by the private practitioners who stood to lose political power to the full-time faculty. When it occurred, many fine private practitioners defected to several community hospitals in the western suburbs of St. Louis, where the population was expanding. Private patients followed their doctors. Thus, the merged Barnes-Jewish Hospital lost a large group of well-paying patients, and became a primary hospital for the inner city and a tertiary care center for the region.

Peck was very effective in the way he handled the executive faculty, which was bent on protecting the interests of their own departments, and the various boards of trustees, shepherding them along in a gentle way toward reaching the goals that had been set. He was about as effective as it was possible to be in managing the frequently contentious relations with our hospital system partner (the Barnes-Jewish-Christian System, BJC).

In early 1996, Peck wanted my opinion on the departmental administration, saying that I was one of several senior faculty members he was consulting. I told him that although I had heard rumors and complaints, my interactions with the chair had always been cordial. He thanked me and I left.

In the fall of 1996, the dean asked me to visit him again. He began by restating the problems, and saying that the situation had grown sufficiently worse—that he and the executive faculty had concluded that a change in the leadership was imperative, and soon—too soon to wait for the usual national search, which can take a year or more—to produce a candidate; a transitional figure was needed. The dean went on to say that some senior faculty of the department, including the associate chairs of internal medicine, were vocal in the chair's defense, but many faculty members were opposed to Atkinson's staying on. Peck feared that the department would split over this issue, and that defections of important faculty members could occur to the detriment of the department and the school. The new chair would have to handle the changeover with conviction, but delicately. I was shocked that the problems had reached this state, and said so.

Peck then asked whether I would take on the job of chair of the department for a sufficient amount of time to quiet the hard feelings, and to set the department on a course of fiscal soundness. Then the search for a permanent replacement would begin. He estimated one to two years.

The offer came as a genuine shock, as the chair of medicine was not a position I had ever aspired to nor expected to achieve, certainly not at Washington University. I believed that the distance between Munkacs, Auschwitz, and a chairmanship at a place like Washington University was a distance simply too great for me to traverse. Furthermore, I was sixty-two years old and had recently been diagnosed with an illness which, although essentially asymptomatic at that time, caused me some concern.

I mentioned the names of others whom I thought the dean should approach, but he said everything had been discussed and the executive faculty felt I was the right person. The offer sounded a lot like an "acting" chairmanship. In my previous role, as acting chairman of preventive medicine in 1983, the dean, Kenton King, had made it clear that I was expected to act as placeholder but not to initiate any new activities or to stir the pot in any way. At the end of that stint, I was debriefed by a committee of chairs. Among the many issues that arose, I was requested to describe my impressions of being an acting chairman. I told them, "It was a lot like catching gonorrhea from a toilet seat—all of the pain, none of the fun."

I feared that accepting another position as an "acting" chair would place me in a position of being merely an emollient (although that, too, is important), without being able to address any substantive issues that might need urgently to be addressed. I told him my concerns, and he assured me that I would be as free to act as a permanent chairman.

Peck gave me two weeks to think about it. It was clear to me that a new chairperson was going to be named. The question was should I or should someone else serve. Mentally, I reviewed the potential intradepartmental candidates and decided that perhaps I was in fact the best person to serve the purposes of the department at that time. Also, I was tempted because I felt honored to have been chosen, at a critical time, to lead the biggest department in my very prestigious medical school whose previous chairs of medicine had been illustrious academicians.

I consulted Miriam, David Kipnis, and others whose opinions I valued, and decided to accept provided I would indeed be given the authority of a permanent chair; including the hiring and firing of staff and faculty and the initiation or termination of "lines of business" consistent with furthering the quality of the department. The dean agreed. Still, I shook his hand with some trepidation. It was a big jump in responsibility from supervising a unit of forty to fifty people to sixteen hundred, with a disproportionate increase in budget. I regretted my father had not lived to see it. He would have been very proud.

The dean announced the change publicly in late October. Without giving me any notice to prepare, he called a special meeting of the department on November 1, 1996, at which he briefly justified the change in leadership and introduced me as the new chair. He then walked out of the room, leaving me to face the amassed faculty on my own. In my extemporaneous speech I attempted to calm the crowd by saying that I had not sought the job. It had sought me. I promised I would do what was necessary to place the department into a good position within the school and nationally, giving it my best effort. I also stressed that the changeover did not presage the end of the world. This was obvious. The department had survived many vicissitudes over its past nearly one hundred years as a premier department, and it would survive this change. I also said that my door was open, and that I would be pleased to hear suggestions on how to proceed.

Several people rose to speak. My predecessor's associate chairs expressed their anger. They considered the change of chairs a plot by the dean to get rid of a troublesome, powerful chair who disagreed with some of the dean's initiatives in the patient practice area. In their opinion, if enacted, the changes would unfavorably affect the department's position within the school. At the same time, they accused me of betraying a chairman who had treated me well in order to gain political power. One angry man even said that in order to save the department we should kill the dean. We who knew him knew this was bluster. Nevertheless, it added to the tension.

Fortunately, others rose in support. As the meeting was ending, a few even came up, patted my shoulder, and thanked me for taking on the job (better you than me). Within the two weeks following the meeting, the resisters fought a rearguard action. They circulated a letter about the unjust action the dean had taken in firing a fine chair and accused him of replacing an eminent personality with a well-meaning mediocrity. Seeing who had signed the letter bothered me, because it came from persons I greatly respected. But there was no time for wound licking; I was too busy. There was much to learn and many faculty to meet, both individually and in groupings. Over the first few days, I met with every division in the department.

One of the first decisions I had to make was whether to retain any associate chairs. I was convinced, after consultation, that there was no need for them, as there was ample staff support and many highly capable people among the faculty of three hundred who could be called on for advice and help. Ad hoc committees could also be created as needed. Within a few days of my officially assuming the post, I called each of the associate chairs in one by one, thanked them for their past service, and sent them back to their labs and clinics full time. Some asked if losing their administrative roles meant they would also lose their sizable salary supplements, and explained how much they had come to rely on the extra funds. I phased the supplements out over time to lessen their pain.

The only exception was Gerald Medoff, the former founding head of the modern infectious disease division, who entered my office asking, "Are you going to fire me, too?"

I said, "No. I want your help with the many interactions to the hospital."

He became "Senior Advisor to the Chair," kept his salary supplement, and served loyally and effectively.

For the next three years life was hectic, with meetings from early morning until late evening, frequently followed by a business dinner dealing with intra- and interdepartmental and schoolwide issues, including the faculty practice plan. Managing the relationship between the department and the Barnes-Jewish Hospital and the BJC system also took time. My learning curve was steep, but the work was fascinating and important.

I learned in some detail how excessively complicated and expensive is the system of delivering medical care and paying for it in America. This is because there is too much variation within and between insurers, e.g., which pre-existing conditions they exclude from coverage, what diagnostic procedures and therapies they cover and to what extent, the sizes of premiums and copays (what the patient pays out of pocket), and which physicians they find acceptable. Even the forms they use differ from one to another.

The insurers have also devised a series of ingenious procedures to contest, and when they can get away with it, deny payments to health providers. Their hope seems to be that the providers faced with the manifold difficulties of collection will yield. But providers also have expenses and are entitled to be paid for their work. Thus, the insurers' bureaucracy engendered a counterbureaucracy on the side of the providers to assure that due payments are in fact received. Needless to say this adds to the cost of medical care, while neither bureaucracy directly benefits the patients. The back-and-forth tussling can result in payments being delayed by several months, a nice "float" for the insurers. In sum, the payment of undeserved excessive salaries to insurance executives and their extensive staffs, and the generation of profits to satisfy shareholders, have added a huge additional burden of cost to the delivery of health in this country.

It is interesting that when business types speak of the excessive costs of medical care, the costs of the interposition of a nonproductive insurance industry are not mentioned. The problem seems to be that doctors order too many tests, give too many drugs, and make too much money; and that they can get away with this profligate behavior because there is insufficient competition in the system and patients are ignorant consumers.

The fact of the matter is that the medical delivery system can certainly use improvement, which is being done by, among other things, the importation of systems-management procedures; but the insurance industry is of no help in either effecting these improvements or in the diagnosing or treating of patients. It merely adds another obnoxious burden, the aggravation and financial cost that all of us must bear.

The reaction of many physicians to this mess is illustrated by a medical school classmate. At our thirty-fifth reunion, he stood up to say that for decades individual physicians and organized medicine feared that controls on medical practice and on payments would come from the left of the political spectrum. "We always cried 'socialized medicine'. Instead, the attack came from the right as the insurance industry, with the support of big business, imposed a business model on us based strictly on economic criteria, without regard for the humane aspects of medicine and the independence of our profession."

With the help and cooperation of a great many people, I was able to meet most of the goals the dean set for me, and a few of my own. I replaced some division heads, recruited some new ones, started some new outpatient ventures, and played a role in the initiation of some intradepartmental and schoolwide activities.

My successor, Ken Polonsky, a premier diabetes researcher, clinician-administrator, and teacher from the University of Chicago, arrived almost to the day three years after I took over. With the turnover I lost my titles of Busch professor and physician in chief, and became a plain professor and physician who was able "to spend more time in his lab and with his family".

A few months later, a gala appreciation dinner for over three hundred colleagues and spouses, hosted by Bill Peck and Ken Polonsky, was held in my honor at the St. Louis Ritz-Carlton Hotel. Miriam, our children and their spouses, my mother, Sandy and Carol Korein, and Kurt and Marilyn Metzl from Kansas City were present.

Many fine words were spoken by retired Chancellor William Danforth, current Chancellor Mark Wrighton, Dean and Vice Chancellor Peck, and Chair of Medicine Ken Polonsky; and I was given a handsome gift.

At the end of the evening, when we were alone with our friends, Marilyn Metzl commented about the party as follows: "You must have really pulled their asses out of the fire for them to have given you such a grand party." She is a sharp clinical psychologist, with whom I would not dare to disagree.

Two years after my leaving the post of chair of medicine, Dr. Samuel Schechter, my father's kindly former resident at the Jewish Hospital of St. Louis (1946-7), who was well into his eighties at that time, told me that he would be endowing a chair in medicine and he wanted me to be its first occupant. Naturally, I was pleasantly surprised and grateful, thinking that it would be wonderful to occupy a third professorial chair at my alma mater. A few months later Bill Peck called to notify me that indeed I would be getting the Samuel E. Schechter chair. Miriam commented that next I should be given a couch. At a gala ceremony, attended by Sam and his family, Miriam, our children, and about one hundred friends and guests, the chancellor hung a medallion around my neck. He, the dean, and the chair of medicine, paid me kind compliments. I gave the professorial lecture summarizing my research of the last eight to ten years.

That evening we had a dinner at the chancellor's home for forty people, where again nice words were said about Sam Schechter and me. Sitting around the table in the chancellor's home surrounded by my wife, children, friends, and distinguished colleagues, I pondered the distance our family had traveled since 1944 when the Germans invaded Munkacs. I quietly thanked God, my metaphorical benign being, about whom I know next to nothing with any certainty, for all His mercies: a wonderful wife, children, grandchildren, friends, and a career; and for having provided me with the accompanying satisfaction and joy. I also thanked Him for children who found it important to continue to assure the survival of the Jewish people in the way they were raising my grandchildren. I hoped my father was seeing his progeny in the United States, and hearing all the wonderful things said about his son.

PART VI

My Conclusions About the Shoah

I have given much thought to my life experiences, and how the Shoah fits into the rest of my life. What follows are general conclusions I have reached that have permitted me to function pretty well, and to accept the world as I perceived it to be.

Killings

In the old days, tribal groups continued to survive through history by defeating their enemies. The losers were killed or sold as slaves, their women taken as wives or concubines. Their languages and religions disappeared, relegated to the province of the archeologist. Somehow the Jews managed to survive as a group.

For the last few hundred years the face of war has changed. Losing nations managed to weather defeat and even to retain some of their lands by paying the victors reparations, or by becoming allies useful in the next round of confrontations against a third party. For example, the Germans were enemies of the U.S. in World War II. After being defeated, they made themselves indispensable to the victorious U.S. by becoming allies in the Cold War against the USSR, thereby gaining many advantages and saving themselves from severe retribution.

The Jews of Europe were in a different position. For the past two millennia, they lived as a more or less tolerated minority, at times able to live quietly and to achieve some prosperity and social status, at other times being forcibly converted to Christianity. At still other times they were exiled or killed and their properties expropriated by the "crown"—their fates always in the hands of others.

After a bloodletting, Jews might be expelled, permitted, or even compelled to remain in place for further exploitation.

If fortunate, they were permitted to try to find tranquility or opportunity elsewhere. Sometimes the Jews had luck; the old ruler died to be replaced by one with a kinder disposition. European nations played this cat and mouse game with "their" Jews for almost two millennia.

Then, in the twentieth century Hitler and his supporters throughout Europe decided to settle the "Jewish problem" once and for all by reverting to a mode of warfare even worse than the prehistoric primitive: namely, the war of *complete* extermination, with the added refinement that the most modern available technology was used to achieve killings on an industrial scale. They were largely successful in the lands they captured in Western and Central Europe, with the active participation or indifference of indigenous populations. Fortunately for the Jews, the USSR with aid from the U.S. defeated the Axis powers on the Eastern Front, saving the three million Jews of Russia from annihilation.

Survivor Anger and Survivor Guilt

In my opinion, too much has been made of "survivors' guilt" and too little of survivors' *anger*. I suspect experts studied a relatively few survivors who happened to feel guilty. Then they inappropriately generalized their findings to the whole group from what I suspect was a biased sample. This "finding" has found favor with the press and become sensationalized to the point of being accepted as established fact. I wish the press would explore the issues of "perpetrators' and bystanders' guilt." It would also be nice to see some journalistic articles on how the succeeding generations of Germans have been educated about the Shoah, and German nationalism.

My experience does not support the contention that a widespread survivors' guilt exists. While many survivors say they do not understand how or why they survived while others did not—and are grateful for their luck or God's good will—I have not heard them say they felt guilty about surviving. Perhaps I have not run into those who should feel guilty because they survived by stealing the food of others, or by unfairly gaining some favored treatment for themselves at the expense of others. But stating that survivors in general feel a sense of guilt seems to me to imply that all the lucky ones survived at the expense of their fellows. This was simply not so.

The survivors I know experience a continuing sense of loss and sometimes anger, without experiencing the so-called "closure", a concept foisted on us by the providers of psychobabble. It is probable that some hurts may never be "closed." One does not always "move on." Politicians routinely and devoutly wish to "move on" after they are caught in an indiscretion or illegality. Not wishing to pay the price, they say, "Let's look toward the future," and, "Let's move on." But not all aspects of life are like politicians' peccadilloes. Some events evoke anger that can last a lifetime. I know survivors who are still angry. I am among them.

How do I as a survivor feel about the perpetrators of the Shoah and their active and passive allies? My early feelings soon after the war were quite bitter, most notably toward the Germans and Hungarians, whose "kindnesses" had affected my family and me most directly. Still, even in my darkest days, I did not imagine myself ordering the wholesale death of the perpetrator nations were I in a position to do so. Though I must admit that had someone else wished to annihilate them, I would probably have been encouraging and certainly would have taken *no* steps to stop it. Nor would I have been too upset had the task been successfully accomplished.

Do not be surprised! Look at the magnitude of their hatred. The Germans and their Axis allies were fighting a difficult war against the Allies. Almost since the beginning they were diverting precious men and materiel toward the task of rounding up and killing millions of Jews. By 1944, after five years of war, they were clearly losing. Yet rather than throwing every possible resource into the battle to stave off the unconditional surrender demanded by the Allies, scarce men and materiel continued to be diverted from the several fighting fronts to maintain the huge system of concentration camps and killing factories. It seems obvious that killing Jews was more important than winning the war. (Parenthetically, one could argue that the Jews helped the Allies to win the Second World War by unwittingly serving as a diversion for Axis resources. Consider it a fourth front, after the eastern and western fronts, and Italy.) In my opinion such hatred is incurable, and attributing it to socio-economic causes is a mistake.

We had hoped that after the slaughter of World War II, the Shoah, and the unconditional surrender there would be a change of heart in much of Europe. Indeed, the first few decades were encouraging. The Germans made sympathetic noises and paid some reparations, and a few other governments said the right sounding words. Avowed anti-Semites kept quiet. We started to say, "Maybe this time it is different. Europe is getting over it anti-Semitic illness," and our anger began to abate in the face of hope. But after a hiatus lasting for perhaps fifty years, the anti-Semitic virus seems to be spreading again. Obviously, it is not easy to alter the natural order of things, such as the passing of long ingrained mental attitudes from generation to generation. In epidemiologic terms there are clearly carrier-reservoirs of the disease that have survived, and these constitute the source of the newly spreading contagion. Our frustration and anger are aroused in response.

Reconciliation and Forgiveness

Are the survivors supposed to "understand" and, ultimately, to forgive the perpetrators and their supporters? Are there any justifications for the Shoah, any extenuating circumstances?

One commonly recited story begins with the notion that the germ of the Second World War was planted at the time of Germany's defeat in the First World War. The defeat was an embarrassment for the proud, martial German nation. In fact, the ruling Junker-military caste did not accept the defeat—to them, an intolerable sign of inferior power and/or generalship. They blamed the Jews for a "stab in the back" and sought to sabotage the terms of the Versailles Treaty. The treaty, forcibly imposed by the victors (rather than arrived at by negotiation with the defeated), forbade German rearmament and retained a French army of occupation in the Ruhr, a further blow to national pride. In addition, there were alleged to be unreasonably large financial reparations to be paid to the victors, which kept the national economy from recovering. The worldwide economic depression and terrible inflation of the 1920s in Germany added to the woe. All of this led Germans to accept a savior in the form of Hitler, who promised to restore their pride and economy, and to avenge the Jews' perfidy.

Are we to accept that the Junkers' hurt pride and Hitler's paranoid delusional anti-Semitism justified their whipping the German people into a frenzy sufficient to start a world war and the killing six million Jews and millions of other "undesirables"? Some temper tantrum!

How different the world would have been had the terms of the treaty been adhered to and the Weimar government been permitted to work in peace! Instead of sabotaging the Weimar government, the Junkers could have retired to their estates and ordered the army to be loyal to the government. This would have obviated Hitler's opportunity to take power. Even a most charitable reading of the actions of the German ruling classes after the First World War provides no extenuating circumstances for their behavior.

What does it mean to forgive, and who is in a position to forgive? To forgive means to welcome the wrongdoer back into civil society. This usually follows genuine repentance of the behavior and the payment restitution. Both repentance and restitution must play out over sufficient time to convince the wronged party that the intent is genuine. The greater the wrong, the longer is the time. Thus, forgiveness, which contains a large element of trust, is earned over time.

I was taught that only the injured person could forgive those who have trespassed against him. I can choose to forgive, or not, one who has harmed me. I cannot forgive someone who has harmed another on behalf of the other. That is, no third party intermediary has the right to intrude on this delicate bilateral relationship, and presume to forgive on behalf of someone else, even if that someone else is God. In the absence of forgiveness by the harmed party, such an intrusion in effect represents a retrospective abetting of a crime by the third party. If the wronged party is dead, the wrongdoer must simply live with his guilt, vis-à-vis the victim, for the rest of his life. This is not as harsh as it sounds. First, he is alive while the victims are dead, with ripple effects on the victim's family. Second, other victims may be ready to forgive. So, the perpetrator may have to live unforgiven by only a fraction of the persons he has harmed.

Some people and institutions, such as those who have no great love for the Jews or who have a "Christian" forgiving nature, are impatient with the pace forgiveness imposes and wish no one to live (or to die) in an unforgiven status. These fine people wish to invoke a rapid and complete pathway toward forgiveness so we can "leave the past behind and move on" toward a better future. In my belief system this sort of wholesale forgiveness is not possible, nor is it desirable. In fact, the contrary is true. To secure a better future one must keep reminding people of the unpleasant past. Is it not preferable to keep unpleasant memories alive, even at the risk of "hurting feelings" than to risk more genocide? Clearly, the lessons of the Shoah have not been learned, as demonstrated by the recent genocides carried out in Africa and the Balkans. Could it be because the horrors of the Shoah have been forgiven, forgotten, or denied by prestigious persons and institutions too soon after the genocide? How else, except by remembering, will anyone learn the lessons of the Shoah and pause before beginning such activities?

The Catholic clergy appeared to be among those in a hurry to forgive. Many priests aided Nazis in escaping just retribution by spiriting them to South America. Further, it appears many tormentors were "forgiven" their sins, restored to the good graces of the Church, and permitted to partake in its sacraments, including last rites that are meant to assure dying people that they were being ushered into eternal life. So far as I know, no Nazi, including Hitler himself, has been excommunicated, much less denied the benefits of clergy.

In effect the Church pre-empted any potential discussion between the Jews and their tormentors about murder, torture, restoration of trust, and restitution. What is there left for a Catholic to discuss with someone he has harmed when he has already been provided God's mercy by a potent, priestly intermediary of the Church?

It requires a lot of hubris, which the Church has never lacked, to behave in this way without so much as consulting the wronged. How would the Catholic clergy feel if Jews arrogated to themselves the forgiving of sins committed by Catholics? Is it my place to do that? Is it the Church's role to forgive the sins their parishioners committed against Jews?

Just as the Church was ready to forgive the murderers, it was ready to overlook the acts of its errant priests. I have seen no reports that Nazi-helping clerics were chastised in any way, at any time in the last sixty years. Since the Church is ordinarily not bashful in expressing its displeasure, I interpret its silence on this issue as tacit approval, perhaps under the heading of "Christian charity" toward sinners. I assume my opinions would be characterized as Jewish "Old Testament" cruelty. Humbug!

My contention is not with individual Catholics; nearly all the ones I know are uncomfortable condoning much less discussing what the organized Church has done or neglected to do before, during, and even immediately in the wake of the war. I speak of the organization, which stubbornly has resisted accepting responsibility for its Shoah-related deeds just as it has refused to accept institutional responsibility for the more recently publicized crimes against boys and young men, cloaking itself in infallibility as an institution.

Obviously, some segment of the population in each country whose Jews had been deported abhorred what was happening. These "righteous Gentiles" helped the Jews. Many of these acts are memorialized at Yad Vashem, the museum of the Shoah in Jerusalem, and in other Holocaust museums, in numerous books, and in films. The stories of twenty-seven thousand righteous Gentiles are recorded, a goodly number. However, if we multiply that number by ten to account for any forgotten anonymous benefactors, that gives us two hundred and seventy thousand in all of Western and Central Europe out of an eligible population of about one hundred million. Obviously there remained a sufficient number of active and passive collaborators to make the Shoah a great success from the Nazi point of view. Is it too harsh to say that the vast majority of adult Europeans of the 1930s and 1940s were more or less tainted by the Shoah? In my opinion, no, it is not too harsh.

It would be startling and wonderful—in the sense of evoking a feeling of wonder—if the current political classes across the whole spectrum of society in several European nations freely and spontaneously spoke some sincere words acknowledging the vicious acts of the previous generations, followed by a pledge not to follow in the footsteps of their ancestors. This may be much to ask. Matters of personal and national pride, filial loyalty, and public embarrassment are involved.

However, in this case such a break from tradition should not be interpreted as an act of disloyalty, or as a wholesale renunciation of national traditions or pride. Rather it would demonstrate renouncing the worst of the nationalist hubristic tradition and selecting only the best concepts and acts for a better future.

Instead, what have we seen from the successor generations of the perpetrators and their allies? How do they feel? Have they been taught by their complicit elders to be welcoming and open-handed with the wronged and their needy progeny? [I do not mean only Jewish sufferers here.] The length and difficulty of the negotiations about statements of regret, restitution of property, and the interposition of all sorts of technical demands on the victims lead me to believe that neither the original negotiators nor their successors were filled with remorse, or bursting with an uncontrollable impulse to right the wrongs done during the war. Nor have the publics from which the negotiators are drawn risen against them to demand swift and generous justice. I conclude that just as most of the perpetrator/bystander generation felt no great regret or empathy for the victims, they also did not teach either empathy or contrition to their offspring.

Additional evidence for the persistence of offensive old attitudes toward Jews comes from well-documented surveys that show significant numbers of Europeans still harbor strong anti-Semitic feelings, even in countries where Jews are now present in insignificant numbers. The antagonisms are manifested by placards, graffiti, and more seriously by assaults on Jewish persons, personal property, synagogues, community centers, and cemeteries.

European governments have been behaving like right-handed persons whose left hands do not know what the right is doing, and vice versa. They have been slapping the Jews with the right hand and mollifying them with the left. They have only recently and reluctantly begun waking up to the anti-Semitic feelings and acts within their borders. Some avowedly anti-Semitic political parties, churches, and civic organizations continue to operate with a wink and a nod from their governments. We the wronged would like to achieve a relationship of trust with the current generation of Europeans, but we sense ambiguous reciprocal feelings, insufficient to allay our mistrust justified by a long history.

Another impediment to amicable relations between Jews and Europeans are their contrasting views of Israel. Whereas Jews tend to support Israel, European governments and many civic and church organizations accept the canard that the West Bank of the Jordan River belongs to the Arabs, whereas in fact it is disputed territory, its status to be settled by negotiation. Having accepted the Arab premise, Europeans are quick to condemn Israel's continuing presence on the West Bank and any military operations by Israel against the Palestinians and other hostile neighbors, whereas terrorist acts by Arabs and their repeatedly stated aims of destroying Israel are tolerated. This is the essence of anti-Semitism. We expected better.

One would have thought that Europeans and their governments would be staunch political and moral supporters of Israel, first as a relatively painless way of paying "reparations" in political coin, and second in their own self-interest. After all the trouble their predecessors took to cleanse Europe of Jews, surely they wish to encourage the Jews to remain in the Middle East, far, far away from Europe. Think, Europe! If through your actions (or inactions) the Arabs and/or Iranians do in future achieve a victory over Israel, how many Israeli Jewish men, women, and children would survive? Where would they go? Would Europe take them back, or would it permit the Arabs/Iranians to do as they pleased with them in return for the incredible promise of free flow of oil to Europe? The experiences of victims during the Shoah, and in Bosnia, Kosovo, Rwanda, and Sudan do not engender hope for any *timely* succor from Europe should the Arabs have their way in Israel. It seems Europe is better at repeatedly speaking a reluctant and belated *mea culpa* than at helping to save lives in a *timely* fashion, which is why Israel has decided to maintain a strong armed force for its own protection.

The constant lecturing of the Israelis by Europeans grows tiresome, because it is inappropriate. By what criteria of morality are the Europeans entitled to lecture the Israelis on what is right and wrong? Europe, are your hands so clean that you can claim to know the morally correct thing to be done in the Middle East? Do you not realize that you are encouraging the Arabs' intransigence, to Israel's detriment, and to the detriment of peace in the region? Have some humility in view of your own past actions. Why do you do it? Is it because you believe this craven, cringing behavior vis-à-vis the Arabs will assure the delivery of oil to yourselves?

Perhaps I am being too harsh with Europe. After all, they do have their problems. Among them is their burgeoning, restless Muslim population. It seems as if Europe's acceptance of large numbers of Muslim immigrants has not worked out too well, if one is to believe news reports of burning cars and neighborhoods, and occasional bombings. More Muslims now reside in Western Europe than Jews did before the Shoah, and their numbers continue to grow. In effect, the western Europeans have traded their Jewish population for a larger number of Muslim Arabs. I wonder if they find the trade to have had a positive effect on the civic peace and progress of their countries. Do they find comfort in contemplating the violence now periodically engulfing their cities following any speech or action perceived as being insulting to Muslims, and in wondering about the terrorist cells they may be harboring in their midst?

Is it not ironic that the lands the Muslims occupied in Europe in the early Middle Ages, and then hundreds of years later lost in battling the Christians, are now being gradually re-occupied at least in spirit, by Arab immigration and biologic reproduction? The Bible states that "the sins of the fathers will be visited upon the sons". This was not meant as a threat but as a prophecy. Perhaps the prophecy is playing itself out on the Europeans.

Israel

Why do people like me support Israel? Do we not believe in the ideal of a single humanity, related to each other by bonds of brotherhood and dealing with each other solely by peaceful means? Do not the atavistic prevailing nationalistic and ethnocentric ways obstruct the world from achieving the long dreamed of "universal brotherhood" and peace that Jewish Bible proclaims as the ideal? Should the Israelis not be ashamed of their "paranoid, xenophobic" insistence on having their own state based on religion and ethnicity?

Idealistic pacifists do take the position that the Jews are retrogressive and obstructionist. Bigots, who use idealism as a stick with which to beat the Jews, level the same accusations. The answer, by ideal standards, is that yes, the Jews are retrogressive. But the world has not yet reached the ideal state of utopia. A simple test suffices. The vast majority of mankind is just as devoted to its own multiple particularities as are the Jews.

In the 1980s a Finnish scientist visited my lab in St. Louis for two years. He was very productive and our families got on famously. They had one young son. When years later we were visiting their home in Helsinki, I asked his wife what sort of woman she would consider to be a suitable mate for her son. She said, "It has to be a Finnish woman because we are a small people and we do not wish to disappear." Should she be admonished for her "narrow" nationalism?

Unfortunately, some particularists in addition to being old fashioned about retaining their own identities have big guns and wish not only to preserve their own particularities for themselves but also to impose them on the rest of us. See your daily newspapers for details.

Should the Jews be the first to test the practicability of the universal ideal of the brotherhood of man by offering to give up their state and blending into the people of the world? I believe the Jews have experienced this experiment for the last two thousand years, with strongly discouraging results. Ask also the opinions of those who have been stateless for a relatively short time or still are without their own states. Have the Kurds enjoyed their stateless status? Did the Irish and the East Indians? Apparently not. They all wished to be free to practice their benighted particularities.

I am as enlightened as the next fellow, and would support a worldwide union of peoples. I would do so immediately *after* others who wish to unify mankind gave up on their own uniqueness. When the utopia arrives, Jews should and will join in. However, given our experience, Jews should not be expected to continue to take the lead utopian position.

Western Europe is now among the foremost preachers of the gospel of the unity of man. They reached that exalted, enlightened consensus after many centuries of mutual bloodletting, capped by the two world wars of the twentieth century. For most of their history European leaders felt themselves to be exalted above all other nations and peoples, since they were the bearers of Christian civilization; and they used their big guns to bring Christianity and civilization (the western particularities) to the "primitives." Their recent conversion may or may not be sincere, but the previous "pupils" are no longer willing to listen to the "master." They prefer to run their own shows. Yet, as is true of all converts to the "truth," the Europeans still believe they have lessons to teach in proper behavior. The irony is that perhaps they do, but by now their instructions are not readily acceptable in light of the internal and external history of Europe.

Israel's basic law includes the "right of return" for all Jews. This right has been exercised by the Jews of the Arab world, who in their hundreds of thousands moved to Israel within a couple of years of its founding, and by a million Jews of the former Soviet Union, who also voted with their feet and left for Israel.

Those Jews living on the edge, between comfort and discomfort, also are happy to have Israel as an option. For example, many French Jews have purchased property in Israel in recent years, "just in case" the Muslim situation there gets out of hand. Perhaps the Arabs have not thought through the consequences of their anti-Semitic behaviors in Europe. If the situation for Jews, for example in France, deteriorates, many more may feel driven to move *to* Israel. This entirely predictable result would be contrary to the aims of the Arabs, namely the driving of the Jews *out* of Israel.

Finally, it is a matter of great satisfaction and pride for Jews to contemplate that nations must now deal with Israel with some measure of circumspection and respect. It is no longer a simple matter to go about persecuting and killing Jews at one's convenience and pleasure. Costs may be involved, and these must be considered. Put bluntly, Israel is capable and willing to exact a cost for the spilling of Jewish blood. This may give some currently active and potential enemies pause. The battle between gazelles and lions has been eternal and one-sided. Since the advent of Israel, the gazelles have acquired some sharp canine teeth and the will to use them. The carnivores are surprised, but slow to learn.

Moving On?

For me, the Shoah will never be forgotten. Nor will I ever forgive the perpetrators and their helpers for what they did to me and my family and my people. I hope there is a Dantean Hell in which they may continue to burn for millennia to come.

However, I have never felt their children were to blame for the acts of the parents, unless they adapted the attitudes of their parents. I wish the ambiguity of Europe's signals toward Israel and the Jews could be replaced by unequivocal support, i.e., my wish and hope is that European governments will acquire the strength of character to stop tolerating indigenous anti-Semitism, and the anti-Semitism cloaked as anti-Israelism.

Perhaps not surprisingly, as I have aged, my sharp anger has been gradually replaced by a degree of acceptance of the fact that the war is long past and people are saying, "Let's move on." To the generation of my progeny, the Second World War and the Shoah are as dated as the First World War is to my generation, a troubling memory on which one need not dwell for too long. People today are exercised about other issues, among them the war in Iraq and Afganistan, the Islamist threat to the West, and the economic recession. Life moves on, although not always in directions to our liking.

Nevertheless, remembering is critical for the reasons enumerated above. Holocaust museums, memorials, and courses serve to remind the people of the world what others are capable of when in the grip of an idea that seems more important than humanity itself. Hopefully, keeping the memory alive will make it *more difficult* for such ideas to be inculcated into publics that seem with dull, recurring regularity to be susceptible to seduction by sociopath, fanatic, would-be leaders singing the beloved, well-rehearsed siren songs of nationalistic and/or religious xenophobia. These self-important nuts are present everywhere. If the publics could learn the lessons of the Second World War, perhaps they would resist the temptations of ceding power to would-be dictators and sociopaths. Stay tuned!

With Gratitude:

This project would not have been started or completed without the consistent, patient encouragement of Miriam Schonfeld, my wife and the love of my life; and Joshua Lawrence and Suzanne Schonfeld; Julia Elizabeth and Michael Zeuner; Jeremy David and Sara Jane Casey Schonfeld; my wonderful children and their spouses. I am eternally grateful for their interest in and sympathetic reading of this text. My children have given me much joy, most notably the unique life-prolonging joy of *nachas* from grandchildren: Rachel, David, Rebecca, Alexandra, Brian, Aaron and Daniel. Their adherence to our customs and values, imparted by our children, gives me some comfort that our lineage will continue within the people of Israel. Several persons have read portions of this memoir and made useful contributions: Mel Hecker, Sandor Korein, Judie and John Larosa, and Anne Roiphe. I am grateful to all of them for their insights. Of course, any errors and misjudgments are mine.

Made in the USA
Middletown, DE
20 February 2018